L. D. Michaels is a London[...] cooking from a West India[...] traditions and a Portugues[...] restaurant owned by a Pole i[...] global travels and present semi-suburban life in an unfashionable but cosmopolitan part of North London have done much to shape his attitudes to food and cooking. He has written, under a variety of pseudonyms, for a number of magazines. This is his first major book and is a direct result of his preoccupation with what he calls 'lost popular technologies'.

L. D. MICHAELS

The Complete Book of Pressure Cooking

PANTHER
Granada Publishing

Panther Books
Granada Publishing Ltd
8 Grafton Street, London W1X 3LA

Published by Panther Books 1977
Reprinted 1978 (twice), 1980, 1982, 1984

Copyright © L. D. Michaels 1977

ISBN 0-583-12779-7

Printed and bound in Great Britain by
Collins, Glasgow

Set in Times

CONTENTS

ACKNOWLEDGEMENTS

Many people gave advice – literary and culinary – to me while I put this book together and, more importantly, passed on their favourite recipes, allowing me to adapt them as I saw fit so as to give the standardized appearance necessary in a cook book.

Thanks are due to Mrs B. Sommer, Francesca Greenoak, Mrs Lorraine Greenoak, Lavinia Trevor, Adrian Shire, Lionel Trippett and especially to Franny Singer who acted as amanuensis/typist for the whole operation.

The errors are mine alone.

L. D. Michaels
London, 1977

1: INTRODUCTION

Almost thirty years after it was first introduced to the public, pressure cooking is still undervalued and misunderstood. The miracles that the manufacturers seemed to promise when the first modern pressure cookers became widely available after the end of World War II eluded many of the early buyers when they came to try them out in their own homes. Until quite recently the pressure cooker has been undeservedly out of fashion – sold almost as a curiosity to a minority.

The fact is that the pressure cooker is one of the most useful kitchen aids around, and one of the least expensive, both to buy and run. A wider public is just beginning to realize what has been under its collective nose for ages.

The pressure cooker enables you to prepare a wide variety of dishes much more rapidly than usual with more conventional techniques. In many cases the result is better-tasting and better-looking and has improved texture and nutritional value. In the years since the equipment first appeared cooks have discovered precisely what they can do – and what they can't. All that is left is to rescue the pressure cooker from the strange prejudices that have surrounded it and to help those cooks who distrust it to make the most of pressure cooking.

That is precisely what this book seeks to do. I've tried to write both for the cook who is just beginning and for the experienced one who probably thinks that pressure cookers aren't any good for 'serious' results. Every pressure cooker comes with its own instruction booklet – my book can be used for all pressure cookers, no matter what make, and leaps the gap between simple instruction and proper explanation. The essentials of pressure cooking are easy but there is no reason why the results should be any less good than the most skilled, proud and fussy cook regards as the best.

I don't believe that pressure cooking replaces entirely other methods of preparing food. I do believe that it provides a number of extra techniques and possibilities which every cook should know about. I know, from my own experience, that it is possible to revive some of the delicious old recipes of yesteryear that have fallen into disuse because modern cooks lack the time for all the lengthy simmerings and skimmings and clarifyings and reducings that they called for. Also, from my own experience, I know I have been able to invent new recipes which would be virtually impossible by any other method.

What I'd like most of all is to take the pressure cooker out of its present 'special' status and let it take its due place in the kitchen with all the other essential sensible appliances that we use. The time isn't with us yet, but I'd like to look forward to when the pressure cooker isn't pulled out of its cupboard either in a half-ashamed fashion or as a gimmick – but simply as the best and quickest way of getting a certain set of foods and dishes cooked – just like that!

What do pressure cookers do? By means of super-heated steam created inside the cooker, considerable savings can be made in the time conventionally taken in cooking a wide variety of dishes. This new technique of cooking, which is more than just an updated version of what cooks have been doing for the last few thousand years, usually manages to preserve the inherent nutritional qualities of the food much more effectively than any other method of cooking. The shorter time taken brings more advantages than simply less slaving over a hot stove, since you'll be using less fuel for heating and will run less chance of greasing up your kitchen.

All these claims were made when pressure cookers first appeared and, with very few reservations, they are all true. Why then did the pressure cooker never become really popular? I think there are two reasons. First, twenty-five to thirty years is not a long time in the history of cooking. Practically everything else we use in the kitchen is merely a modernized form of something that has been around for hundreds, even thousands, of years. New recipes, when they have appeared, have been more often the result of the clever combination of ingredients rather than new techniques. So mistakes were made. Second, the hopes of the manufacturers and of those cooks who bought the early appliances were wildly optimistic, so much so that disappointment was inevitable. Alas, because a few things were a little less miraculous than had been anticipated, the general public started to believe that nothing good could ever come from a pressure cooker. They were wrong.

Pressure cooking isn't a miracle that completely suspends what happens in the ordinary course of cooking processes – it won't give you a perfectly roast joint in minutes (though I've seen that claimed), barbecue you a steak or fry you a fish. However, used and understood properly, it will transform the way you think about cooking.

This book is designed to help you integrate the pressure cooker into your normal cooking routines, habits, likes and dislikes. Everyone knows that good cooking is a mixture of knowledge, imagination and instinct. By the time you've been using this book for a while, I hope your own skills will be developing rapidly and you'll know instinctively when to turn to your pressure cooker for the best results.

Each of the main chapters (I have followed the traditional cookbook practice of writing about foods in the order in which they would normally be eaten in a meal) begins with a simple 'how-to-cook-it' section which contains the basic principles. I then give my own versions of traditional favourites cooked by the pressure method and finally there are some more sophisticated ideas for the more ambitious. I want to show that, despite its speed, pressure cookery is by no means 'cheating' and that it is perfectly capable of the highest *cordon bleu* results. The range of recipes is wider than you will find in most conventional cookbooks, but everyone should find several favourites as well as some things they may like to experiment with cautiously – my own tastes are probably excessively cosmopolitan. The range of basic ingredients is also wide. Our shops are offering us new foods – new varieties of fish, textured vegetable protein (synthetic meat) and exotic vegetables.

I've also included my own adaptations of Caribbean, Mediterranean, Indian and Chinese cooking, not only for adventurous Anglo-Saxon readers but also for those who eat like that all the time. Vegetarians are usually poorly catered for in 'general' cookbooks, yet pressure cooking can be of special help to them, not only in retaining the maximum goodness in fresh vegetables but also in making the handling of dried ingredients much more simple. Many non-vegetarians simply don't know the variety of textures and tastes that vegetarian food offers – perhaps this is their chance to learn.

Pressure cookers can also be used to steam certain cakes, puddings and emergency breads, so there's a chapter on that – another neglected area of modern-day cookery.

If you own a freezer, then the pressure cooker can help you prepare the food for safe hygienic freezing – probably more effectively than any other method available to the domestic user. At every stage I'll be telling you how to cope with the cooking of pre-frozen foods and how to adapt the instructions on the packet.

At the very end of the book you'll find a quick reference guide both to ingredients and their basic methods and to the places in which the book gives more detail. I've also included a more-than-usually thorough measurement guide as the variety of standards (old Imperial, newer Imperial, metric and American) appearing in cookbooks and recipes is very confusing. Sooner, probably, rather than later, you'll want to turn to your own favourite recipes in other books and want to know how to convert! The practice I've adopted throughout the book is to quote metric and put an approximate Imperial measure in brackets afterwards – thus: 75 g (3 oz), 750 ml (1½ pts), 122 °C (252 °F). The equivalents I have used vary slightly throughout the book – I have gone for ease of use rather than mathematical accuracy, but they all work. If you want to convert from American-style cup measurements, check in the back;

you'll also find a reference to the old-style Imperial measures like gills. When I refer to pints I mean the Imperial measure of 20 *fl oz*, not the American one of 16 *fl oz*. Similarly an Imperial quart is 40 *fl oz*, not 32 *fl oz*. One day, we'll all measure things the same way . . .

Finally, by way of reassurance and whetting the appetite for what is to come (and that is half the secret), let's dispel a few of those myths about why one shouldn't use a pressure cooker:

1. PRESSURE COOKERS ARE DANGEROUS
Nonsense. All appliances on the market should be able to withstand a minimum internal pressure six times in excess of anything required for normal use. All pressure cookers have a safety valve which blows well before danger point. The safety valves are sensitive both to excess pressure and to excess heating. If you over-heat, the food may get spoiled and if the appliance boils dry the bottom may eventually warp. However, the pressure cooker is a good deal safer than a frying pan, much safer than a deep-fat fryer and much less likely to create a mess than an out-of-control saucepan.

2. PRESSURE COOKERS ARE DIFFICULT TO CONTROL
Well, they do work fast – that's the idea, but with foods that cook rapidly anyway there's no need to cook at full pressure. With the valve or weights off, the pressure pan is a superb steamer at ordinary temperatures – one of the best ways of cooking vegetables and fish. If you follow the timings you should have no trouble. In any case, one of the first things you learn is when to under-cook certain foods and then finish off under careful control at normal conditions. The rest of it takes as much practice as learning any other sort of cooking method.

3. IT'S DIFFICULT TO FLAVOUR AND SEASON
Not true. Pressure cooking uses less liquid than ordinary methods (when you steam, in fact, the liquid you put in

doesn't touch the food at all) so that your spices and herbs will not be diluted as much as they are ordinarily – so you simply use less. By finishing off a dish at ordinary temperature and pressure you can control everything normally. And as far as herbs are concerned – the pressure cooker actually encourages you to use them properly. Most people put herbs in far too early in the cooking process – the heat simply dispels into the atmosphere the aromatic oils that constitute the flavour, or breaks them down, leaving a bitter taste. The majority of herbs are best added, finely rubbed between the fingers if they are dry, towards the end of the cooking period, and with the heat down low. With pressure cooking, you simply speed up the normally long period of cooking the main ingredients and then finish off slowly, adding herbs and correcting seasoning as good cooks have always done.

4. PRESSURE COOKING SPOILS THE FOOD'S TEXTURE

True, up to a point, if you are careless. But if you think ahead, don't expect impossible results and follow the instructions, the texture of some foods may be even better than you are used to – vegetables, rice and cereals, for example. Most pressure-cooked foods are spoilt through careless pressure reduction by too rapid cooling.

5. CLAIMS MADE ABOUT THE RETENTION OF NUTRITIONAL VALUES ARE EXAGGERATED

The human body needs a wide variety of nutrients to sustain it – not only carbohydrates, proteins, vitamins, minerals and various sorts of fats but enzymes also. The nutritional value of some of our foods goes into decline the moment the food is picked, the vegetable lifted from the ground or the animal killed. Heat kills some of the other ingredients in the foods we eat – in some cases fortunately for us, as the bacteria in some raw meats are harmful to humans. But the greatest losses in food values stem from three common happenings in the kitchen – long cooking times, open-pan cooking and the leaching away in water or stock or gravy which is then discarded. Pressure cooking minimizes all of these.

6. PRESSURE COOKING MAKES FOOD SOGGY AND COLOURLESS

Not true. It's all a matter of following the instructions carefully and applying a little common sense. Provided you are not too slap-happy (in which case you'll never be a good cook, whatever method you try) you should have no trouble.

7. THE PRESSURE COOKER HAS BEEN REPLACED BY THE MICROWAVE OVEN. THE PRESSURE COOKER HAS BEEN REPLACED BY THE SLOW-CROCK

We can take these two objections together. The pressure cooker can handle a wide variety of foods – some of them supremely well. The microwave cooker, which costs about fifteen times as much, also offers speed. However, some foods are cooked even more rapidly in the pressure cooker – most vegetables and some meat dishes, for example. The real value of a microwave cooker is that it can defrost quickly and safely and can also reheat cooked foods. The slow-crock, which is essentially an earthenware pot with an electric element supplying a small amount of heat, is also a useful culinary gadget. At the moment it is slightly more expensive than a pressure cooker and offers a smaller range of results. The slow-crock is marvellous if you have the time and forethought to be able to use it. It cannot cope with emergencies and is not much good for vegetables – you do get good results with meat. So the pressure cooker, far from being replaced, is still the best and most sensible kitchen appliance after the cooking stove and refrigerator and basic pots and pans have been purchased!

8. PRESSURE COOKING CAN'T BE USED FOR GOURMET RESULTS

Just you wait till the end of this book and see!

2: HOW TO USE AND CARE FOR YOUR PRESSURE COOKER

Pressure cookers vary quite a bit in their appearance and the precise manner of working so that you should always consult the instruction book that comes with your appliance before using it. The usual material from which they are made is spun aluminium which has strength and lightness, though some are made from stainless steel. The early models were all in shiny aluminium but some of the more modern ones now have coloured exteriors and a few have an interior coating of PTFE or Teflon which gives non-stick qualities.

All pressure cookers have certain features in common:

1. A PAN which is usually much thicker than an average saucepan. It will resist high pressures and withstand the effects of sudden cooling.

2. A LID which is similarly thick and which can be fastened down tightly. The lid will contain —

3. A PRESSURE VALVE OR WEIGHTS which control the pressure inside the pan. Some models have a spring-loaded flip-up valve, some have a spring-loaded indicator and some have a series of weights which fit over a small escape vent. The escape vent must be kept clear of food particles at all times; if it becomes clogged, even slightly, pressure will build up inside the cooker and at the very least you will find the food gets over-cooked. If your pressure cooker has weights, then don't be surprised if they are considerably lighter than the markings on them: the 15 *lb* weight with my old Prestige cooker weighs 126 *g* (about 5 *oz*) – it's the combination of the weight sitting over a vent and having steam forced through it from underneath that causes the pressure build-up inside. Most 'weight' systems consist of three sections, an inner (L) weight, a sleeve making the

pressure up to (M) and then an outer sleeve to make up the normal operating pressure (H) or 15 *lb*. Another device is the valve which revolves slowly when the cooker is at the right pressure. This gives you a visual check on what you are doing. Such a device is found on one of Europe's best selling models. The lid will also have —

4. A SAFETY VALVE. This is to prevent the inside from becoming over-pressurized or over-heated. Most valves have two components: one which is sensitive to pressure and which blows out at around three-and-a-half to four atmospheres; and one which melts suddenly and rapidly if the heat becomes excessive. The valves are usually of rubber composition with a metal core, or of one sort of rubber on the outside with an inner plug of a different type of rubber composition.

Under normal circumstances and with proper use, the safety valve should never 'blow' unless after a time it becomes worn.

'Blowing' occurs if
(a) The pressure valve has become blocked and steam can't escape at the rate at which it should. This will happen if the pressure valve isn't cleaned regularly or if you are cooking foods that froth up and your saucepan is over-filled (to more than two thirds).

(b) You have let all the moisture leave the pot, either by not putting in enough to begin with, or by over-cooking. In these circumstances the pan ceases to be a pressure cooker and starts acting like an oven. The food will be spoilt and the safety plug will melt to prevent too much damage.

You hear dreadful stories about safety valves blowing and directing a stream of extremely hot mashed plum at the kitchen ceiling. Most of the stories are apocryphal. The more recently made models tend to 'blow' at a lower pressure than the earlier ones, so that the cook has enough warning and the worst that happens is a messy dribble.

5. A TRIVET. This is a small inverted tray with holes in it which almost exactly fits the bottom of the pan. The water that makes the pressurized steam is placed underneath the trivet and food can be placed on top of it so that at no stage does the food touch the water. The food is then properly steamed and the valuable nutrients that could dissolve in the water are retained in the food. The trivet is not used for all recipes, of course.

If you use the pan with the trivet and with another pan resting inside, but with the lid *off*, you then have a double-boiler – suitable for making delicate sauces (see p. 281). Some makes offer you a wire basket, or pannier, which does the same job but is easier to lift out.

6. DIVIDERS AND SEPARATORS. These are containers, some of them solid, some punctured with small holes, which rest on top of the trivet. You can put different sorts of food in them and, because the cooking is done by steam, the flavours do not mix. You can easily cook three sorts of vegetable together and not have them all taste like one another.

The separators with holes in them should be used wherever possible so that the steam can penetrate freely all around the food. It is only food that is liquid or in very small particles (like rice) that should be cooked in a solid separator. Since the steam can't get at the food that easily, the cooking is done largely by the heat of the pressure cooker, and not the pressure, so cooking takes a little longer.

7. A GASKET. This is a rubber-composition seal which fits between the lid and the pan, depending on the precise mechanical means of closure. The gasket ensures that the cooker is sealed tight. If steam is seen escaping from beneath the lid, then the gasket is faulty and will need replacing. Almost certainly you will find that you have been cooking at a lower temperature and pressure than you intended and, as a result, your food will be under-cooked.

8. A MEANS OF CLOSURE. A pressure cooker needs to be mechanically secure. There are a number of different mechanical devices used. Some require you to twist the lid carefully into a series of locking lugs on the top of the pan, some have massive handles and springs, some depend on an eccentric oval fitting lid slotting into place, and with some there are twisting handles over the lid which are then screwed up to tighten into lugs on the pan.

Most pressure cookers are designed so that you cannot open them under pressure, though a few are.

Most early mistakes in pressure cooking come from incorrect closure of the appliances. Read your instruction manual carefully!

HOW TO USE YOUR PRESSURE COOKER

Pressure cookers are used in two ways:

1. As a pressure steamer.
2. As a pressure boiler.

In the first method, the trivet is placed in the bottom of the pan and the food is laid over it, or in separators. Water placed below the trivet is boiled up under pressure and converted into high-pressure steam. Food and water do not come in contact. In the second method, the trivet is not used and the food is cooked in the fluid which may be either water or stock.

When cooking solids the appliance should never be more than two-thirds full in order to let the steam percolate and penetrate thoroughly. *When cooking with fluids the appliance should never be more than half full* in order to avoid boiling and frothing up which would clog the escape vent on the pressure valve.

In the ordinary course of pressure cooking you insert the food, close the lid and place the pan over a high heat. After two or three minutes there will be a strong sound of steam coming from the escape vent. At this point all the air will have been evacuated from the appliance and the inside filled with steam at ordinary pressure and the internal temperature will be 100 °C (212 °F).

You then bring the pressure up either by moving the appropriate lever or by putting on the weights. Your instruction book will tell you how. For a while the cooker will be silent; then you should hear the escaping steam again. Some cookers have a special indicator, or the valve starts to murmur or rotate. This means that the internal pressure is now up at 2 atmospheres (15 *lb*) or (H). *You should then reduce the heat* to keep the process just ticking over.

Applying more heat is not just wasteful: it does not speed the process any further and only results in the more rapid boiling away of the water. If you are pressure steaming you could run the risk of boiling dry, and if you are pressure boiling, you could leave your pieces of food without any stock around them and risk burning.

THE TIMING OF ALL RECIPES STARTS FROM WHEN THE COOKER IS FULLY UNDER PRESSURE

Pressure cooking times only are given at the head of each recipe.

In general, you should always put as little liquid as possible in the appliance. Firstly, if you over-fill, the water takes longer to boil and thus the cooker takes longer to come under pressure. Secondly, if you are going to use the fluid at the end of the process, say to make a sauce or a stock, then the more water there was to begin with, the more dilute will be the nutrients that have dissolved in it.

The calculation of the amount of water to be used is always very simple. Provided you keep the appliance just ticking over and are not over-heating, then at 15 *lb* (H) weight or normal operating conditions, 140 *ml* ($\frac{1}{4}$ *pt*) *of liquid is expelled as steam for every* 15 *minutes of cooking time**.

* If you use the U.S. cup measurement (8 *fl oz* – 234 *ml*) you would work on half-a-cup per 12-minute period.

Most manufacturers recommend that the minimum amount of liquid you put into your appliance should be 140 *ml* plus 140 *ml* – i.e. 250 to 280 *ml* or ½ pint. You add a further 140 *ml* for each additional 15-minute segment. Thus for an hour's pressure cooking you would need: 4 × 140 *ml* + 140 *ml* = 700 *ml* (1¼ *pts*) of fluid. By contrast, if you were to leave the valve off and keep the heat high 120 *ml* (4 *fl oz* or ⅓ *pt*) of water would be driven off as steam in 5 minutes.

Remember the timing always starts once the cooker is under pressure. *As a very rough guide, once the cooker is under pressure cooking time is only one-fifth of conventional times*, though an actual recipe will often involve more than just cooking at full pressure.

One thing that will affect the length of cooking time is the degree of freedom the pressurized steam has to circulate. Food cooked on top of the trivet or in the perforated separator will cook more rapidly than food in a solid separator or in some other vessel like a boilproof bowl or one of heatproof glass. The recipes will tell you how to adjust.

At the end of the cooking time you must *reduce pressure* to bring the contents of the pan down to the same pressure as the atmosphere. There are two ways:

1. Rapid cooling, which involves placing the pan in cold water or, if necessary, under a running cold tap.
2. Slow cooling, which merely means taking the pan away from its source of heat.

The pressure cooker will be able to withstand the violent changes in temperature arising from the first method. In the interest of speed the rapid method is usually the better and should only be avoided if the contents are very fragile like vegetables, soft fruits, rice, etc. What normally happens when pressure is reduced rapidly is that there is a turbulence inside the cooker. Delicate foods and large quantities of liquids would be upset, but most solid foods would be unharmed.

Do not try to remove the lid before pressure is reduced. In most cases it will be impossible anyway.

COOKING SEVERAL ITEMS SIMULTANEOUSLY

Since cooking by pressure steaming means that particles of food need not be touching or have their juices conveyed to each other by liquid, you can easily cook several items together. If they have different cooking times put in the longest-cooking item first, cook for a short while, reduce pressure, add the next ingredient, raise pressure again and begin timing. Thus if you are cooking whole new potatoes, cauliflowers in quarters, and spinach, you would —

    1. Load up with potatoes (cooking time 8 minutes) and pressure cook.
    2. Four minutes later, depressurize, load up with cauliflower (cooking time 4 minutes), pressure cook, and
    3. Three minutes after that, depressurize, load up with spinach (cooking time 1 minute), pressure cook for 1 minute, and
    4. Depressurize and serve.

In fact this is as complicated as it is ever likely to be! (See p. 65)

A FEW QUESTIONS AND ANSWERS

WHAT TYPES OF HEAT SOURCE CAN BE USED?
Almost any.
    1. GAS. The flame should be as high as possible while bringing to pressure and should then be lowered until the cooker is just muttering over.
    2. ELECTRICITY. For a solid hot plate, switch the plate to high to bring to pressure and, if cooking time is less than 15 minutes, switch off and place the cooker on the edge of the plate as it cools down naturally. When the plate has

cooled down a little, the cooker can be moved back to cover the plate completely.

For a radiant plate, start high in order to bring to pressure and then reduce to simmer when pressure has been reached.

3. SOLID FUEL. Follow the instructions given for solid hot plates above.

4. BUTANE (CALOR) STOVES normally do not generate as much heat as a mains gas stove so bringing to pressure will take a little longer. You should be able to reduce the flame once pressure has been reached.

5. OPEN FIRES. These need watching carefully as they vary a great deal in their heat output. A fresh damp log will temporarily lower the heat of a camp fire or barbecue. In general, start on a high heat, and once pressure is achieved, keep the appliance muttering. Watch your fire carefully so that the cooker neither starts boiling too rapidly nor depressurizes when you don't want it to.

WHEN DO YOU ADD AND ADJUST SEASONING?

Before and after cooking time. Since pressure cooking uses far less liquid than ordinary cookery, any seasoning you use will be less diluted by the end of cooking time, so you use quite a bit less. In pressure steaming, using the trivet, you can add seasonings (salt, pepper and spices) and herbs before cooking starts. Remember that dried herbs are far more concentrated than fresh ones, but that they need rubbing in order to activate them.

In pressure boiling, when you are cooking without the trivet and placing the food in a liquid such as stock, it is best to season first but to leave the herbs till after. Herbs can't tolerate prolonged high temperatures – the aromatic oils that provide the flavour simply get dispersed or chemically broken down.

For cooking periods in excess of 10 to 15 minutes I usually prefer to take the pressure off a little before the correct cooking time is up, open up the pan and then add herbs and check the seasoning by tasting, using a spoon. I then finish off with ordinary cooking in the open pan, so that I have perfect control. This method takes only a little longer.

If you are cooking with some of the more exotic additives used in vegetarian cooking like garam masala, *miso*, other soy derivatives or sesame oil, then these should be added at the very last moment when the dish is actually cooling down.

WHAT TYPE OF PRESSURE COOKER SHOULD ONE BUY?

Buy the biggest you can reasonably afford. The bigger ones take no longer to cook food than the smaller ones. A very small one is useful only because of its portability if you are carrying a back-pack. The very big ones are used largely by people interested in preserving, canning and jam making. If you intend to do bottling or jam making or make steamed puddings, a variable pressure control is a definite asset. Buy a cooker by a well-known manufacturer so that you can be sure to get spare parts and service facilities. Some people have more than one pressure cooker – they are very useful and not that expensive!

ARE THERE ANY EXTRA ITEMS OF EQUIPMENT?

Choose from the following:

1. A timer, if you haven't one already. A pinger or buzzer is best.

2. An extra set of separators.

3. An extra trivet so that you can stack food inside the cooker.

4. A wire basket or pannier.

5. A few teacups for individual portions of sweets or infant foods.

6. A stainless steel or aluminium bowl for cooking large quantities of rice or for using, with the trivet but without the lid, as the basis of a double boiler.

7. Boilproof bowls (plastic or china) for puddings.

8. A casserole dish (make sure it fits inside and can be pulled out again conveniently).

9. Spoons, forks, ladles, strainers, mashers, all with

suitably long handles so that you can reach inside the cooker.

10. A seamless cake tin.

11. A strainer or mouli for soups and purees.

12. A blender, a good one with a heat-resistant goblet, helps a great deal with instant soups and stocks.

13. A meat thermometer – in general a very under-rated kitchen aid.

WHAT ADJUSTMENTS DO YOU MAKE FOR COOKING AT HIGH ALTITUDE?

Once you are 600 metres (2000 feet) above sea level, you should add one minute to each period of pressure-cooking time for each 300 metres (1000 feet) above sea level. This is because atmospheric pressure drops the higher one gets, and with it the boiling point of liquids decreases too. You have to compensate by increasing cooking time. At 2200 metres (7000 feet) water boils at 93 °C (199 °F). If you are climbing very high mountains, then you will need to have the valve on the cooker adjusted; write to the manufacturers and make enquiries.

CARING FOR THE COOKER

Keep your appliance clean and sweet. Before using it wash it out with hot soapy water and after each use wash thoroughly. Do *not* use washing soda, especially with aluminium models, as it reacts chemically with the metal.

Always inspect the escape vent beneath the pressure valve to make sure it has not become clogged. Follow the maker's instructions about inspecting the sealing gasket and the safety plug periodically.

After cleaning, it is preferable that the appliance should be left to dry or dried with a cloth. Do not put it away while it is still damp. Store with the lid on *upside down*. If you store the pressure cooker sealed up, mustiness will occur.

Aluminium vessels tend to pick up stains from food that is

cooked in them. The stains are not harmful, but are unsightly. Periodically boil up some vinegar, dilute solution of cream of tartar, lemon juice or other *very* mild acid with which to remove the stains. From time to time you can use a pan scourer or soap-filled steel-wool pads, but don't do this too frequently as you could leave small pits in the metal which will merely collect small fragments of stain all over again. Pits can be smoothed out with wet-and-dry papers. Teflon models of course should be less likely to pick up stains and should never be scoured.

One tip sometimes offered is that, before using for the first time, you season the pan by boiling a dilute milk and water mixture in it for 5 minutes or so. I am not personally convinced that this has any effect; on the other hand it doesn't do any harm. You can attempt to make your pressure cooker non-stick by using a proprietary non-stick aerosol: usually this involves spraying on a special chemical and then baking it on in the oven. I once did this with a pressure cooker, but the do-it-yourself method is less effective than the factory product – inevitably the trivet and separators cause scratching. The solid PTFE, if it comes off, is not harmful or poisonous. You simply have to recoat, if you think it worth while.

The outside of the cooker needs little attention; but remember that aluminium does not improve if it stands too long in soapy water – you could lose the shiny mirror finish. Don't let carbon deposits from gas or open fires accumulate on the outside.

If the cooker has over-cooked and has accidentally boiled dry or the safety valve has 'blown', check:

1. The safety valve and replace if necessary.
2. The gasket, by filling the appliance with a small amount of water, sealing, and watching for escapes of steam along the edges of the lid. Renew the gasket if necessary.
3. The bottom of the pan. Under extreme conditions of heat the base of the pan may bulge and distort. In that

event, do not use the pan any further but see if the manufacturer can service it. If the pan has a distorted base, then
the food will be heated unevenly and troubles of all sorts
will multiply.

A SUMMARY OF STEP-BY-STEP PROCEDURE

1. Prepare the food in the usual way. Small pieces cook
more rapidly than larger ones. Place in cooker on the trivet
(if the method so requires). Season now or at the finish.

2. Fill the cooker no more than two-thirds to prevent
clogging safety valve. Half fill the cooker if cooking with
liquids.

3. Add amount of water called for. Minimum of 140 *ml*
($\frac{1}{4}$ *pt*) plus 140 *ml* for every 15 minutes of pressure-cooking
time or part thereof.

4. Seal down lid according to instructions.

5. Place on high heat with steam vent open until steam
can be seen and heard coming through the vent.

6. Close pressure valve by placing weights or flipping
valve.

7. Reduce heat so that cooker mutters or indicator is just
visible. You are now cooking at the required pressure and
cooking will be maintained at low heat. Excessive heat will
disperse moisture too rapidly.

8. Start timing, keeping a careful watch.

9. When cooking time is up, reduce pressure either by
plunging cooker into cold water or, if the food is very
delicate, by allowing the cooker to cool naturally.

10. Open steam vent or remove weight to break vacuum.

11. Remove the lid. Do not attempt to remove the lid
while there is still pressure in the pan. (N.B. One or two
models are specially designed to let you do this: follow the
instructions carefully.)

12. Season or dress. If necessary complete cooking at
normal temperature and pressure. Remove food and serve.

THE RECIPES

In the next chapters of this book, which follow the usual
'menu' order of foods and dishes, I have followed a set
pattern:

1. BASIC METHOD AND TIMINGS. Usually I will cover not
only fresh food but also frozen, dried and freeze-dried.
Dried foods are those that have had their moisture taken
away from them naturally, by exposure to the sun, like
pulses. Freeze-dried (dehydrated) foods have been treated
to a rapid freezing technique and include things like 'instant'
dried peas, peppers, onions and so forth. Usually dried foods
take longer to reconstitute than freeze-dried ones.

2. TABLES

3. STANDARD FAVOURITE RECIPES.

4. SPECIAL METHODS OF COOKING including nutritional
recommendations.

5. MORE ADVENTUROUS RECIPES which you may like to
try or which will inspire you to adapt and invent your own.

Good cooking begins with good buying. Pressure cooking
can sometimes rescue slightly stale or 'old' food, but the
best results, as with the best of conventional cookery, come
from fresh, good ingredients. Buy clear, lively looking
vegetables, properly hung meat and firm fish.

Timing is for cooking under pressure, after proper
preparation, and begins when the cooker has been brought
to the right internal temperature and pressure. Unless
otherwise stated, this is at 15 *lb* (H), the normal operating
level.

What governs cooking time most of all is the speed of
heat and steam penetration. Small pieces cook more rapidly
than big ones. It is not the total weight of the ingredient but
the size of the individual pieces that counts: 2 *kg* (4½ *lb*)
of carrots thinly sliced, diced or cut into matchsticks
(allumettes) will cook more rapidly than a single carrot,
whole and uncut, weighing 250 *g* (9 *oz*). Make all the
portions of any one ingredient roughly the same size.

Usually only pieces of meat and fish that are served entire (and of course cooked whole) are timed by weight.

Adjust all cooking times slightly for personal preference.* Some people prefer their vegetables crisp (*al dente*) while others like them plump and juicy; the latter result takes a little more cooking time – you'll soon learn.

I think it is worth paying a little attention to the final appearance of the food. The saving in cooking time gives you more time to cut up the vegetables into nice-looking pieces and shapes – carrots can become circles, ellipses, long thin sticks; celery can be cut into comma-shapes. The extra effort required is minimal, the effect on the final appearance on the serving plate dramatic. Quick recipes don't mean that the food has to be sloppy or unattractive.

Most of the recipes are for four people unless otherwise stated.

* Tefal cookers operate at a lower temperature and pressure than others. Compare the timing in their instruction book with the ones here.

3: SOUPS AND STOCKS

I really can't remember when I last made a soup merely by opening an aluminium-foil pack or tin can – and that isn't just cookery writer's snobbery. There simply hasn't been any point; not only are home-produced soups vastly better in every respect, but with a pressure cooker they need take hardly any longer to fabricate than the so-called 'convenience' versions.

Soups need not be the thin, ghostly apologies we are used to; they are marvellous appetizers when taken as clear hot liquids at the beginning of a meal, clearing the taste-buds for the things to come. They can provide a meal in themselves when thickened-up with vegetables and meat chunks and with croutons floating on them. They can be used as an instant restorative after hard physical work, exposure to cold weather, or illness – the hot fluid rapidly warms the body and the constituents are usually easily digested. The Chinese have broth at the end of a meal – to clear the mouth and aid settling the stomach.

Soups can be made from all manner of scraps that would normally be thrown away. Most of the costs of commercially packaged soups go into the aluminium foil or the tin can and the colourful wrapping; then there is the advertising the food-processor has to expend in order to get you to buy his product rather than his rivals', the costs of distribution, warehousing and the retailer's mark-up. Precious little of what you pay goes into the food itself.

Normally soup-making in the home, particularly if it involves meat, is a long process. The pressure cooker, optionally joined by the blender, has changed all this. No single category of food illustrates the versatility of the pressure cooker as well, or the variety of ways in which it can be used.

The pressure cooker can make you meat soups in 7 or 8

minutes, vegetable soups in 5 minutes; it can produce
first-rate meat stock in 40 to 50 minutes, and even a marrow-
bone stock in 2 hours (against 12 hours by other methods).
You can have clear soups and thick ones – and you can
try your hand at unusual fish soups and even ones based on
fruit (a particular favourite of mine). Soups can be hot, cold
or jellied.

INSTANT SOUPS

Clear Chicken Soup   3–4 minutes

*Pre-cooked chicken pieces in bite-size, chicken stock (or good
quality cubes) to make 1 l (1¾ pts). Onion finely diced, carrot
finely diced. Handful of rice or broken noodles. Scraps of
vegetable tops (e.g. outer cabbage leaves, brussels tops,
cauliflower, celery; but not too many different ones). Seasoning. Chopped parsley for garnish.*

1. Use cooker without trivet. Bring stock gently to boil.
2. Throw in solid ingredients and let liquid boil again.
3. Close lid, let steam build up and escape steadily
through vent. Pressurize, reduce temperature so that cooker
is just ticking over and cook for 3 to 4 minutes.
4. Depressurize by cooling carefully under a tap. Open
lid. Add salt and pepper and perhaps parsley to taste. Serve.

Slightly-less-instant-but-better Clear Chicken Soup
3–4 minutes

Use the same ingredients plus 1 *tablespoon of oil*.

1. Use cooker without trivet. Heat oil in bottom and let
carrots and onions 'sweat' for a bit. The onion should
become clear, not brown. Remove from heat.
2. Carefully pour stock over sweated carrots and onion,

replace on heat and bring to boil. Add rice or noodles and vegetable scraps. Return to boil. Close lid. Bring to steam-escape point. Add weight/valve. Bring to pressure. Reduce heat to make cooker tick over and cook for 2 minutes.

3. Remove from heat. Cool to depressurize. Open lid. Add chicken pieces and close lid. Bring up to pressure again and pressure cook for 2 more minutes.

4. Depressurize as before. Open lid and add seasonings as before. Serve.

The first recipe gives quite acceptable results, but the extra trouble taken with the second makes a marked difference. Frying the onion and carrot first gives a much stronger base to the broth, and by delaying the addition of the cooked chicken pieces you ensure that, while they become thoroughly warmed-up (all that is called for), there is no chance that they become over-cooked or the slightest bit mushy or stringy.

Clear Brown Vegetable Soup   5 minutes

Brown stock or cube to 1 l (1¾ pts). 3 rashers of streaky bacon. Onions, carrots, turnips, finely diced. 1 tablespoon flour. Celery pieces, skinned tomatoes (or tinned tomatoes, or dilute puree). Bay leaf or bouquet garni sachet. Salt, pepper.

1. Cut bacon into very small pieces and cook gently in base until all the fat has run out. Add onion, carrots and turnips, and fry until a golden brown. It doesn't matter if the bacon starts looking very crisp. Keep pieces moving on base to prevent sticking. Add flour and let it turn gently brown, but do not burn.

2. Add stock carefully, and then other ingredients, including bouquet garni. Don't put in too many distinctive vegetable scraps. Heat till boiling. Skim lightly with a spoon if necessary. Cover and pressure cook for 5 minutes. Depressurize, preferably by allowing the cooker to cool

itself. Remove bouquet garni or bay leaf. Correct seasoning.
Serve.

Thick Brown Vegetable Soup   **5 minutes**

Use the same ingredients as above plus 2 *medium-size unpeeled potatoes*. Proceed exactly as above except that, before
using the stock, place stock mixture in blender, turn it on
and drop in the potatoes, rough cut. The whole effect will
look like a dirty snow-storm. When you add the stock
and proceed as before, the potato will cook almost instantly
and form a very effective thickener.

Lentil Soup   **20 minutes**

1 *large onion*, 1 *carrot*, 2 *leeks* (*all diced*), *bacon bone scraps*
(from any grocer who cuts his own bacon), *celery*, 125 g
(4 *oz*) *lentils* (soaked for an hour), 1 *l water* (1¾ *pts*), *bouquet
garni sachet*, 1 *tablespoon margarine*, 1 *tablespoon flour*,
140 *ml milk* (¼ *pt*), *assorted root vegetables* or *boiling sausage*.
(Instead of ordinary tap water, you could use vegetable
water.)

1. Place diced vegetables, bacon scraps, water, soaked
lentils and bouquet garni in cooker. Bring to boil, close lid
and cook for 20 minutes.
2. In the meantime prepare a classic plain white sauce
with the margarine, flour and milk – heat the margarine in a
saucepan so that it begins to dissolve, add the flour, stirring
all the time to make a white paste (what the French call a
roux) and then, before the colour changes, slowly add the
milk so that the whole mixture becomes a smooth, thickish
liquid. Cook for a few minutes.
3. Take contents of pressure cooker, remove bacon bone
scraps, then puree or mash contents. If you have a blender,
do it in that. Add white sauce and blend thoroughly. Check
seasoning.

4. Return contents to open pressure cooker and add either root vegetable scraps or boiling sausage. Close lid and cook for 1 to 2 minutes under pressure.

5. Depressurize, remove lid and serve.

Alternative Lentil Soup   **20 minutes**

Ingredients as above, plus 1 *tablespoon of oil* and 1 *tablespoon of curry powder*.

Heat oil in bottom of cooker, add curry spices, and, as they sizzle, add onion, carrot and leeks. Fry gently to impregnate. Then add water and lentils and proceed as before – this will give a mildly curried bite. You could also add —

(a) *tomato puree* to give the soup a redder colour and a sweeter taste.

(b) *a smidgin of chili sauce* or *Tabasco* right at the end to give a hot undertaste.

(c) *a few drops of sesame oil* (from oriental and health food shops) just before serving to give a nutty flavour.

All these soups will be more or less familiar. You can make an instant meat soup by using the chicken soup formula, but substituting a meat or brown stock cube and scraps of pre-cooked meat. You could make a thick tomato soup by using the vegetable soup formula but basing it on chicken (white stock) and adding tomatoes and a thickener like the blended raw potato or the white sauce. Leave out the tomato and put in more asparagus and you have cream of asparagus; substitute mushroom and you have the beginnings of cream of mushroom; and so on.

REAL SOUP

You should be able to get a fair variety of soups simply by manipulating the ingredients but 'real' soups are even better.

They take a little more trouble but only a little more time. Thanks to the pressure cooker, very high-quality home soup-making is entirely feasible, even for people who haven't got all day for the preparations – and once you have started liking 'real' soup, you won't be able to bear the ready-made alternatives.

Soup consists of up to three elements:

a base or stock – usually brown or white meat, fish or vegetable;

a thickener (if required) which can be flour or corn-starch, potato, bean, grain, egg, cream;

solid ingredients – which can include everything under the sun.

STOCKS

The French for stock is *fond* or base and every classic cookbook will tell you that the basis of a good soup is a good stock. Stocks are made by the intensive cooking of scraps of food-bones, tough meat, fish flesh, vegetables. The aim of the cooking process is to produce a strong-tasting fluid, low perhaps on vitamins, but high in concentrated minerals and certain proteins. A good stock, or even an indifferent one, gives a bottom undertaste to soups that water simply can't provide and which cannot be added during a normal cooking process.

Most classic cookbooks start off by describing the foundation brown stock – made from meat scraps, bone and certain vegetables. I'll follow precedent because there is a certain logic in doing so, but I also feel that some readers may think it a little unrealistic to open a book about a relatively instant cooking method by describing an hour-long process. Other readers may like to feel reassured that I frequently avoid making meat stocks for precisely that reason. I have three recommendations:

1. Use stock cubes. But buy good-quality ones – free from mustiness and a floury taste. You need two sorts –

white (chicken) and brown (meat or beef). Try several brands before settling on one. I've experimented with the 'herb'-, 'onion'- and 'curry'-flavoured stock cubes available and haven't been impressed.

2. Rely on vegetable stock (see p. 40) which takes a far shorter time to prepare from scratch. Vegetable stocks usually don't have the lasting qualities of meat-based ones, which is why they tend to get relegated in the classic cookbooks. There are vegetable stock cubes and pastes on the market, but I have yet to find one which I like.

3. Get to like fish soups. Fish stock is quick and easy to prepare as well. Again, good fish stock cubes or powders are rare.

Foundation Meat Stock   **40–50 minutes**

1 *kg* (2 *lb*) *bones* (fresh or cooked). *Onions, carrots, celery, swedes, turnip* (not too much – it has an overpowering taste) *salt, pepper, mace, bay leaf.*

1. Wash the bones and chop finely.
2. Put in open cooker with 500 *ml* (1 *pt*) water, boil and skim off the scum that rises with a spoon or ladle.
3. Add vegetables and the herbs (don't use parsley or any herb that dislikes prolonged cooking). Half-fill with water (no more than half).
4. Close cooker, bring to pressure and cook for 30 minutes for pre-cooked bones, 45 minutes for fresh.
5. Reduce pressure, strain solids through sieve, then degrease* and cool.

---

* *Degreasing:* meats throw off a lot of fat when cooking. To remove grease while still hot, roll up a paper towel and mop the surface of the fluid, snipping off the end of the towel as it becomes soaked. Better, let the liquid cool thoroughly in a refrigerator (not a freezer) and the fat will float to the surface and solidify, when it can be scraped off with a big shallow spoon. You can buy special jugs which are supposed to help you, but I wouldn't bother.

6. The stock will probably be slightly jellied, which is a good sign.

7. On re-use, dilute with an equal quantity of water and heat. Add herbs, like parsley, sage, fresh or freshly rubbed. Adjust seasoning.

All stocks tend to concentrate flavour, so do not over-season or put too much in to begin with.

This stock will keep 3 to 4 days under refrigeration. After that it should be brought to the boil briefly and allowed to cool again to kill off bacteria. Without refrigeration, boil every day or so.

Freezer Foundation Stock   50 minutes

This, as the name implies, is specially formulated for freezer storage – it is more concentrated, has fewer additives and omits those that might decay early.

Bones, fresh or cooked; root vegetables (but not green vegetables). *No herbs. Pinch salt and pepper*.

1. Wash bones and chop fine. Salt any meat to assist the release of juices. Most cookers will take up to 2 *kg* (4½ *lb*) of meat and bones.

2. Cover with water (but no more than half-way up the pressure cooker wall). Boil and skim off scum.

3. Add vegetables and a bit of seasoning. If some water has boiled away, make up to half-full.

4. Bring to pressure. Cook 35 to 40 minutes for pre-cooked bones, 45 to 50 minutes for fresh bones and meat. Cool to reduce pressure.

5. Strain off solids. If you wish you could now return the fluid to the open pan for rapid boiling to reduce and further concentrate the fluid. Cool and degrease by skimming off solid fat.

6. Freeze. Keeping time is about three months.

7. On re-use this stock will need diluting by 2 or 3 times

as much water. Bring to boil for safety. Add vegetables at this point, pressure cooking green vegetables into the stock for 4 to 5 minutes.

Check seasoning.

Marrow Bone Stock   **2 hours**

Marrow bone. Water. No vegetables. No herbs. No salt.

1. Chop bones as small as possible.

2. Put into pan with $1\frac{1}{2}$ *l* (3 *pts*) of water but do not more than half-fill cooker. Bring to boil and skim off scum.

3. Cover, pressure cook for 2 hours, cool to reduce pressure. Strain bones. Degrease. (The fat is dripping and can be used for flavoursome frying – it even makes a good spread for bread or toast, but only if you are not very figure-conscious!)

4. Dilute before using. Add vegetables, seasoning and herbs with care.

Brown Stock   **40–50 minutes**

Use the same procedure as for Freezer Foundation Stock (p. 37) but start off with *a tablespoon of oil* or *butter* in the base of the pan, and fry some *finely diced onion* in it, including the *onion skin*. The onion should be allowed to become clear and then turn brown (as the sugar in it caramelizes and then begins to burn). Keep onion moving in base before adding the other ingredients as indicated before. The onion and especially the skin add a fine colour as well as taste. Instead of oil or butter you could use some scraps of *very streaky bacon* and heat them until all the fat is running out. You can then fry your onion in that. You will, of course, need less *salt* than in the original recipe.

Chicken Stock   **20–30 minutes**

Cooked or uncooked left-over chicken fragments, including skin, bones, neck, stomach, heart, but excluding too much liver. You could use a really old bird which would not be suitable for anything else.

1. Chop up meat and bones very finely. Add enough water to cover ingredients. Boil in open pan. Skim off scum.

2. Add more water to no more than half-full, depending on degree of concentration required. Pressure cook 20 minutes for cooked meat, 30 minutes for uncooked.

3. Depressurize, strain out solids, cool and degrease.

4. On re-use, dilute to taste (at least an equal amount of water), add parsley and other herbs, e.g. chervil, thyme, sage.

If you use an entire stewing hen, the pressure-cooking time is 40 minutes. This stock will keep 3 to 4 days in a refrigerator, after which it will need boiling up again. If a concentrated stock is required for freezing, omit all vegetables and use more meat. The vegetables are then added on re-use. The carrot is especially important as it gives sweetness and freshness to the fluid. Life of the freezer stock is three months.

White Stock   **25–35 minutes**

A white stock can also be made from *veal – using neck, knuckle and trimmings*. You can use these in conjunction with *chicken* if you wish. Pressure-cooking time is 25 to 35 minutes, depending on whether the meat is pre-cooked and the size of the pieces. It is often important that a white stock retains its colour. Careful skimming helps. For this reason also, when adding to a frying onion, the onion must merely be allowed to go transparent – it should not be allowed to brown. When white stock is added to a mixture of heated butter and flour (a *roux*) and slowly stirred in you get the classic *velouté* sauce which is often the basis of thick soups (see p. 43) and sauces for vegetables and meat dishes. If you add to a *velouté* sauce a small amount of warm cream you get a sauce supreme. Chicken supreme is cooked chicken pieces smothered in sauce supreme – it all fits in, doesn't it? (See p. 208.)

Vegetable Stock   **10 minutes**

Vegetable scraps – almost anything, especially potato peelings, lettuce, cabbage and cauliflower outer leaves, celery, roots (but go easy on strong tasters like *turnip*), *carrots* (for sweetness), *onion, broccoli tops, limp 'old' vegetables,* etc. *Salt, pepper, bouquet garni.*

1. Fill cooker base with scraps and water up to half-way mark. Use a greater proportion of water to solids if your vegetables are 'dryish' – either a bit old or mostly root. Bring to boil. Cover, pressure cook for 10 minutes. Cool at room temperature to reduce pressure. Remove bouquet garni.

2. For a thick soup – mash the remaining solids or put in a blender. For a clearer stock – strain.

3. All vegetable stocks should be carefully tasted at the end of cooking time. Adjust seasoning. Add crushed herbs like parsley, sage, chervil as the liquid cools. Occasionally one vegetable can become overpowering, particularly when the cooking time has been long. You'll soon develop a sense of what to avoid.

4. This stock will keep about 24 hours. On re-use: adjust seasoning. Adding *soy sauce* or *miso* (fermented soy paste – from health and oriental shops) will give a meatier taste. Adding *sesame oil* (from the same specialist outlets) will give a nutty taste. These additions are made right at the end of the cooking process – thus, if you are using the vegetable stock as the basis of a vegetable soup, you would cook your vegetable fragments in the vegetable stock for the appro-

priate period, depressurize, open up the lid and add the *miso* as the soup cools down and just before serving. (N.B. If you try *miso* you will need less salt, as the paste is already very salty.) You can add *grated cheese* at the end of the cooking period as well.

Brown Vegetable Stock   10 minutes

Ingredients as before plus one large diced onion, oil and 1 tablespoon of sugar. Tomato puree (optional).

1. Heat oil in base and turn into it the diced onion (which should include the skin) and the sugar. Fry until the onion and sugar caramelize and turn brown. (If you wish, you could add scraps of *ginger root* at the same time to give an oriental flavour.)

2. Then proceed as before. The onion colours the fluid as well as flavouring it. Tomato puree will make the result look redder and taste sweeter.

Fish Stock   15 minutes

Fish scraps, including head, tail, bones, skin (if not too scaly), but be wary of very strong-tasting or oily fish like mackerel, herring or mullet. Water to cover. Diced onion, carrot, leek, salt, pepper, lemon juice. Bay leaf and bouquet garni.

1. Wash fish and bring to boil in base of cooker. Remove scum, add vegetables, bring to boil, making sure that fluid does not more than half fill the cooker. Add bay leaf and bouquet garni, cover, bring to pressure and cook for 15 minutes.

2. Reduce pressure at room temperature. Strain off solids. Remove bay leaf and bouquet garni. Adjust seasoning. This stock should be used on the day on which it is made.

Basic Chinese Broth   **20–30 minutes**

Raw or cooked chicken or pork. Sugar, salt, sliced ginger root. Water.

1. Proceed as for chicken stock (see p. 39) but omit all the vegetables and replace with the ginger. This recipe gives a basis for a large number of Chinese soups; a small quantity of the broth, together with a trace of soy sauce, can be added to most quick stir-fry* dishes at the end of the cooking process.

How to Clarify a Meat Stock

It is often not necessary to clarify meat stocks unless you wish to make a special feature of a very clear appearance – as in classic consommé. However, here is the way to do it – the secret is never to let the soup boil; it must only simmer.

For every *litre of fluid* you need *one slightly beaten egg white* and a *crushed egg shell*. (Reserve the egg yolk for some other purpose.)

Let stock settle and add egg white and shells very carefully. Slowly heat up, avoiding any turbulence in the fluid. A thick crusty foam will form and in this you should clear a small opening to check that no boiling takes place. Simmer for 10 to 15 minutes and then remove from heat source. Push foam to one side and ladle out stock carefully, pouring

* Quick stir-fry is an often-used Chinese cooking technique. A small quantity of *cooking oil* is heated almost to smoking point in that frypan with a round bottom called a *wok*. The finely chopped ingredients – usually *thinly sliced meat* and *vegetables* and *bean shoots* – are then added bit by bit. They are rapidly cooked in the oil and then dragged to the side to let the oil drain while further pieces are cooked in the hot oil. Then all the pieces are returned to the centre. *Broth* and *soy sauce* are added. They turn to steam, fluffing up the food, which is then eaten.

it through a muslin cloth into a bowl while it is still hot. Cool and refrigerate. If the mixture boils up at all, cloudiness will result and you'll have to start all over again.

SOUP THICKENERS

If you want a thick soup there are various ways of achieving the desired result. The recipes which follow will give some practical applications, but here are the principal methods and the ways in which they are of use:

1. *Pureeing a thin soup.* You simply pass the entire fluid and the meat and vegetable fragments through a sieve or into a blender. If you decide to buy a blender, don't get the very cheapest sort – one with a heat-proof goblet will allow you to blend your soups straight from the cooker.

2. *Adding flour.* You can use any sort of ordinary (i.e. not self-raising) flour at the rate of 25 g to $\frac{1}{4}$ l (1 oz to $\frac{1}{2}$ pt) put in at the beginning of cooking time.

3. With a *roux* which is equal parts of butter or margarine and flour cooked into a white paste and then added. Or, if you add milk to the *roux* first to make a thickish fluid which is cooked for a few minutes thoroughly, you get a *velouté* or plain white sauce which is used for cream of tomato and cream of asparagus soups (see pp. 47–9).

4. The same results, with rather more ease, can be obtained from *cornstarch* (or *cornflour*) and also from *arrowroot*, neither of which are quite so prone to lumpiness as ordinary wheat flour. Flour acts as a binder for bean soups.

5. *Potato.* I referred to the 'dirty snow-storm' trick on p. 33. A medium-sized potato cut up and blended while still raw into a litre (2 *pts*) of water will make a very effective thickener. You can increase the amount of potato if you wish, but it bulks out in the cooking process. The effect, usually called *parmentier* in French cooking, gives a bulky reassuring sense to meat and vegetable soups. Potato and

leek soups are of course well known (see pp. 46–7). If you don't have a blender, the best thing to do is to use pre-cooked mashed potato which is then whisked into the soup with a fork either before or after the soup-cooking process. Alternatively, a single tablespoon of instant mashed potato in a half litre of hot soup will have the same effect.

6. *Egg*. This gives a very rich velvety finish to the soup. The egg is always added at the end of the cooking process – eggs heated above 70 °C or so will curdle. As the cooked soup is cooling down, whisk in the egg – white and yolk, if you wish. I like to place the soup in a blender, whizz it around and then drop in the egg which cooks instantly. Try it especially with a green vegetable soup.

7. *Cream*. Like egg, cream does not take kindly to being over-heated – protein hardens too rapidly. Cream can be whisked in lightly at the end of the process. One nice effect to go for is to ladle the soup into individual bowls and then set the liquid gently turning around inside the rim of the bowl. You pour thin cream onto the surface and it leaves a galactic spiral trace as it sinks into the soup.

8. *Grains*. Oatmeal and barley and rice can all be used as thickeners – the first two being familiar in many Scottish soup recipes. The right proportion is about 12 g per litre – 1 tablespoon to half a pint.

9. *Bean puree*. A lentil soup will lose its texture quite easily in the course of cooking, particularly if you are using the more common red split lentils as opposed to the green or brown varieties. The lentils can then be mashed or blended into the fluid.

Most thick soups are the better for having some contrasting solid ingredients as well – so if it is a vegetable soup, reserve some of the pieces while you mash the rest and add them afterwards. Alternatively you can add croutons – either tiny pieces of bread fried crisp or bits of streaky bacon almost burned. Coarse grated cheese of the Cheddar type can look attractive as well as taste good, and so can fresh-cut garnishes of herbs, parsley being the most popular.

CLEAR SOUPS

Chicken and Rice Soup   7 minutes

Chicken stock to 1 l (1¾ pts). Finely chopped onion, carrot. As much long-grain rice as you can easily cup in your hand. Nutmeg, parsley, salt and pepper.

Method A

Bring stock to boil in open pan. Add onion and carrot and grated nutmeg. Throw rice into boiling liquid and bring back to boil. Close pressure pan. Bring to pressure and cook for 7 minutes. Reduce pressure at room temperature. Season. Add parsley. Serve.

Method B

Lightly fry half the onion and half the carrot in a little fat or butter till clear. Don't let them burn or caramelize. Then add stock, bring to boil, add remainder of carrot and onion and proceed as in Method A.

Beef and Mushroom Soup   7 minutes

Beef stock to 1 l (1¾ pts), 2 tablespoons of margarine, butter or cooking oil, onion sliced in rings, 200 g (½ lb) of minced (ground) beef (or spun vegetable substitute),* 150 g (¼ lb) thin-sliced mushrooms. Salt, pepper, chopped parsley.

1. Heat oil in base of cooker and gently fry first the onion rings till they are transparent and then add the ground meat. The meat should end up looking brown and not grey. (Add garlic or garlic powder, or cayenne powder or chili powder if a *hot* result is wanted. Add a pinch of curry powder for a slightly Indian taste.) Stir to prevent sticking and burning. Add mushrooms a little later and fry and sweat gently.
2. Add the stock and seasoning. Bring to boil. Pressure cook for 7 minutes. Reduce pressure.

* See pp. 21–9 ff.

3. Taste and correct seasoning. Add tomato puree for a sweeter and fuller taste and for a redder final appearance. Correct seasoning again. Add parsley, chervil or basil (if tomato used).

4. Rice can be added at the beginning of the recipe or noodles after 2 minutes of cooking time to add bulk. In this way the dish can become a complete meal.

Avgolemnon Soup   10 minutes

1 l (1¾ pts) of strong vegetable stock, 2 eggs, 1 lemon, 60 g (2 oz) long-grain rice, salt and pepper.

1. Make a vegetable broth (see p. 40) and at the same time cook the handful of rice in the fluid. By the time the vegetable stock is ready the rice will have cooked in it. Drain rice, blend stock smooth, and then recombine. The stock should have plenty of potato in it which should of course be pulped.

2. Beat the eggs in the juice of the lemon. Take a small portion of the cooked stock and add to the beaten eggs. Stir vigorously and then return the whole to the main pot. Heat the open pressure cooker for a few minutes so that egg mixture is smoothly melded into the broth. Do not overheat or the egg will curdle.

This is a classic Greek soup.

THICK SOUP

Potato Soups   7–8 minutes

Chicken stock to 1½ l (2¼ pts), 1 medium leek fine-chopped, 1 medium onion fine-chopped, 1 medium carrot fine-chopped, 600 g (1¼ lb) potatoes cut up fine,* 50 g (2 oz) butter or fat, 1 clove of garlic, salt, pepper; optional: cream.

* If a white potato soup is wanted remove the peel; if you want a health-giving soup leave the peel on.

1. Heat fat and sauté the garlic, leeks, onions and carrots until the leeks are soft, do not brown. Add the stock and potatoes.* Bring to boil. Cover pan. Pressure cook for 7 to 8 minutes.

2. Cool and depressurize, open pan. Adjust seasoning. For a richer taste add a small quantity of cream.

This is a very basic soup which tastes good in itself. The suggestions on p. 34 for additives like Tabasco, chili, sesame oil will all work well. The final dish should look white and clean unless you have used potato peelings. A finer finish to the soup can be obtained by blending for a couple of minutes. The appearance of the soup is aided immensely by the use of a garnish like chopped parsley or chopped chives.

A number of interesting variants are possible using carrot, cucumber, peas, parsley, watercress, sorrel and mushroom and indeed any vegetable that happens to come to hand. The general method is to take a small portion of the finished soup and leave on one side. Take the carrot, cucumber, peas, etc. and sauté together with a small amount of celery in butter until soft. Add the now sautéed vegetables to the reserved portion of the soup, whisk it in and then add to the main portion of the soup. Simmer in the open pan for five minutes, or if you prefer close the pan and pressure cook for 2 minutes. Marjoram goes well with a carrot soup; dill well with a cucumber soup; some pea soups are improved by the addition of a little sugar to the sautéed mixture; fried onion may be added to broccoli and to watercress; paprika to the sorrel and parsley. The possibilities for experimentation are almost endless. But don't go wild!

Basic Cream of Vegetable Soup   7–8 minutes

1 *l* (1¾ *pts*) *of water or vegetable water*, 1 *diced potato and assorted scraps to make stock or* 1 *l* (1¾ *pts*) *vegetable stock*.

* If you have a blender use the 'dirty snow-storm' formula (see p. 33).

4 *large carrots* or 2 *to* 3 *large onions,* or *cut-up celery stick,* or 2 *green peppers,* or 125 *g* (4 *oz*) *mushrooms,* or half *a cauliflower cut up,* or *corn from* 1 *cob* (or *small packet or tin*), or 6 *asparagus spears,* 2 *tablespoons of oil, butter* or *margarine,* 2 *tablespoons of flour,* 250 *ml* ($\frac{1}{2}$ *pt*) *milk, water* or *vegetable stock. Salt and pepper. Herbs. Additives.*

1. Prepare the vegetable stock in the usual way. This will take 8 to 10 minutes of pressure-cooking time, or a little bit more if the pieces are large. Use the potato in the 'dirty snow-storm' way or mash the potatoes as much as possible before adding.
2. Sauté the vegetable which is to form the basis of the soup by heating in a small amount of oil.
3. Prepare the white sauce by cooking the flour in the oil for 3 or 4 minutes but avoid browning; then add milk or vegetable stock. Different flavours can be obtained by using different oils – for example a soy oil or a safflower oil or an olive oil as opposed to the usual corn oil. And a different flavour again can be obtained by using a different flour. In addition to white flour or cornstarch you could use cracked wheat, barley, rye or buckwheat as available or even cornmeal which would give a yellow finish.
4. Combine the heated stock, the sautéed vegetables and the sauce and simmer for a few minutes. You can blend together all the ingredients and get a smooth finish. If you reserve a small amount of the chosen vegetable, preferably cut up into attractive shapes like rings, or half moons or matchsticks, this can then be added as a form of garnish. Other garnishes that can be used would include grated cheese, green onion (scallions), chives, parsley, watercress. The soup can be made richer by the addition of a small amount of pouring (single) cream added in the attractive galactic spiral way mentioned on p. 44. Ground celery seed or celery salt sometimes makes an additional interesting taste for certain otherwise rather bland vegetable soups.

In addition to the vegetables specified above you could also use lettuce, mustard greens – that's the top of the mustard plant – bits of cabbage, brussels sprouts and of course the very popular tomato.

Cream of Chicken Soup   7–8 minutes

The same thickening technique can be used on a chicken soup: while a clear chicken soup (see p. 45) is cooking prepare a butter-and-flour thickener using equal quantities of butter (or margarine) and flour – say 2 tablespoons each. Cook for 2 or 3 minutes till blended. Keep the result white-looking – the mix must not burn. Add 140 *ml* (¼ *pt*) of milk, and mix to make the basic white sauce. Having cooked the chicken soup in the cooker, add white sauce and correct seasoning. Add herbs like parsley to taste. To give textural contrast and bulk add some small pieces of fried chicken. As with a lot of soups it's better to keep a number of small chicken pieces to float around. A chicken and tomato combination can be very pleasing but there should not be too much tomato as it has a very strong taste all of its own. Similarly leek and celery in small quantities go well with chicken.

Cream of Red Meat Soups

These are not nearly as successful. Beef seems to work much better with grains and oatmeal as in Scotch broth or with potato (see below, pp. 58–9).

Minestrone Soup (To serve 8)   20 minutes

1 *kg* (2 *lb*) *mixed green vegetables including shredded cabbage, celery, peas, soaked beans,* 250 *g* (½ *lb*) *shin beef or other cheap cut,* 1½ *l* (3 *pts*) *of stock* (*meat or vegetable*), 250 *g* (½ *lb*) *rice or spaghetti. Seasoning. Parmesan cheese.*

1. Dice meat and vegetables. Place in stock. Bring to boil. Skim if necessary.

2. Bring to pressure and pressure cook for 20 minutes.

3. Add rice or spaghetti and cook rapidly in open cooker. Adjust seasoning.

4. Serve with Parmesan cheese.

A more 'authentic' feel to the soup can be obtained by adding a small quantity of tomatoes and by adding upwards of two cloves of garlic. There is no definitive recipe for minestrone!

Cheese and Onion Soup   **10 minutes**

1 l (1¾ pts) vegetable stock or water, 1 tablespoon of flour, 4 large Spanish onions, 125 g (4 oz) butter, piece of bay leaf, lemon juice, grated Gruyère cheese (or Cheddar for a stronger cheese taste), thyme, sage, paprika, salt, pepper, Worcestershire sauce and Tabasco or chili.

1. Using all the butter except for one tablespoon, sauté the sliced onions in the base of the cooker until they go first clear and then turn brown. If you keep the skin with the onions you will get a deeper brown appearance more rapidly. Pour over the vegetable stock or water and include the bay leaf and lemon juice. Bring to pressure and pressure cook for 10 minutes.

2. Combine the remaining tablespoon of butter with the tablespoon of flour in a separate saucepan and cook well. Allow to turn slightly brown. At the end of cooking time open up the pressure pan, remove the bay leaf and mix in the butter and flour mixture. (It might be a little easier if you sop a little of the cooking fluid from the pressure pan into the saucepan containing the flour and butter and mix together first.) Now add your other herbs – the thyme, the sage, some paprika powder, also salt and pepper. Seal the pan again and cook for a further minute. Open the pan and check seasoning. At this stage if you wish you may add

Worcestershire sauce and Tabasco or chili. Now add the cheese and stir until melted. It's really a matter of individual choice how much you put in.

To serve:

1. In the bottom of each soup bowl put a slice of thin fried bread. Pour the soup over and sprinkle with more grated cheese.

2. Put soup into each bowl and then place a slice of processed cheese (it need not be of the same variety as you've put into the body of the dish) over the top of the bowl so that it covers it. Place the bowl under the grill briefly so that the cheese melts and turns stringy and forms a type of crust. A rather flashy but very effective result!

Mulligatawny Soup   7 minutes

Pieces of cooked chicken (could be left over from making stock), *chicken stock to make* 1 *l* (1¾ *pts*), *big handful of rice*, 2 *tablespoons of margarine or butter*, 2 *tablespoons of flour*, 1 *cooking apple*, 1 *medium-sized onion*, 1 *tablespoon of curry powder, juice of* ½ *lemon*, 2 *tablespoons of cream, salt, pepper, bouquet garni;* optional: *garam masala.*

1. Bring the stock to boil. Add the rice, seasoning, bouquet garni and pressure cook for 7 minutes. Reduce pressure at room temperature.

2. During cooking, melt the margarine or butter (or you could use *ghee* which is Indian clarified butter). Fry together the curry powder, diced onion and chopped apple (you can add a carrot if you wish). The mix should be kept on the move. Be careful not to let the curry spices burn otherwise they will become bitter. Add the flour after 5 minutes and cook the mix thoroughly for a further 5 minutes. Do not allow too much discolouring and certainly no burning.

3. Lift the bouquet garni from the stock. Strain the rice and keep warm on one side. Add the stock to the curried apple and onion, slowly stirring all the time.

4. Add the cooked chicken pieces and the lemon juice. Adjust the seasoning. Bring to boil, skim if necessary. Throw in rice. Add cream and a pinch of garam masala if you wish. A final check on the seasoning and serve.

Thick Spinach Soup   5–6 minutes

½ *kg* (1 *lb*) *fresh spinach finely chopped,* 2 *tablespoons of green onions finely minced,* 1 *clove garlic,* 3 *tablespoons of butter, a pinch of nutmeg,* 1 *l* (1¾ *pts*) *of chicken or beef stock,* 250 *ml* (½ *pt*) *thin cream* (use half pouring cream and half milk), *sugar, salt, pepper, lemon juice,* 1 *hard-boiled egg finely chopped, paprika.*

1. Sauté the spinach, green onions and garlic in the butter. The spinach will wilt rapidly.
2. Add the stock and the nutmeg. Bring to boil. Cover and pressure cook for 5 to 6 minutes. Puree the results in a blender or pass through a mouli. Add cream and the seasonings. Adjust to taste. Add the egg and paprika.

The paprika or chili is important because it provides an interesting contrast to what turns out to be a surprisingly bland soup. Instead of the cooked egg you can pour in one or two raw eggs while the blender is pureeing the spinach fragments. This will give an even richer and smoother taste. By way of contrast, you can add cut-up bits of streaky bacon that have been crisp-fried to make croutons. It provides an interesting taste as well as crispness. The cream can of course be put to decorative use by swirling in at the very last minute. A similar soup could be made with chervil. And if you are very experienced you may like to attempt an experiment with dandelions. If you do so, choose your dandelion leaves with great care. They should be young and fresh otherwise they will be extremely bitter and it may be necessary to add a certain amount of sugar or carrot puree to sweeten and lighten the result. Good luck!

FISH SOUPS

North Sea Soup   5 minutes

2 *cutlets or large steaks of cod or haddock or any other white fish,* 1 *l* (1¾ *pts*) *of fish stock,* 1 *glass white wine;* optional: 3 *tablespoons of tomato puree,* 2 *tablespoons of flour blended with* 125 *ml* (¼ *pt*) *milk, salt, pepper, parsley.*

1. Place the fish stock and the seasoning in the cooker. Bring to pressure. Cook for 5 minutes. Allow the pressure to reduce at room temperature.

2. Lift out the fish. Remove the skin and bone and cut the fish into large flakes. Strain the liquid, stir in the wine, tomato puree if desired, and the blended flour. Return to the heat and cook for 1 minute.

3. The soup ends up being rather smooth and not thick. Correct seasoning.

Fish soups gain from the addition of fennel or caraway or chives or dill.

Instead of flour one can use a small potato for thickening and this will give an altogether more filling result.

Smoked Haddock Soup   6 minutes

½ *l* (¾ *pt*) *of fish stock (or chicken stock if you prefer),* 500 *g* (1 *lb*) *smoked haddock,* 1 *onion,* 400 *ml* (¾ *pt*) *of milk,* 125 *ml* (¼ *pt*) *double cream, salt, pepper, parsley.*

1. Skin the fish by placing in a shallow dish and pouring over boiling water. Remove the bones and break up the flesh neatly.

2. Place chopped onion and flaked fish in the bottom of the pan. Pour over the stock and bring to the boil. Skim. Pressure cook for 6 to 7 minutes. Blend or puree the fish and put back in the pan. Pour over milk and heat through,

seasoning with salt and pepper. (You should remember that haddock is salty already so go easy.) Blend in the cream lightly. Serve in bowls garnished with a few prawns.

You can sharpen up the soup either with the use of cayenne pepper or by adding a single anchovy before cooking time. This soup can be served chilled in hot weather.

Red and White Soup   5 minutes

2 pieces of cod, fresh haddock or other white fish, 1 l (1¾ pts) fish stock, small glass of white wine, 3 tablespoons of tomato puree or 2 large canned tomatoes, 2 tablespoons of flour blended in 125 ml (¼ pt) milk, salt, pepper, parsley for garnish.

1. Flake fish lightly. Place in stock with seasoning. Pressure cook for 5 minutes. Allow pressure to reduce at room temperature.
2. Lift out a few large pieces of fish and keep on one side. Place the remainder of fish in a blender (or pass through sieve). Add puree of canned tomatoes together with the blended flour and milk. Add wine. Return to the pan. Bring very rapidly to a simmer and cook for 1 minute in the open pan. If the soup appears to be too thick add a little more milk, or fish stock.
3. Correct seasoning. Serve in individual cups. Garnish with the portion of fish saved, and parsley. The liquid part of the soup should be a pleasing reddish-pink colour, and the reserved fish should be clean and white.

Mediterranean Soup   12–15 minutes

250 g (½ lb) each of three different sorts of fish (e.g. 1 white fish, sardines, eels, squid, red mullet, whiting), 1 onion, 2 cloves garlic, very large pinch of mixed herbs, 2 tomatoes

(or *tomato puree*), 4 *tablespoons of butter, pinch of saffron,*
$1\frac{1}{2}$ *l* ($2\frac{1}{2}$ *pts*) *of water or fish stock,* 2 *tablespoons of salt,*
pinch of pepper, handful of pasta, handful of stale bread
crusts.

1. Fry the chopped onion lightly in the butter so that it
becomes clear but not brown. Add tomatoes or tomato
puree, then the garlic. Finally sauté the fish in the mix.
Simmer for 8 to 10 minutes in the open pan in order to
break the fish down.

2. Add the assorted seasonings – salt, pepper, mixed herbs,
saffron. Pour over the stock. Seal pan and pressure cook for
approximately 12 to 15 minutes.

3. At end of cooking time mash the soup including any
bones. Pass through blender if available. Then return to
pan and bring to simmer. Add the pasta (e.g. vermicelli) and
pressure cook for a further 2 minutes. The soup can be
served with the toasted bread crusts rubbed with garlic.

Quite obviously this outline recipe can be used in a number
of different ways!

If a reasonable proportion of shellfish is included,
e.g. shrimp, clams, mussels, the recipe is known as
bouillabaisse.

You can also adapt the recipe using freshwater fish like
bream, tench, perch, trout, carp, in which case the soup is
known as a *matelote.*

If you add milk and a couple of small potatoes you then
have a *chowder*!

Bisque   10 minutes

The secret of bisques is to cook very gently and briefly
and add the milk ingredient at the very last moment. You
can use this recipe with crawfish, lobster, clam, shrimp,
oyster, mussels or any other shellfish available.

½ *kg* (1 *lb*) *of cooked shellfish removed from the bone and de-veined if necessary*, 1 *l* (1¾ *pts*) *of fish or chicken stock*, 1 *diced onion*, 4 *stalks of celery including leaves*, 2 *cloves*, *bay leaf*, *pepper or peppercorns*, *parsley*, *salt*, *paprika*, *carrot*, *butter*, *flour*, *milk*.

1. Reserve a small amount of the shellfish meat for the final garnish. Take the remainder and place in cooker with the stock, the onion, the cut-up celery and seasonings. Pressure cook for approximately 10 minutes and after removing bay leaf sieve or blend the result.

2. Prepare a white sauce with equal parts of butter and flour and a small amount of milk. Season lightly and add gently to the mix.

3. Add the reserved bits of shellfish meat. Adjust seasoning.

4. You can vary the results by adding paprika or cayenne. If an alcoholic result is desired, use either dry sherry or a white wine added at the end. If the final taste is rather bland add a minced anchovy fillet. The use of carrots along with the other vegetables will sweeten the result and may get rid of some of the salty taste. Finally add chopped parsley or chives for a contrasting garnish.

VEGETABLE SOUPS

Green Garden Soup   5 minutes

Fresh green vegetables (e.g. peas, beans, assorted vegetable tops), plus small carrots, turnips, spinach to the weight of about 300 g (12 oz), 1 l (1¾ pts) white stock. 2 tablespoons of thickener like sago or cornstarch, butter, salt, pepper, and a few tasty green leaves for garnish: parsley, lettuce, mint, watercress, chervil – anything to hand.

1. Bring stock to boil, add vegetables with mint and parsley for flavour. Re-boil.

2. Pressure cook for 5 minutes. Depressurize with cold water.

3. Add green-leaf garnish. Add small knob of butter, adjust seasoning and serve.

4. If you wish, strain the liquid as soon as it is cooked. Reserve some pieces of solid vegetable and pass the remainder through a blender or sieve until absolutely smooth then reheat and add the reserved vegetables as a garnish.

The final taste and appearance of this dish can vary considerably, depending on the quality of the ingredients and your skill as a blender. If the result is not sweet enough don't be afraid to add a small amount of sugar. The main thing is not to cook for too long, otherwise some of the ingredients, particularly members of the cabbage family, may start to break down and you'll get a 'boiled cabbage' taste and smell.

Fresh Pea Soup   4 minutes

300 g (¾ *lb*) *of fresh shelled peas* (you can use frozen ones if you wish), 1 *l* (1¾ *pts*) *white stock, mint, parsley, salt, pepper, cayenne and cream.*

1. Cook peas in the stock with the herbs for 4 minutes under pressure. Allow pressure to reduce at room temperature. If available, use a few pea pods for flavouring.

2. Strain out the soup removing herbs and pods. Puree the peas or blend with the stock in the blender and return to open cooker. Re-boil, watching the consistency of the soup; if it turns out a little too thin and watery you could add flour and butter in the form of a *roux*, or alternatively mashed-up, cooked potato.

3. Correct seasoning and whirl in a little light cream. Cayenne pepper may then be added. (As an alternative you could add croutons of crisp-fried bacon.)

Basic Bean Soup   12–30 minutes

This is the basic recipe for cooking lentils, split peas, beans, limas, chick peas, etc. The shortest time should be used for the smallest and softest beans (e.g. split peas) and the longest time for hard varieties like chick peas. On the whole the lentil (cooking time from dried 20 minutes) is by far the most successful.

200 g (6 oz) beans, 1½ l (2½ pts) water or vegetable stock, assorted diced and sliced vegetables (e.g. onions, peppers, celery, carrots, potatoes, tomatoes, vegetable tops, mushrooms, greens, etc.), 2 tablespoons butter, salt, pepper, bouquet garni, herbs, garlic.

1. Pressure cook beans in stock for 20 minutes or longer (see table of cooking times for dried vegetables, pp. 104–5, 294–5).
2. Sauté the vegetables in the butter till the onions become transparent. Add to cooked beans and stock and pressure cook for 2 minutes. Season carefully. If a smooth result is wanted, pass through sieve or blender.

Note that once bean soups are thick they burn easily, so keep the heat low.

Most beans gain immeasurably from the presence of a bit of meat, particularly bacon.

A curried effect may be obtained by frying curry spices in the oil while you sauté the vegetables. A very rich meaty effect may be obtained by the addition of *miso* at the very end of the cooking process. A nutty effect is produced by the judicious use of sesame oil.

Basic Grain Soup   10–15 minutes

Grain soups can be built up in the same way as bean soups. The recipes are very similar, the only difference being that the grains will not mash up as well as beans. Usual pressure-cooking time is between 10 and 15 minutes. Appropriate grains are rice, barley, kasha, wheat, oatmeal, cornmeal, buckwheat, barley, etc. (See pp. 233–4, 305–6 for timings and tables.)

200 g (6 oz) dry grain, 1½ l (2½ pts) water or stock.

1. Wash the grain in running water. Drain and then add to the boiling stock. Pressure cook for the appropriate period (see pp. 233–4, 305–6).
2. Open up pan and add sliced and diced vegetables (e.g. onions, celery, carrots, tomatoes, cabbage tops – anything to hand) and pressure cook for a further 3 minutes. (You could sauté the vegetables first in a separate pan if you wished.)
3. Blend the final soup and adjust seasonings. These can be varied quite extensively. In addition to salt and pepper, such herbs as rosemary, thyme, sage, parsley, tarragon, chervil and chives, are all interesting; garlic can be added for sharpness and soy sauce for an exotic flavour.

In general grain soups are best given a very pronounced 'regional' flavour so be cautious with your inventions! Grated cheese is a particularly useful addition.

COLD SOUPS

Many vegetable soups can be served chilled in the summer. Consommé, of course, turns to a delicate and pleasing jelly.

Vichyssoise   **7 minutes**

White stock to 250 ml (½ pt), 2 tablespoons butter, 4 sliced leeks, 1 medium onion, sliced, ½ kg (1 lb) potatoes cut up, 2 medium carrots, 250 ml (½ pt) milk, 125 ml (¼ pt) double cream, chopped chives (or chervil), salt and pepper.

1. Fry leeks and onions in butter till golden brown.
2. Add potatoes, stock, carrots and seasoning.
3. Pressure cook for 7 minutes in the usual way. Depressurize.
4. Add milk and half the cream and bring just to boil. Remove instantly from heat and allow to cool. Strain, sieve or blend. Correct seasoning.
5. Chill. Check seasoning again. Pour on remainder of cream and add chopped chives or chervil for garnish.

Trembling Tomato Soup

140 ml (¼ pt) fresh or tinned tomato juice, 1 teaspoon sugar, clove garlic, sprig of mint or basil, 570–850 ml (1–1½ pts) rich chicken stock, salt and pepper, Worcestershire sauce, green pepper or green tomato.

1. Boil tomato juice, garlic, mint or basil, and seasoning gently in a saucepan for 5 minutes. Strain and add enough stock to allow gelatinizing to give a 'trembling' set (the chicken bones will provide enough gelatine for this).
2. Add Worcestershire sauce, adjust seasoning, reheat; allow to cool, chill in fridge. To serve, garnish with strips of green pepper or tomato.

Another method:

1. Instead of stock use stock cube and proprietary gelatine (follow instructions on packet).

FRUIT SOUPS

Fruit soups are little known outside East Europe and Scandinavia, which is rather a pity. They are all served very cold in chilled bowls. You use the pressure cooker to stew the fruit of your choice to a syrupy pulp. Add sugar and lemon juice to taste, bring out the subtleties of the fruit with spices like cinnamon, cloves and ginger then thicken with cream, either sweet or sour. A dry white wine or a sparkling dry cider can add a luxurious kick and luminescence – marvellous for summer.

Plum Soup   10 minutes + cooling

500 g (1 lb) stoned and chopped plums, 60 ml (2 fl oz) each of dry white wine and apple juice or 120 ml (4 fl oz) dry sparkling cider, pinch of cinnamon, cloves, ginger, 2 table-spoons thick cream, 1 teaspoon castor sugar, ½ teaspoon lemon juice, 1 small tart apple.

1. Pressure stew plums in wine and apple juice or cider for 10 minutes. Puree and sieve or, better, pass through a blender. Add sugar and lemon juice and spices to taste after cooking period. Chill for several hours.
2. Blend in thick cream to give over-all consistency. You could add more wine or sparkling cider at this point. Check spicing, sugar and lemon juice to taste.
3. Cut apple into very thin matchsticks to provide garnish.

This gives a more-or-less basic method: in some cases (e.g. cherry), you can reserve some uncooked fruit, chop it up and use that as garnish. Fruit soups should not be *too* sweet. Castor sugar and lemon juice are used for adjustment and cooling.

Apricot and Orange Soup   12 minutes

10–12 dried apricots, 1 medium diced cooking apple, 280 ml (½ pt) water, 1 can orange juice concentrate (frozen), 150 ml (5–6 fl oz) cider, 120 ml (4 fl oz) white wine, 60 ml (2 fl oz) sour cream, sugar, lemon juice, mint sprigs.

1. Pressure stew dried apricots and diced apple in 250 ml (½ pt) water for 12 minutes or until pureed. Sieve and/or blend. Chill.

2. Add orange juice concentrate (you could use freeze-dried whole orange drink using only ¼ of the amount of water recommended to reconstitute), cider, white wine, and blend in cream. Adjust taste with sugar and lemon juice. A great deal will depend on the type of apricot, apple and orange juice concentrate used. Add more water if the consistency is too thick.

3. Garnish with fresh mint sprigs.

4: VEGETABLES AND VEGETARIAN SPECIALITIES

Ever since I learnt how to cook them properly, I have adored vegetables. Anyone brought up at the time I was found it easy to think of vegetables as mushy greenish additions to the real business of eating: namely the joint of meat – and perhaps if that was the best cooks could do with greens and roots we would be right in down-valuing them.

But most people, alas, still don't know how to cook vegetables – the most favoured method is to dump them in water with salt and pepper, boil them up for a bit, drain and then serve. This virtually guarantees that the end product will be soggy and that all the nutritive elements will either have been destroyed by heating (e.g. the vitamins) or thrown away with the vegetable water (e.g. the minerals and trace acids). What you are eating is all too often a cellulose container of mildly flavoured water. In fact, if you heat for too long even the mild flavourings will break down and you'll get that distinctive 'boiled cabbage' smell rushing through the kitchen. The great thing about pressure cooking is that you are compelled to look at your vegetable cooking techniques afresh – and you'll find that the pressure-cooking method not only preserves the goodness in the vegetable but also vastly improves the taste and texture.

The secret is that, since pressure cooking works by high-pressure steam, the vegetables are never in contact with the water at all, but are suspended above it, either on the trivet or in a perforated basket. This means that when you lift the vegetables out, what liquid there is in them is the cooked sap, no more and no less, and with most of the original goodness and taste intact. Further, by watching the timing carefully (which is not all that difficult) you can control the degree of 'doneness', so that if you want your cabbage or cauliflower to be crisp and crunchy as opposed to limp and floppy, it is all within your power.

There is also another important nutritional point – pressure-cooked vegetables are prepared in an atmosphere of *steam* not air, so that losses of vitamin C are minimized (see p. 273). Food that tastes good and does you good can often be one and the same!

GENERAL TECHNIQUES

1. Use the trivet. For most purposes the vegetables, in a basket or laid across the trivet, are above the boiling water in the base of the cooker.

2. Take care in buying your vegetables. The first rule of all good cooking is to use the best ingredients – vegetables start deteriorating the moment they are picked. It is true that pressure cooking can sometimes fluff up tired-looking leaves, but that is very much second-best. Greens should be firm, cauliflower and broccoli curds should be clear and unmarked. Only buy shrink-wrapped packs from a supermarket in an emergency – the vegetables will have been grown for their keeping qualities and cosmetic and uniform appearance rather than for their taste and value.

3. Prepare vegetables as short a time as possible before cooking. Many vegetables, when cut, release an enzyme which breaks down the vitamin C content. The smaller the pieces into which the vegetable is cut, the more rapidly it will cook – the process depending on the speed of heat and steam penetration. For the same reason, individual pieces should be uniform in size, otherwise small pieces will be over-cooked while the insides of larger ones are still raw. Take some trouble over the shapes into which you cut the vegetables. Simply because pressure cooking is a rapid method is no excuse for an unappetizing sloppy jumble when it comes to serving. For a 'country' or 'peasant' look, rough-cut chunks are effective and 'natural' but a more elegant appearance can be obtained by cutting roots like carrot and parsnip into long thin matchsticks (allumettes or juliennes) or circles or ovals (by cutting on the slant).

Celery and cabbage can be made into commas and half-moons. The result needn't look prissy.

4. Use as little water as possible. Nearly all vegetables can be pressure cooked in under 15 minutes, so use the minimum quantities – 250 *ml* ($\frac{1}{2}$ *pt*) water or less. If you use more you merely prolong the time necessary to bring the cooker up to pressure and the resulting vegetable water (which you may like to reserve to use for stock at a later date or to make a sauce (see below p. 76)) will be more dilute than necessary.

5. Under-season. Since most of the flavour of the pressure-cooked vegetables will come from the cooked sap and since in any case the vegetables will not be immersed in water, you need very little seasoning. Freshly ground black pepper is more important, often, than salt. Some cooks believe that salt should not be added till afterwards as it has the effect of drawing out the sap by osmosis so that, while the vegetables end up looking attractively deep-coloured, some of the goodness has gone into the water at the bottom of the cooker. It is all a matter of preference.

6. Obviously, straining and draining of vegetables is not necessary – they can be lifted straight from the cooker to the plate or serving dish with only the addition of seasoning, garnish, butter or sesame oil.

7. You can cook several vegetables simultaneously since they have no direct contact with each other. You can either depressurize and repressurize so that you get the timings right (a somewhat messy process, see p. 22) or, better, adjust the size of the lumps of vegetable accordingly. Largish pieces of cauliflower, medium chunks of carrots and small pieces of potato will all cook in about the same time – 6 minutes or so.

8. DO NOT OVERCOOK. I prefer my leaf-vegetables fairly crisp (*al dente*) and they are certainly more nutritious. Cook slightly longer if you like your vegetables soft and juicy. To be cautious, cook for less time rather than more. If the vegetables are under-cooked slightly, reseal the lid, but LEAVE THE WEIGHT/VALVE OFF. You can then finish off at ordinary temperature and pressure.

9. Not all vegetables are worth pressure cooking as they take so little time in any case. A few, like spinach, merely need bringing up to pressure (seal pan, let steam escape fiercely, close weight/valve, let pressure build up) and then the cooker should be removed from the heat source at once; the spinach will be cooked. Alternatively, use your pressure cooker as an ordinary steamer – let the steam escape from the top vent but do not use the weight/valve. The vegetable will now cook more slowly at ordinary temperature and pressure. Your ordinary cookbook will give you timing. The pressure cooker is, in fact, a first-rate steamer!

10. Flash pressure cooking. This is a more sophisticated technique for people concerned to preserve the maximum vitamin content. Use it with fresh green vegetables. Instead of placing the vegetables in the cold cooker, heat up the water beneath the trivet, separators or pannier first and let it boil, filling the pan with steam. Then lower the basket of prepared vegetables into what is already an atmosphere of steam, and seal the lid. Bring to pressure in the ordinary way and use the standard timing. The advantage of this technique is that the deterioration of vitamin C that takes place in heated air is prevented by immersing the vegetables as soon as possible in steam!

TABLE OF FRESH VEGETABLES

All vegetables to be cooked with the trivet and with 250 *ml* ($\frac{1}{2}$ *pt*) water in the base of the cooker unless otherwise specified. The timings are varied according to the size and age of the ingredients.

Vegetable	Cooking Time (mins)	Cooking and Serving Instructions
ARTICHOKE (French, Globe)		Wash, remove discoloured leaves, cut stems short, stand heads upright
Small	6	on trivet. Serve with melted

Vegetable	Cooking Time (mins)	Cooking and Serving Instructions
Large	10	(browned if preferred) butter, lemon juice and salt – or with Hollandaise sauce (see recipe p. 76).
ARTICHOKE (Jerusalem)	4–5	Wash, peel, cut into uniform pieces (quarters if large, halves if small). Serve with: melted butter, white sauce and golden egg crumbs. Pepper and salt.
ASPARAGUS		Wash and cut up. Serve with melted
Tips	1	butter or Hollandaise sauce. The cut
Cut	2–3	pieces may take 4 minutes or more and should be saved for soups or stocks.
Whole stalks*	2	Arrange in bundles of 6 to 8 in perforated container which should stand in 10 *cm* (3½ *in*) water. The bundles should be placed on the slant, stems in the water. Using this method, which approximates the classic culinary technique, the stems are super-*boiled* and the tips super-*steamed*. Serve with melted butter or Hollandaise sauce (see recipe p. 76).
AUBERGINES (Egg-plant)	1–2	Wash but leave purple skin intact. After cooking, lift from trivet, dry lightly on kitchen paper and fry in hot butter or olive oil. The pressure cooking ensures a juicy interior.
BEANS		Shell. Older beans will need longer
Broad		cooking time. Serve with butter or
On trivet	2	herb sauce.
In container	4	
French, runner, string, snap, princess		Slice on the slant. Remove the strings from older beans. Young beans will
On trivet	2–4	need hardly any cooking at all. Serve
In container	4–5	with butter. A sprig of mint will add variety.
Soya (Fiskeby), see SOYABEANS		
Lima	1–2	Shell. Serve with butter or a sauce made from vegetable water and *roux*.

* Remove the trivet.

Vegetable	Cooking Time (mins)	Cooking and Serving Instructions
BEET		Wash well leaving some stem.
Tiny, whole	10	Remove trivet. Cook. Remove skins.
Large, fresh	15 or more*	Serve buttered, spiced or cold in salads with vinegar and sugar.
Greens	2–3	Treat like spinach. Until recently this was purely an agricultural crop; it is now sometimes called leaf-beet or perpetual spinach.
BROCCOLI White Purple sprouting	2–4	Wash, season with salt and place on trivet. Separate from other vegetables with greaseproof paper. Serve with butter or Hollandaise sauce (see recipe p. 76).
BRUSSELS SPROUTS		Wash. Remove wilted yellow leaves.
On trivet	2–3	Season with pepper. Serve with
In container	3–4	melted butter or sauce made from vegetable water and *roux*. Alternatively, take cooked sprouts and lightly toss in hot butter so as to crisp-fry the outside.
CABBAGE Green White		Remove discoloured pieces. A quartered cabbage will take 5 minutes – older cabbages still longer. Serve
On trivet	2–3	well peppered and with melted
In container	3–4	butter.
Red		Cook separately. See recipe p. 80.
On trivet	2–3	
In container	3–4	
CARROTS		Remove tops. Peeled carrots look
Cut	2–3	cleaner, scraped carrots are more
(depending on age or size)		health-giving. Cut into matchsticks
Whole	4 or more	(very short cooking time required) or thin circles and ovals instead of the usual chunks. Serve with butter, gently fried in butter or with *velouté* sauce.
CAULIFLOWER		Remove all except inner leaves.
Flowerets	4	Separate from other vegetables with
Quartered	4	greaseproof paper. Serve with butter,
Whole	4	with parsley sauce, with cheese sauce or quick crisp-fried on outside.
Leaves	2–3	Treat like asparagus (p. 67).

* The very large ones may take 30 minutes: if cooking time exceeds 15 minutes remember to add another 150 *ml* (¼ *pt*) or so of water.

Vegetable	Cooking Time (*mins*)	Cooking and Serving Instructions
CELERIAC (Celery-Turnip)	3–4	This is the root of the celery plant. Peel thickly. Cut into 2 *cm* (1 *in*) thick slices. Drip lemon juice over. Serve with white sauce garnished with crumbled hard-boiled egg.
CELERY	3–4	Scrub, remove leaves (save for garnishing soup or putting into stock), de-string tough stalks. Cut into allumettes or crescents. Serve with white or parsley sauce or *roux* and juice.
CHICORY (Endive)	4–6	Do not cut as this makes for a bitter taste. Cook alone in the cooker without trivet. Melt 50 *g* (2 *oz*) butter with 2 tablespoons of water, 1 tablespoon of lemon juice. Cover with buttered greaseproof paper. Cook over low heat for 4 to 6 minutes. To serve, remove endive and reduce cooking liquid to make sauce.
CORN, see SWEETCORN		
COURGETTES (Zucchini, Baby marrow)		Leave skin on. Serve with melted butter or crisp-fry in melted butter. Add garlic and tomato puree for an Italian taste.
Whole	4	
Sliced	1–2	
CUCUMBER	1–2	Use older fruit. Slice lengthways and remove pips. Or dice. Serve with a white or onion or parsley sauce. Large cucumbers can be stuffed like a marrow. Paprika can offset the taste. Can be sautéed after pressure steaming.
DANDELION LEAVES	Cook to pressure only	Use only very young leaves. Toss in butter with light seasoning.
KOHL-RABI		Select small ones: remove leaves and cut into very thick matchsticks. Serve with cheese or Hollandaise sauce or deep fry as for French fried potatoes. Can also be baked with sour cream sauce, or stuffed. They taste like turnip cabbages.
Sliced	4	
Whole	8	

Vegetable	Cooking Time (mins)	Cooking and Serving Instructions
LEEKS	4–6	Cut off roots and most of green leaves. Very large leeks are tasteless. Serve with white, cheese or parsley sauce or paprika. Leaves can be used in soup or for garnish.
MARROW (Squash, Gourd) (for COURGETTES, see separate entry)	4	Skin and slice. Serve with white or cheese sauce or *roux* and vegetable water.
Stuffed	10–12	Gouge out centre and fill with cooked minced meat, add onion and vegetable. (See recipes pp. 92ff.)
Vegetable spaghetti	8–10	(See recipe, p. 114.)
MUSHROOM	1–3	The smallest (button) mushrooms need hardly any cooking at all. It is doubtful if it is worth cooking mushrooms by themselves.
OKRA (Lady's Fingers)	3–4	Choose tender young pods. Remove stems and cut into 15–20 *mm* ($\frac{1}{2}$–$\frac{3}{4}$ *in*) slices. Wash well. Serve with butter and seasoning. Or fry in butter till crisp.
ONIONS		Steamed onion avoids bad smells. Remove the outer skin to preserve clear colour. The pre-cooking period is for when onions are to be finished off with a roast.
Sliced	3–4	
Quartered	6	
Whole	8–10	
Pre-cooking	4	
PARSNIPS		Parsnips need careful cooking and flavouring if they are to be more than just starch and roughage. Fry lightly in butter to finish, adding garlic, nutmeg or cinnamon for an unusual 'medieval' taste. Parsnips to accompany a roast should be pressure par-boiled for 2 minutes.
Sliced } On trivet	3	
Whole } On trivet	10	
In water beneath trivet	3–4	
Pre-cooking	2	
PEAS		Shell and cook with mint and a few pods (and a bit of sugar if peas are very old). Serve with butter or mixed with other vegetables, e.g. carrots, sweetcorn.
In perforated container	2–4	
In solid container	5	
Mange-tout	2	Mange-tout are cooked whole in their pods – some people even prefer them raw!

Vegetable	Cooking Time (mins)	Cooking and Serving Instructions
PEPPERS (Bell peppers, Capsicum) Green or Red	5	Slice off tops at stalk and and remove pips and centre. Peppers can either be cut into short strips or into very long continuous ones. See separate recipe for stuffed peppers (pp. 92ff.)
PLANTAIN	6–8	These are the large yellow or green bananas used in West Indian, African and 'soul' cooking. Remove skin and fibrous strings. Can be rapidly fried after cooking to crisp up. Serve with crackling or with streaky bacon.
POTATOES Sliced Whole	4–6 6–10	Large potatoes should be sliced. Make sure all pieces are roughly the same size. Leave the skin on for better health. You can toss in hot butter or fry or roast afterwards. Add mint or dill or parsley and pepper for flavour.
Sweet, see SWEET POTATOES		
PUMPKIN	10–15	Longer time is for chunks of whole pumpkin. The inner flesh is for pumpkin pie.
RUTABAGA, SWEDE (Yellow Turnip) Quartered Whole	12 20*	This is a root crop usually served mashed with salt, pepper and butter. It can be served diced with a cream sauce.
SALSIFY (Vegetable oyster, Scorzonera) On trivet In water	25* 15	Soak salsify in water to remove earth from root – then peel skin. *Either* pressure steam and serve with butter or sauce. *Or* remove trivet, place 1 *l* (1¾ *pts*) water in bottom and boil up with 1 tablespoon of flour and 1 tablespoon of lemon juice. Add a pinch of salt. Pressure cook for 15 to 20 minutes and then serve with butter or bechamel sauce.
SORREL	Bring to pressure only	This spinach-like leaf is very strong-tasting and is seldom cooked by itself but can be mixed with other green leaves. It needs hardly any cooking. Serve tossed in butter.
SOYABEANS (Fiskeby)		Soyabeans have an unusual number of 'animal protein' amino acids and

* Use 350 *ml* (¾ *pt*) water.

Vegetable	Cooking Time (mins)	Cooking and Serving Instructions
In pods	2	so are prized by vegetarians. Varieties that grow in temperate zones are now more readily available. The problem of blandness of taste remains. Serve younger specimens in their shells, older ones as individual beans. Toss with butter and experiment with herbs like chervil, parsley, tarragon, mint, depending on what else is to be eaten at the same time.
Shelled	1	
Textured, Spun, see MEAT SUBSTITUTES (pp. 219 ff.)		Soyabeans can be processed to make meat substitutes; for handling – see pp. 219ff.
SPINACH	Bring to pressure only	Wash well and remove the spines from the thickest leaves. If you forbear from draining the leaves you needn't add any water at all to the base of the cooker. It is however doubtful whether pressure steaming is worthwhile. I use the pressure cooker without the weight and steam for 2 to 3 minutes – a little longer if the spinach is to be pureed. Serve with melted butter or pureed in a small quantity of pre-cooked mashed potato and butter.
SPRING GREENS (Kale, Beet tops, Brussels tops, Chard, Turnip tops)	4	Wash, tear to shred. Serve tossed in butter with plenty of pepper. Experiment with herbs as suitable combinations.
SQUASH, see MARROW SWEDES, see RUTABAGA		
SWEETCORN (Corn, Sugar Corn)		Remove leaves and stalk; top and tail. Serve with melted butter, salt and pepper; cinnamon for variety. Loose sweetcorn can be served like peas, perhaps in a sauce made of vegetable water and *roux*.
Loose	1	
On cob: small	3	
On cob: large	5	
SWEET POTATOES		Peel after cooking – it is much easier. Sweet potatoes can be mashed with butter or milk and butter. Cinnamon can sometimes be added.
Whole large	12–15	
Whole thin	8	
Halves	8–10	
Slices	5–7	

Vegetable	Cooking Time (mins)	Cooking and Serving Instructions
TOMATOES		It is usually not worth pressure
Juice	½–1	cooking tomatoes by themselves
Stewed		unless for juice. Remove skins by im-
Whole		mersing briefly in boiled water. Puree
		result in sieve or blender. Serve with
		salt, pepper and, optionally, sugar.
		Basil is the traditional herbal accom-
		paniment.
TURNIPS		Wash and peel. Serve with butter.
Whole	4–5	Turnips are best mixed with other
Sliced or diced	4	vegetables like peas, carrots and
		sweetcorn.
YAMS		Cook unpeeled. Serve either mashed
Sliced	10–12	and seasoned, or slice and sauté.
		Yams benefit from adventurous
		seasoning: brown sugar, cinnamon,
		lemon juice, sherry, grated orange or
		lemon rind, etc. They can be flambéed
		in brandy!

FROZEN VEGETABLES

Most frozen vegetables need a shorter cooking time than their fresh counterparts. In the first place, vegetables are nearly always part-cooked before freezing – they are either blanched (dropped briefly in boiling water) or may be parboiled (boiled for a short time). Secondly, the freezing process sometimes breaks down the texture of the food a little, so that if they are to retain the crispness of the fresh original, the less cooking the better. The other thing to remember is that with some vegetables a fair amount of water is frozen at the same time – as a result you need add very little when you come to pressure steam.

Opinion is divided as to the value of part-defrosting before cooking. A solid chunk of ice with vegetables imbedded in it is a poor proposition for a pressure cooker. Since the process depends on rapid penetration of heat and moisture, solidly frozen chunks will go soggy with over-cooking while the inside is still icy. If the food can be broken up easily (e.g. peas, beans, purees), then do so, using a wooden spoon and then pressure cook straight from the freezer. If, however, the vegetable has to remain intact (e.g. cauliflower flowerets, asparagus spears, broccoli), then partial defrosting for 45 minutes to an hour is recommended. Corn on the cob should be allowed to defrost completely ($1\frac{1}{2}$ to 2 hours). For convenience the following table gives timings for both completely frozen and partially defrosted vegetables. The general rule is that pressure-cooking time is one-seventh to one-sixth of the time specified on the manufacturer's packet. In each case you need 150 *ml* ($\frac{1}{4}$ *pt*) water only beneath the trivet.

TABLE OF FROZEN VEGETABLES

Vegetable	Cooking Time (mins) (Frozen)	Cooking Time (mins) (Part-defrosted)	Cooking and Serving Instructions
ASPARAGUS			Break up carefully before cooking to allow steam to circulate. Serve with creamy butter or sauce.
Pieces	$3\frac{1}{2}$	1	
Tips or Stalks	3	Pressure only	
BEANS Broad, French, Runner, Snap, Wax, Soya, Lima	4	2	Break up solid blocks.
BEET Red	5	2	Usually only very small beet are frozen by commercial undertakings. Break block carefully.
BROCCOLI	$4\frac{1}{2}$	$1\frac{1}{2}$	Partial defrosting is recommended. If vegetable looks soggy – serve in *velouté* sauce.
BRUSSELS SPROUTS	4	$3\frac{1}{2}$	Break up block carefully. Cook in a separator, lowering into pan when water is already boiling and pan filled with steam. Sprouts should be crisp.

Vegetable	Cooking Time (mins) (Frozen)	Cooking Time (mins) (Part-defrosted)	Cooking and Serving Instructions
CARROTS	3	1½	Break block. Serve with butter or sauce. Some commercial types are sold already in a sauce, in which case, cook in solid separator for 3 to 4 minutes.
CAULIFLOWER Flowerets	3	1	Partial defrosting recommended – the flowerets are easily damaged.
MIXED VEGETABLES (Carrots, Peas, Beans, Sweetcorn, Turnip)	4	2	Break up roughly. If provided with a frozen sauce, cook in solid separator for 4 to 5 minutes.
PEAS	2½	Pressure only	Break up roughly. Commercial frozen peas are often very sweet and sometimes have mint added to the seasoning. Go easy on the seasoning.
SPINACH	4	Pressure only	Break block up. Leaf spinach is usually a waste of time frozen as it ends up pureed.
SWEETCORN Loose	1½	Pressure only	Corn on the cob should be completely defrosted and then just brought up to pressure.
On cob		Pressure only	

I am personally unconvinced that it is worth pressure cooking many frozen vegetables!

THE RECIPES

These recipes are, roughly speaking, in ascending order of sophistication. Like quite a number in this book, they have been selected partly to show you basic ways of using the pressure cooker and partly to give you ideas for interesting dishes. Timings refer to fresh ingredients; check tables for frozen ingredients.

The recipes at the end of the chapter are really rather adventurous. Most vegetables, if fresh, benefit from simple steaming. You can serve them either by themselves as accompaniments to the main dish, or tossed lightly in melted butter. If you like to serve with a sauce try the following ideas:

1. A simple *white* sauce with equal parts butter (or margarine) and flour heated together to make a white paste (a *roux*) and then cooked with a little milk. This gives you the basic *bechamel* of French cooking. You need to stir well to avoid lumps and must not over-heat or the sauce will lose its white colour. Add seasonings. If you add grated cheese at the end you have a *cheese* sauce – good with cauliflower, for example. If you add chopped parsley you have *parsley* sauce and minced fresh onion gives you *onion* sauce – much better than from a packet, and cheaper too.

2. A *velouté* is *roux* plus vegetable juice. If you take the vegetable water beneath the trivet after cooking time (it contains trace minerals and soluble vitamins) and add it to your flour and butter paste you get a delicate sauce. This method, incidentally, ensures you get as much goodness as possible from every vegetable.

3. A *Hollandaise* sauce is a classic haute-cuisine sauce: whisk 3 egg yolks in a double boiler and 1 tablespoon of lemon juice (you can use your pressure cooker as a double boiler, see pp. 281–2) for 3 minutes. Add 150 g (6 oz) butter in tiny pieces one by one so that they dissolve, and finally add 1 tablespoon of hot water. Whisk lightly and it's ready. Use this with expensive vegetables.

4. A *mousseline* is made with Hollandaise plus a dollop of thick beaten cream. Very rich and extravagant!

Some vegetables benefit from braising – cooking in a stock (e.g. celery) and the larger vegetables can be stuffed with meat, rice or cooked lentils (see pp. 92ff.), to make a complete dish.

Braised Celery **4 minutes**

140 ml (¼ pt) *brown stock or cube, 1 or 2 heads of celery depending on size, 2 tablespoons of tomato puree, pinch of sugar, seasoning, chopped parsley.*

1. Use cooker without trivet. Bring stock gently to boil.
2. Cut celery sticks in half and add to stock. Add seasoning.
3. Close lid, let steam build up and escape steadily through vent. Pressurize, reduce temperature so that cooker is just ticking over and cook for 4 minutes.
4. Depressurize by cooling carefully under tap. Open lid.
5. Lift out celery and place it in a heatproof dish in a warm oven.
6. Boil stock in open pan until reduced by half. Stir in tomato puree, add the sugar, taste and correct seasoning then pour over the celery. Garnish with chopped parsley. Serve.

Braised Cabbage **20 minutes**

1 kg (2 lb) *cabbage, 5 slices smoked bacon, 1 strip pork rind, 1 carrot, 1 onion,* 140 ml (¼ pt) *water, salt, pepper, bouquet garni.*

1. Cut off damaged or yellow outer leaves. Wash cabbage.
2. Remove trivet from pressure cooker. Add the water and bring to boil. Plunge cabbage into the boiling water. Close the lid. Bring to pressure and cook for 5 minutes. Depressurize. Drain the cabbage.
3. Empty and clean the interior of pressure cooker, reserving the liquid. Slice carrot and onion, quarter the cabbage, dice the bacon and place in cooker. Add the strip of pork rind and the bouquet garni. Pour back the cabbage water. Add seasoning.
4. Close lid. Bring to pressure and cook for 15 minutes.

Depressurize. Open lid. Remove bouquet garni and adjust seasoning. Serve.

Authentic Asparagus   2 minutes

This breaks all the rules – you pressure *boil* the bottoms and *steam* the tops.

Asparagus bunch, salt, pepper, butter.

1. Remove trivet. Take separator (one or more) and place on bottom of pan. Lay asparagus tips sideways in separator. Fill bottom of pan with water to cover up to $\frac{1}{3}$ the length of asparagus stalks (but do not let cooker become more than half-full).
2. Season water liberally with salt and pepper.
3. Bring slowly to pressure. Reduce heat and pressure cook for 2 minutes.
4. Reduce pressure carefully. Lift separator from the water.
5. Serve with melted butter.

(This method can also be used for cooking the outer stalks of cauliflower and some kinds of cabbage.)

Broccoli   2 minutes

Cook broccoli in the ordinary way (see p. 168). Remove from cooker. Sprinkle grated cheese (Cheddar for mild effect, Parmesan for stronger) and then cover with hot melted butter.

Artichoke   steamed 10 minutes
                                                 boiled 12 minutes

*4 artichokes, 250 ml ($\frac{1}{2}$ pt) water if steaming or 570 ml (1 pt)
water if boiling, salt, pepper, olive oil, lemon juice, fresh
herbs, melted butter, mustard, vinegar.*

1. Wash artichokes and remove outer leaves which are
usually tough and discoloured. Cut stem to allow heads to
stand in an upright position for serving.
2. Bring water to boil in pan. Remove or leave trivet
depending whether you are boiling or steaming. Add salt, a
little olive oil and a few drops of lemon juice to the water.
Place artichokes upright on the trivet or in the water. Close
lid. Bring to pressure. Cook for 10 minutes if steaming or
12 minutes if boiling.
3. Reduce pressure. Take out the artichokes and allow
them to drain.
4. To serve, place them upright on a plate. A sauce should
be available in a bowl for dipping. A dish of melted butter
with a few drops of lemon juice added is the simplest,
although lemon butter with fresh herbs is also very good. A
sauce vinaigrette goes well too (1 tablespoon of vinegar,
3 tablespoons of oil, salt, pepper, mustard and chopped fresh
herbs to taste).

Browned Parsnips   10 minutes

*250 g ($\frac{1}{2}$ lb) parsnips, 120 g (4 oz) brown sugar, 2 tablespoons
of butter; optional: garlic, nutmeg or cinnamon, seasoning.*

1. Wash parsnips and place on trivet in pressure cooker.
Cover trivet with water. Bring cooker to pressure for
10 minutes.
2. Reduce pressure. Open lid. Remove trivet and remaining water. Add butter and sugar to parsnips in pressure
cooker and heat. Stir occasionally. Remove from heat when

lightly browned. Add garlic, nutmeg or cinnamon while heating. Adjust seasoning and serve.

String Beans and Bacon   1 minute

1 *kg* (2 *lb*) *string beans, bits of crisp-cooked bacon, butter, salt, pepper;* optional: *horseradish or minced onion, water to cover trivet.*

1. Cut beans in half lengthways. Place on trivet. Add water. Add seasoning and if desired also add the bits of crisp bacon, the minced onion or horseradish. Close lid. Bring to pressure. Cook for 1 minute.
2. Depressurize. Open lid. Place beans in a dish and add the butter. Adjust seasoning. Serve.

Red Cabbage   5 minutes

1 *small red cabbage*, 1 *medium onion*, 2 *tablespoons of red wine vinegar*, 2 *tablespoons of water or ham stock*, 2 *cooking apples*, 2 *cloves*, 1 *tablespoon butter*, 1 *tablespoon of flour for thickening*, 1 *tablespoon of brown sugar*, *seasoning and nutmeg*, 2 *slices of streaky bacon.*

1. Remove trivet from pressure cooker. Cut bacon into small pieces and gently fry in bottom of cooker until the fat runs out. Chop the onion thinly and fry with the bacon until soft but not brown. Then add the vinegar, water or stock, finely shredded cabbage, cloves and sliced apples. Bring to pressure and cook for 5 minutes.
2. Reduce pressure at room temperature. In a separate pan melt the butter and add the flour slowly and cook without colouring the thickener. Strain the liquid from the pressure cooker into the pan stirring all the time. Add the cabbage and other vegetables. Add sugar to taste (at least 1 tablespoon). Sprinkle well with pepper and nutmeg. Adjust seasoning. Reheat before serving.

Mashed Potatoes **6 minutes**

toes of any size, milk, butter, salt, pepper.

Cut potatoes roughly into 2·5 *cm* (1 *in*) chunks and pressure steam in separators for 5 to 6 minutes. The smaller the potato pieces, the more rapidly they will cook. There is no need to season at this stage. Place cooked potatoes in mixing bowl and mash by hand, using the remaining steaming fluid and/or milk to moisten the mix, if required (a lot will depend on the variety of potato being used). Season with salt and pepper to taste. Add a nut-sized dollop of butter if wished. This recipe seems – and is – absolutely obvious, but it shows how the pressure cooker can be used, without any pretension or self-consciousness, to speed up a necessary process in cooking. Once you have mashed the potatoes, instead of serving them simply as they are, you may have time to try the following variants:

Potatoes Duchesse

You need a 'thinnish' mashed potato mix for this (a little more milk). Make a cone of greaseproof paper as you would for squeezing cake decoration, only rather larger. Chop off the end to make a spout and fill the bag with hot mashed potato. Squeeze through the small end into dollops of potato which you deposit on a baking tray. Brown in very hot oven (245 °C, 475 °F, GM 9) until crisp on top.

Latkes

While you are mashing your steamed potatoes, add some minced onion and, if you like, about half a grated carrot. Add salt, pepper and, if desired, more exotic seasonings such as the Indian condiment – garam masala. Make largish patties out of the mix, keep well shaped by lightly flouring, and then fry gently in shallow oil until brown and crisp on the outside. This is a well-known Eastern European and Jewish side-dish.

Chantilly Potatoes   6–8 minutes

350 g (12 oz) *mashed potato,* 1 *carton whipping cream,* 60 g (2 oz) *grated cheese, salt, white pepper, cayenne.*

1. Pre-heat oven to 190 °C (375 °F, GM 5). Prepare mashed potato (see p. 81). Whip cream until stiff and add the seasoning. Combine cheese and cream.
2. Shape the potatoes into a mound on an ovenproof plate. Cover with cream mixture. Place in the oven and bake until cheese is melted and potatoes are lightly browned.

Browned or 'Roast' Potatoes   6–8 minutes

6 *steamed potatoes about* 5 *cm* (2 *in*) *diameter, butter and cooking oil,* 2 *tablespoons of finely chopped parsley.*

1. Prepare and cook potatoes in pressure cooker (see p. 71) but give them about 1 minute less than the normal cooking time so that they are slightly resistant to the fork.
2. Pre-heat oven to 180 °C (350 °F, GM 4). Melt a mixture of butter and cooking oil in a small pan. The mixture should be about 6 *mm* (¼ *in*) deep and heated well and nearly crackling.
3. Put the potatoes in an ovenproof or casserole dish (one that has a lid) and pour the hot fat mixture carefully over them. Let the potatoes cook *covered* in the oven for about 20 minutes. Turn them occasionally for even colouring. On the final turn sprinkle with chopped parsley and proceed to bake the potatoes *uncovered* for a further 10 minutes.

Potato Salad   15 minutes

6 *medium potatoes*, 6 *eggs*, 2 *medium onions*, 280 *ml* ($\frac{1}{2}$ *pt*) *salad dressing*, *salt*, *pepper*, *paprika;* optional: *diced cucumber or radish slices, lettuce leaves.*

1. Choose potatoes of equal size. Wash well but do not peel. Place them on trivet, add water, close lid, bring to pressure and cook for 8 minutes. Reduce pressure quickly under cold running water.

2. At the same time hard-boil the eggs. Put eggs in cold water before shelling them. Drain and peel potatoes. Slice the potatoes, eggs and onions thinly, keeping them in separate piles.

3. Select a salad bowl that is fairly deep and arrange the ingredients in alternating layers as follows: potatoes, salad dressing, onion, egg, seasoning, until all the potatoes are used. Reserve some egg slices for the top garnish. Diced cucumber and radish slices may be incorporated in the layers of ingredients.

4. Refrigerate until chilled thoroughly. Immediately before serving mix all together carefully with two spoons gently lifting and stirring without breaking the slices. Decorate the edge of the bowl with lettuce leaves and the top with slices of egg.

Sprinkle paprika over the dish.

Hot Potato Salad   15 minutes

6 *medium potatoes*, 4 *eggs*, 4 *slices of bacon*, 1 *large sweet onion*, 175 *g* (6 *oz*) *celery*, 50 *ml* (2 *fl oz*) *vinegar*, 2 *tablespoons of sugar, salt and pepper, paprika.*

1. Prepare and cook potatoes whole in pressure cooker (see p. 71). Hard-boil eggs at same time. Drain, peel and dice potatoes into 13 *mm* ($\frac{1}{2}$ *in*) pieces. Shell and slice eggs. Keep warm (while preparing remaining ingredients),

preferably in ovenproof dish on low heat. Reserve one egg for garnish.

2. Cut bacon into small pieces and fry in a pan until crisp. Cut celery finely and mince onion. Remove bacon from heat and allow to cool slightly then add the sugar and vinegar. Return to heat and stir in the celery, onion and seasoning.

3. When all ingredients are hot remove pan from heat and pour the contents over the dish of potatoes and eggs. Garnish with the egg slices. Serve at once or keep hot until ready to serve.

Chicory Endive   12–15 minutes

1 *kg* (1¾ *lb*) *chicory*, 4 *tablespoons butter*, *salt and pepper*, *juice of half a lemon;* optional: *grated cheese or slices of ham and grated cheese.*

1. Remove discoloured or old leaves from chicory. Hollow out the stump with a pointed knife to avoid a bitter-tasting dish that is unpleasant especially for children. Wash and drain thoroughly.

2. Remove trivet and melt butter in the pressure cooker. Add the chicory. To retain the whiteness squeeze out the juice of half a lemon and sprinkle over the chicory. Add salt and pepper to taste.

3. Close lid. Bring cooker to pressure. Reduce heat and simmer for 12 to 15 minutes. To serve, drain the chicory and arrange on a dish.

4. Grated cheese topped with a few pats of butter can be sprinkled on the chicory then the whole dish left in a hot oven for 5 minutes before serving. Another variation to this provides exciting contrast: roll chicory in slices of ham sprinkled with grated cheese and warmed in the oven.

This recipe does not use water because the chicory is allowed to simmer in its own juice and is able to retain a greater amount of its vitamin content.

Cauliflower – Fry 'n' Steam   **6 minutes**

Cauliflower, oil, salt, water.

1. The green leaves of the cauliflower can be used in the dish or not. Separate the leaves from the rest of the head. Cut stem near to core. Slice the flowerets into medium-sized chunks. Wash and drain thoroughly.

2. Young, fresh cauliflower is best-tasting when it is cooked to a crunchy texture. Longer cooking brings out its cabbage or mushy taste. Remove trivet and pour oil in base of pan. Stir-fry cauliflower for 3 to 4 minutes. Replace trivet and add water; bring cooker to pressure and steam for another 2 minutes. Reduce pressure. Open lid and check the seasoning. Serve.

N.B. If using the leaves as well, add them after stir-frying the cauliflower.

Cauliflower Cheese   **4 minutes**

1 *large cauliflower*, 250 *ml* ($\frac{1}{2}$ *pt*) *cheese sauce (see p. 76), small amount of grated cheese*, 2 *large tomatoes*, 12 *bacon rolls, sprigs of parsley, salt and pepper*, 140 *ml* ($\frac{1}{4}$ *pt*) *water.*

1. Choose a firm, white cauliflower head. Wash, trim and divide it into two. If very large, cut a triangle in the core to permit penetration of heat. Put water in the pan. Lay the cauliflower, cut sides down, on the trivet.

2. Close lid. Bring to pressure in the usual way. Cook for 4 minutes and reduce the pressure by holding under a cold, running tap.

3. While cauliflower is cooking make the cheese sauce (see p. 76) and keep it hot, and also grill the bacon rolls.

4. Skin and slice the tomatoes and lay them on the bottom of a large ovenproof dish. Season them with salt and pepper and dot with butter.

5. When cauliflower has been removed from the pressure cooker and drained, divide it into four and place on top of the tomato slices. Pour the cheese sauce generously over the cauliflower and sprinkle lightly with grated cheese. Place under the grill and allow to brown.

6. Before serving, garnish the dish with the bacon rolls and the sprigs of parsley.

Leeks and Ham   8 minutes

1 kg (1¾ lb) leeks, 4 slices cooked ham, 120 g (4 oz) grated Gruyère cheese, 4 tablespoons butter, 2 tablespoons flour, 275 ml (½ pt) milk, salt and pepper.

1. Prepare and steam leeks (see table pp. 75, 287) on the trivet using 140 ml (¼ pt) of water. Drain thoroughly after cooking. Quarter leeks lengthways.

2. Fold each piece of leek in two and roll in the grated cheese. Wrap each piece of leek in a slice of ham. Put them in a dish lined with butter. Cover the dish with a plain white sauce (see p. 76). Sprinkle the remainder of the cheese over the dish.

3. Place in hot oven for 15 minutes. Serve.

Zucchini Piquant   4 minutes

1 medium-sized marrow, 1 sliced onion, 2 rock-hard salad tomatoes, 1 tablespoon butter, salt and pepper; optional: 1 clove garlic, chopped parsley.

1. Scrub marrow. Slice it finely, removing the seeds.

2. Remove trivet from pressure cooker and melt butter on a low heat. Add the marrow slices and fry slowly for 1 minute or so, stirring gently. Add the onions, tomatoes, seasoning and water (also garlic if desired).

3. Bring cooker to pressure in usual way and cook for

4 minutes. Reduce pressure at room temperature. Taste and correct seasoning.

4. Serve hot, garnished with chopped parsley.

Creamed Carrots   **10 minutes**

8 *medium carrots*, 1 *medium onion*, 2 *tablespoons of butter*, 1 *clove garlic*, 1 *teaspoon flour*, 1 *tablespoon fresh cream*, *salt and pepper*, *spice cloves*.

1. Scrape and wash the carrots then dice them. Peel the onion and cut it into fairly large pieces.

2. Remove trivet from pressure cooker. Fry the onion lightly in the butter but do not allow it to brown. Add the carrots, garlic, clove, salt and pepper. Sprinkle a teaspoon of flour over the ingredients. Mix together.

3. Close lid, and 5 minutes after bringing to pressure (i.e. after initial turn of valve) remove from heat. Let the pressure cooker stand for another 5 minutes before lifting valve and removing lid. This makes for extra tender carrots.

4. To serve, mix in a tablespoon of fresh cream or you can sprinkle the carrots with chopped parsley.

N.B. Carrots benefit from a light sprinkling of sesame oil just before serving. The oil imparts a nutty flavour which contrasts well with the sweetness of the cooked vegetable.

Other Greens

Spinach, onion, lemon juice, nutmeg, salt and pepper.   1 *minute*

1. Wash and section the spinach. Place on the trivet with finely chopped or sliced onion, add juice of half a lemon and seasoning and spices to taste. Add a dash of water for safe cooking.

2. Bring to pressure only and then remove from heat and let stand a minute to give the onion a chance!

Mustard greens, mushrooms, egg slices.   **2** *minutes*

1. Wash and section greens. Place on trivet with a small amount of water. Add the mushrooms. Bring to pressure and cook for 2 minutes.
2. Garnish with egg slices. Serve.

Dandelion leaves, olive oil, mushrooms, garlic.   **1** *minute*

1. Brown the garlic in the bottom of the pressure cooker with the olive oil.
2. Select young dandelion leaves only and toss them into the cooker. Sauté them for a second or so. Add the mushrooms. Bring cooker to pressure only. Remove from heat and let stand for 1 minute to soften the mushrooms to perfection.

N.B. Depending on the size of the mushrooms either cook them whole if they are 'button' or chop them up if they are larger.

Ratatouille   **10 minutes**

2 *medium onions, 3 medium courgettes, 1 medium aubergine, 3 medium tomatoes, 1 green pepper, 2–3 cloves garlic, ½ cucumber, 4 tablespoons olive oil, 250 ml (½ pt) vegetable water or stock or 'dirty snow-storm' potato water, 140 ml (¼ pt) vinaigrette, salt and pepper.*

1. Skin and coarsely chop the onions. Wash aubergine and dice into uniform-size cubes. Quarter and slice the green pepper. Cut courgette into small slices. Peel and dice cucumber. Peel and crush the garlic.
2. Remove trivet from base of pressure cooker and heat

up the olive oil. First add the garlic and onion and stir-fry for 2 or 3 minutes. Then add the courgettes, aubergines, green peppers, tossing and stirring until all ingredients are evenly coated in oil. Pour the vegetable water or stock over the ingredients in the pan and also add the cucumber. Add seasoning to taste.

3. Close lid. Bring to pressure gently and cook for 10 minutes. While cooking, cut the tomatoes into eighths. Reduce pressure and open lid. Stir in the tomatoes well. Close lid again. Bring cooker to pressure only.

4. To serve hot off the stove, omit the vinaigrette. To serve cold, chill the mixture thoroughly then pour over 140 *ml* ($\frac{1}{4}$ *pt*) vinaigrette and toss lightly.

Rutabaga/Turnip

All but the smallest and youngest turnips benefit from pre-cooking (about 3 minutes). Usually turnips are not eaten by themselves, but are an ingredient in 'mixed vegetables' or stews and casseroles.

To eat by themselves pre-cook in the pressure cooker for about 3 minutes and then stir-fry with green turnip-tops for a minute or so. Season with salt and pepper. Cook until greens wilt. You can roast turnips in a very hot oven for 10 minutes with grated-cheese topping, or bake with minced onion and carrot for 15 minutes in a very hot oven.

Spiced Beet   10 minutes

220 ml (7 fl oz) vinegar, 2 tablespoons of sugar, 6 cooked beet, salt and pepper, ground cloves or cinnamon, garlic or ginger.

1. Prepare and cook beet (see table pp. 68, 287). While still warm slice them into the vinegar which should be spiced with sugar and ground cloves or cinnamon, garlic or ginger.

2. When cool, add seasoning to taste. Serve this dish as a relish or in a salad.

Buttered Beet   **10 minutes**

8 *medium beet, salt and pepper*, 3 *tablespoons butter*, 140 *ml* ($\frac{1}{4}$ *pt*) *water*.

1. Wash beet. Prepare them by cutting tops to within 5 *cm* (2 *in*) of stem. Place on trivet, add water, seal and cook.
2. Reduce pressure under running water. Remove cover and allow cold water to run over beet. Slip the skins off by tugging the stem gently and squeezing out the beet.
3. Depending on how they are to be served either slice, dice or leave beet whole. Return them to the pressure pan.
4. Cover pan without sealing and reheat just enough to serve the beet really hot.

Cooking beet brings out their sweetness. Beet greens including the red stems are quite edible, tender and mild tasting and can be cooked with the beet or as a separate greens dish. The cooking time of the beet itself depends on size and if cut up will be further reduced. Beet are among the few vegetables that retain much of their delicate flavour even when over-cooked. To calculate the amount needed for cooking, allow an average of 1 *kg* (2 *lb*) per 4-person serving.

In addition to the recipes above here are some hints for adding bite to your dish of beet:

To dress: use light dressing of vinegar or lemon juice.
To season: use cinnamon, ground cloves, garlic, ginger.
To garnish: use minced parsley, thin slices of green onion, watercress or grated cheese (Parmesan or Cheddar).

Sorrel   **To pressure only**

The bitter-sweet taste of sorrel makes it an exciting vegetable
to serve with a plain dish such as roast chicken or grilled
fish. Its young leaves can be added to salads or can be used
as the base of a sauce. It can be used in addition to or as a
substitute for chervil and parsley and is therefore good as a
garnish for soups, salads, etc. This old-fashioned vegetable –
originally cultivated by the Romans – has many undis-
covered possibilities for cooks who have chosen to ignore it.
It is sometimes difficult to buy at a city grocer's but it grows
freely in the countryside, or in the vegetable patch or flower
garden.

*¾ kg (1½ lb) fresh sorrel, 2 teaspoons French (Dijon) mustard,
4 tablespoons olive oil, 1 tablespoon white wine vinegar, salt
and pepper.*

1. Remove any tough stalks from the leaves. Rinse sorrel
in fast-running water and while still moist place in bottom
of pressure cooker. Bring to pressure and remove instantly
from heat. Sorrel will be cooked. Drain well. Clean out
pressure cooker thoroughly.
2. Mix mustard with oil and vinegar. Return sorrel leaves
to pressure cooker, add the vinaigrette dressing, season to
taste with salt and pepper.
3. Over a medium heat, toss lightly until thoroughly hot.
Serve.

Tomato Green Beans   **6 minutes**

*¾ kg (1½ lb) green beans, 1 small onion, 3 medium tomatoes,
120 g (¼ lb) grated Cheddar or Parmesan cheese, 2 tablespoons olive oil; optional: garlic, herbs (thyme, basil,
marjoram, dill), sesame oil.*

1. Skin, slice and dice onion. Wash and string the beans, cut them either lengthways or diagonally. Section the tomatoes. Grate cheese.

2. Remove trivet from pressure cooker. Heat up olive oil in base of pan and stir-fry onions for a minute. If using garlic, add it to the onions. Add the green beans and continue stirring for another 3 to 4 minutes. Place the tomato wedges on top of the beans. Seal and cook for 2 minutes.

3. Reduce pressure and remove cover. Adjust seasoning. Mix in some of the grated cheese and sprinkle the rest on top when serving. Sprinkle herbs such as suggested above (and if desired, sesame oil) over the tomatoes. Serve.

Aubergine (Egg-plant) Casserole   1 + 45 minutes

¾ *kg* (1½ *lb*) *aubergine, 1 small chopped onion, 2 large thin-sliced tomatoes, 50 g (2 oz) grated Cheddar cheese, 25 g (1 oz) grated Parmesan cheese, 2 beaten eggs, salt and pepper, paprika, 2 tablespoons melted butter, 4 tablespoons dry breadcrumbs, ½ teaspoon oregano.*

1. Wash, peel and slice aubergine. Pressure steam for 1 minute. Drain and mash aubergine. Mix in with it the beaten eggs, melted butter, salt and pepper, onion, oregano and breadcrumbs.

2. Grease a shallow 1 *l* (2 *pt*) baking dish and spread half the sliced tomatoes over the base. Then spread the aubergine mixture evenly over the tomato slices. Arrange the remaining tomato slices on top. Mix the cheeses together and sprinkle over the tomato slices. Sprinkle paprika over lightly.

3. Bake at 190 °C (375 °F, GM 5) for 45 minutes. Serve.

STUFFED VEGETABLES

Almost any reasonably solid vegetable can be stuffed. You scoop out the middle and replace it with a stuffing made variously from minced meat, breadcrumbs, vegetable scraps, rice and other grain, or even fish. Good vegetable hulls to use are aubergines (egg-plant), peppers, tomato (the larger variety), marrow and squash. You can also hollow out potatoes and onions and use the leaves of cabbage or, if you can get them, vine leaves.

Outline for making stuffing

You need a basis, a complement, possibly a moistener, and seasonings. Stuffings are a marvellous way of using scraps, but don't go for too many ingredients as the result will be a confused jumble. The hull of the vegetable to be stuffed will provide one flavour and then you want a reasonably simple combination like a basis of quick-fried minced meat or textured vegetable protein (see chapter 8, p. 219) with a complement of cooked rice, *or* lentils plus bacon pieces plus vegetable fragments, *or* breadcrumbs plus vegetable pieces, *or* cheese plus vegetables, *or* hard-boiled egg (finely chopped) plus vegetables, *or* pre-cooked fish broken into flakes plus one or two vegetables.

Watch the texture of the stuffing – everything should be cut down as fine as possible.

Some mixtures will end up too dry – you can moisten with vegetable juice from the hulled-out vegetable, with sour cream, raw egg, lemon juice or vinegar, depending on the type of ingredients. If the mixture is too wet it will take too long to cook satisfactorily, and you should add breadcrumbs, which will absorb some of the moisture, as will rice and other grains. You can use any of the usual seasonings: salt, pepper, herbs, garlic, curry powder, Tabasco.

Stuffed Marrow   **12 minutes**

1 *medium marrow*, 170 g (6 oz) *cooked minced meat*, 1 *medium onion*, 2 *medium tomatoes*, 1 *tablespoon of rice*, 1 *tablespoon butter*, *mire-poix* (see pp. 153–4 for details),

brown stock or vegetable water, seasoning, sheet of grease-proof paper.

1. Peel marrow. Cut a slice from the stalk end and scoop out centre pulp containing the seeds. Use a knife with a long blade or a long-handled spoon.

2. Remove trivet from cooker. Melt the butter and slowly fry the chopped onion, the sliced and peeled tomatoes and the washed rice for about 5 minutes. Remove pan from heat and add the minced meat and the seasoning. Mix all the ingredients together thoroughly.*

3. Fill the marrow with the mixture, tapping it occasionally to check that the mixture is evenly packed inside.

4. Wash out pressure cooker thoroughly. Prepare the *mire-poix* adding the required amount of liquid. Put the marrow on top and replace the cut-off slice to close the end. Cover with greasepr oof paper.

5. Seal cooker, bring to pressure and cook for 12 minutes. Reduce pressure with cold running water. Lift out marrow and cut into thick slices, overlapping them on a deep serving dish. Keep hot.

6. Mash or sieve the *mire-poix* vegetable. Taste and correct seasoning and if necessary add a little gravy colouring. Reboil with the liquid in the open cooker, then pour round the sliced marrow.

Stuffed Aubergine   10 minutes

3 *small aubergines* ($\frac{1}{2}$ *kg* (1 *lb*)), 2 *red peppers*, 3 *tomatoes*, 4 *tablespoons olive oil*, 2 *cloves minced garlic*, 2 *small onions*, 3 *sprigs fresh parsley, sweet basil, salt and pepper;* for topping: 120 *g* (4 *oz*) *walnuts*, 25 *g* (1 *oz*) *wheat germ*, 50 *g* (2 *oz*) *grated Parmesan*, 2 *tablespoons melted butter*, 220 *ml* ($\frac{1}{3}$ *pt*) *milk or cream.*

* If you start with *raw* minced meat, melt butter and an equal amount of oil in cooker and gently fry onion in it, then add the raw meat. Stir-fry for 3 to 4 minutes till thoroughly browned. Then add tomatoes and rice and carry on as before.

1. Slice each aubergine in half lengthways. Scoop out the centre leaving 1 *cm* ($\frac{1}{4}$ *in*) shell. Cut the centre pulp into chunks. Finely dice two thirds of the red peppers, reserving about a third for decoration.

2. Remove trivet and heat olive oil in base of cooker. Sauté the aubergine chunks and red peppers tossing until evenly coated with oil and until aubergine begins to soften. Season with salt and pepper and half the minced garlic, if desired. Divide this mixture evenly between the six aubergine shells pressing down firmly but gently.

3. Chop onion, parsley and tomatoes. Sauté the onions in the remaining olive oil adding the chopped parsley, sweet basil and remainder of garlic, if desired. When onions become soft, add the tomatoes. Simmer for a few minutes, then spread the mixture on top of the aubergine preparation and pat down. The shells should be full but not overflowing.

4. Wash out the pressure cooker. Place trivet and 140 *ml* ($\frac{1}{4}$ *pt*) water in the cooker. Lay the stuffed aubergines on top and cover with greaseproof paper. Seal and cook for 10 minutes.

5. While aubergines are cooking pre-heat oven to 180 °C (350 °F, GM 4). Prepare topping by combining the wheat germ, minced nuts and Parmesan cheese. Moisten with the melted butter and enough milk or cream to make a soft paste. Remove aubergines from pressure cooker and place on an oiled baking tray. Spread a thin layer of the topping on each aubergine half, and decorate the crust with the reserved red pepper sliced in thin strips. Heat the dish in the oven for 8 to 9 minutes. Serve very hot.

STUFFED TOMATOES

There are a variety of fillings for tomatoes and a selection is included here. The preparation of the fillings differs in each case. However, the basic pressure-cooking principle for the stuffed tomato is the same throughout and is explained below.

Basic preparation and pressure-cooking method for stuffed tomatoes

280 *ml* ($\frac{1}{2}$ *pt*) water with lemon juice or vinegar for cooker.

1. To prepare cases for hot food slice off cap and cut large hollows in very firm unpeeled tomatoes. Wash them.
2. Salt them and invert them on a rack to drain for about 15 minutes.
3. Stuff the tomatoes with the filling and put each in a buttered cup. Put water and trivet in cooker, then cups covered with a piece of buttered greaseproof paper.
4. Seal and bring cooker to pressure for 5 minutes. Reduce pressure with cold water. Lift out cups and scoop underneath each tomato with a tablespoon so they can be served instantly. Replace cut-off slice as a cap.
5. If more than 4 or 5 tomatoes are to be cooked at one time put one set of cups in the water covered with greaseproof paper, then place trivet on top with another set of cups covered with greaseproof paper, making two layers.

N.B. Adjust ingredients for filling according to the size of the tomatoes used.

Fish-Stuffed Tomatoes   **5 minutes**

4 *large, rock-hard tomatoes*, 1 *tablespoon of butter*, 2 *small fillets of cooked white fish, or haddock, or kipper, or* 1 *small tin of tuna fish*, 120 *g* (4 *oz*) *cooked beans (lentils, chick peas or black eye)*, 1 *green pepper*, 1 *anchovy fillet*, 1 *raw egg*, 1 *small minced onion, parsley or basil, salt and pepper;* optional: *garlic, tabasco, curry powder*.

1. Fish should be pre-cooked (a small fillet takes 3 to 4 minutes' pressure-cooking time). In a bowl, flake the fish and add the beans, minced onion, diced green pepper, chopped anchovy fillet, raw egg. Season to taste.

2. Prepare tomatoes as above (p. 96). Fill them with stuffing mix and place cut-off slices of tomato on top.

3. Pressure cook for 5 minutes.

Sweetcorn-Stuffed Tomatoes   **5 minutes**

4 *large, rock-hard tomatoes, 4 slices of bacon, 170 g (6 oz) cooked and drained sweetcorn or a tin of sweetcorn tidbits, 2 chopped pimentos, ½ chopped green pepper, 2 tablespoons chopped celery, 75 g (3 oz) breadcrumbs, 2 tablespoons of corn liquor or cream, salt, paprika, sugar if corn is green;* optional: *grated Parmesan or Cheddar cheese.*

1. Prepare tomatoes as above (see p. 96). Sauté and mince the bacon. Combine the sweetcorn, chopped pimentos, green pepper, celery, breadcrumbs, seasoning and corn liquor. Add the minced bacon.

2. Fill the tomatoes with the mixture. Pressure steam for 5 minutes. Sprinkle with grated Parmesan or Cheddar cheese and brown under grill if desired. Serve.

Onion-Stuffed Tomatoes   **5 minutes**

4 *large, rock-hard tomatoes, 75 g (3 oz) finely chopped onion, pulp from tomatoes, 2 tablespoons of butter, 1½ teaspoons brown sugar, 1 tablespoon celery seed, breadcrumbs, grated Parmesan or Cheddar cheese.*

1. Prepare tomatoes as above (see p. 96). Melt the butter and add the chopped onion, tomato pulp, brown sugar, salt and celery seed. Stir well and thicken if necessary with breadcrumbs. If too dry add cream or milk. The ingredients should be simmered for 3 minutes.

2. Fill the tomatoes with the mixture and pressure steam for 5 minutes. Sprinkle with grated Parmesan or Cheddar and brown under grill. Serve.

Anchovy-Stuffed Tomatoes   5 minutes

4 *large, rock-hard tomatoes*, 230 g ($\frac{1}{2}$ *lb*) *mushrooms*, 2 *tablespoons chopped onion*, 2 *tablespoons chopped green pepper*, 4 *chopped anchovies, tomato pulp and equal amount of breadcrumbs, brown sugar, chopped parsley*.

1. Prepare tomatoes as above (see p. 96). Season the tomato cases with brown sugar. Combine the tomato pulp with the breadcrumbs. Sauté the mushrooms, chopped onions and pepper, and anchovies. Correct seasoning remembering that the anchovies are salty already. Add this to the tomato-pulp mixture.
2. Fill tomato shells with the mixture and pressure steam in the usual way for 5 minutes. Garnish with chopped parsley. Serve.

Shrimp-Stuffed Tomatoes   5 minutes

4 *large, rock-hard tomatoes*, 150 g (5 *oz*) *chopped* (*cooked or canned*) *shrimps* (*or crab-meat*), 1 *tablespoon butter*, 2 *tablespoons finely chopped onion, tomato pulp, chopped parsley*, 3 *tablespoons breadcrumbs, paprika, salt*.

1. Prepare tomatoes in the usual way (see p. 96). Melt butter in a pan and sauté onion in it for 2 minutes. Add the tomato pulp and shrimps. Stir well and then add the chopped parsley, breadcrumbs, and seasoning to taste.
2. Fill the tomato cases with mixture and pressure cook in the usual way for 5 minutes. Serve, perhaps garnished with grated cheese.

Sweetbread-Stuffed Tomatoes   5 minutes

4 *large, rock-hard tomatoes*, 120 g (4 *oz*) *sweetbreads*, 120 g (4 *oz*) *mushrooms, Bechamel sauce* (see p. 76), *breadcrumbs for thickening, butter*.

1. Prepare the tomatoes in the usual way (see p. 196). Sauté the mushrooms in butter. Cook the sweetbreads (see p.190). Simmer the Bechamel sauce and add the ingredients. Thicken with breadcrumbs.

2. Fill the tomato cases with the mixture and pressure cook in the usual way for 5 minutes. Garnish with grated cheese if desired. Serve.

Other suggestions for stuffed tomato fillings

1. Creamed ham or sausage and mushrooms.
2. Bread and devilled ham.
3. Chestnuts and rice seasoned with salt and brown sugar.
4. Creamed green peas, parsley or mushrooms.
5. Mashed potatoes and nuts.
6. Creamed spinach or Florentine.

Haddock-Stuffed Potatoes   **10 minutes**

4 *large potatoes*, 1 *small smoked haddock (or packet of frozen smoked haddock)*, 2 *tablespoons butter*, 3 *tablespoons grated cheese*, *seasoning*, *chopped parsley*, 140 *ml* ($\frac{1}{4}$ *pt*) *water for cooker*.

1. Scrub and prick potatoes well but leave skins on. Put water and trivet in cooker. Add potatoes and haddock in separators. Seal, bring to pressure and cook for 10 minutes. Reduce pressure at room temperature.

2. Cut a slit lengthways in each potato. Carefully scoop out centre and mix this while still hot with the butter, flaked cooked haddock, seasoning and most of grated cheese.

3. Fill potato cases with mixture and place them on a baking tray. Sprinkle remainder of cheese over potatoes.

4. Bake for 7 to 10 minutes until crisp, on middle shelf of oven at 190 °C (375 °F, GM 5). Serve.

Stuffed Onions   **3 minutes**

4 *large Spanish onions, 1 tablespoon butter, 120 g (4 oz) minced beef or veal, chopped ham or fried bacon, 3 tablespoons fresh breadcrumbs, 1 skinned, chopped tomato, pinch of nutmeg, salt and pepper, 1 beaten egg, 140 ml ($\frac{1}{4}$ pt) water for cooker;* optional: *golden breadcrumbs or brown sauce.*

1. Wash onions. Cut off roots but do not peel. Put water and trivet in cooker. Add onions. Seal, bring to pressure, cook for 3 minutes. Reduce pressure at room temperature.

2. While onions are cooking, heat the butter in a small pan and fry the meat gently, stirring and turning to brown evenly.

3. Skin onions when cooked, slice off cap at stalk end and lift out centres. These should be chopped and mixed with the meat, tomato, seasoning, parsley, beaten egg and breadcrumbs. Fill onions with the stuffing mix and replace caps.

4. Place the stuffed onions in an ovenproof casserole dish and sprinkle the tops with golden breadcrumbs or pour over brown sauce to baste while baking. Bake for 30 minutes at 180 °C (350 °F, GM 4).

Stuffed Cabbage   **10–15 minutes**

1 *medium head of cabbage, $\frac{1}{2}$ kg (1 lb) minced meat, 140 g (5 oz) cooked rice, 1 medium onion, 2 tablespoons fat, salt, paprika, 1 small can of tomato puree, 250 ml ($\frac{3}{8}$ pt) tomato juice, 3 tablespoons flour, 1 carton of sour cream.*

1. Heat fat in an open pan, add meat and brown evenly. Add the cooked rice, onion, salt, paprika and tomato puree. Heat well and stir.

2. Prepare cabbage by removing outer leaves. Cut a slice off the top and hollow out centre with a sharp knife. Leave a 1$\frac{1}{2}$ cm ($\frac{3}{4}$ in) shell. Fill cabbage with meat mixture.

3. Place stuffed cabbage on trivet and pour tomato juice into the cooker. Seal and bring to pressure for 10 to 15 minutes depending on size of cabbage.

4. Remove cabbage and place on serving dish. Keep hot.

5. Remove trivet from cooker and thicken the liquid in the base with flour paste. Stir in the sour cream and heat to boiling. Pour sauce over cabbage. Serve this dish with rice, macaroni or potatoes.

Stuffed Vine Leaves   **15–20 minutes**

The Greeks call this Dolmades and the dish can be found all over the Eastern Mediterranean. Vine leaves may be bought fresh or in tins from specialist grocers. Ingredients otherwise are as for stuffed cabbage but omit the flour and sour-cream sauce.

Unwrap the vine leaves and pour meat, rice and onion mixture into the middle. Make a small parcel out of each vine leaf and wrap carefully. Pressure cook 15 to 20 minutes in tomato juice and proceed as before. This dish can also be eaten cold as part of a salad.

STUFFED PEPPERS   **5 minutes**

Basic preparation and pressure-cooking method for stuffed peppers

1. Cut pepper cases in half lengthways and remove stem, seeds and pith from each half.

2. Tap the pepper halves gently on the cutting board to dislodge stray seeds.

3. Wash thoroughly and drain for 10 minutes.

4. Fill each pepper with stuffing and place on trivet in pressure cooker with 140 *ml* ($\frac{1}{4}$ *pt*) water in base. Pressure steam for 5 minutes. Can be served with grated cheese if hot, or mayonnaise if cold.

Rice-Stuffed Peppers   **5 minutes**

4 green peppers, 170 g (6 oz) cooked rice, 140 ml ($\frac{1}{4}$ pt) stock, cream or tomato pulp, salt and pepper, cayenne pepper, $\frac{1}{2}$ teaspoon curry powder or pinch of oregano, 120 g (4 oz) grated cheese.

1. Wash and prepare green pepper cases (see p. 101).
2. Mix together all the remaining ingredients. Adjust seasoning. Fill the pepper cases and pressure steam for 5 minutes.
3. Sprinkle with grated cheese and brown slightly under grill before serving.

Peppers Stuffed with Meat or Fish   **5 minutes**

4 green peppers, 340 g (12 oz) cooked fish or meat, 430 ml ($\frac{3}{4}$ pt) cream sauce (see p. 76), Worcestershire sauce or lemon juice or sherry, 2 tablespoons of chopped parsley, mayonnaise (if served cold).

1. Wash and prepare green peppers (see p. 101).
2. Prepare cream sauce. Mix in the meat or fish. Season to taste. Fill the pepper cases and pressure steam for 5 minutes.
3. Serve hot garnished with chopped parsley or serve cold with mayonnaise.

Peppers Stuffed with Meat and Rice   **5 minutes**

4 green peppers, 225 g ($\frac{1}{2}$ lb) minced beef, 170 g (6 oz) cooked rice, 3 tablespoons minced onion, 2 tablespoons butter, 2 beaten eggs, salt, paprika, celery seed or curry powder or dried herbs or Worcestershire sauce.

1. Wash and prepare peppers as above (see p. 101). Melt the butter in a pan and add the minced beef and the minced onion. Sauté and stir. Add the cooked rice, the eggs, and seasoning to taste. Mix well and fill pepper cases. Pressure steam for 5 minutes.

2. Serve hot.

DRIED VEGETABLES

Traditional dried vegetables are dried by leaving them out in rows under the hot sun or in special evaporation chambers. All the moisture is evaporated away before the plant juices, enzymes and micro-organisms can make the plant decay and go mouldy. To reconstitute, you simply add water. Usually you have to soak for some time. The most common form of dried vegetable is various sorts of beans – known as *pulses* – though dried mushrooms are available sometimes. The Chinese mushrooms available in Chinese supermarkets and delicatessens are worth having even if you do not intend to cook specifically Chinese dishes; only remember that they taste much stronger than their European and North American counterparts.

More recently there have come on to the domestic market *dehydrated* or *freeze-dried* vegetables. These are subject to what is in fact an abuse of normal deep-freezing techniques so that all the water is frozen out. When the vegetables are allowed to return to normal temperatures they have no moisture in them so that, like their dried counterparts, they do not go bad. Dehydrated vegetables, which include peas, beans, onions, peppers, sweetcorn and turnips, have the advantage that they do not need prolonged soaking in order to reconstitute them. Some of them are called 'instant'. However, they are usually less nutritious so far as vitamins are concerned and they are often more expensive. The packaging normally makes clear which is which.

Under normal conditions, pulses need 8 to 12 hours soaking to reconstitute them properly. Some exceptionally hard ones, like chick peas, require 24 hours. Incidentally, once they have been reconstituted, a high proportion of the beans will actually be alive and can be germinated and sprouted. A more rapid means of reconstituting is to soak for 1 to 2 hours in very hot water. Never use soda to speed the process.

With pressure cooking it is possible to cut down on the need for soaking, though if you do not soak at all the texture of the beans may be affected and they will take on a shrivelled, prune-like appearance. In addition, if you cool the beans too rapidly, they may actually explode slightly from within making them mushy and floury.

Dried vegetables are cooked in the bottom of the pan, in water, not with the trivet or in a separator. Beans will absorb a great deal of water in reconstituting and cooking – 1 cup of dried beans will yield 2½ cups of cooked reconstituted beans. Do not add salt until the very last stage – salt tends to draw the moisture out of the beans. The idea is to force moisture into the bean but to retain all the goodness – salt will make the proteins and trace minerals leach out into the cooking fluid.

Pulses must always be pre-washed, even if not soaked, and picked over to remove stray stones. Drop beans into water that is already boiling in the pressure pan. Skim surface if necessary before sealing on lid.

Individual recipes are given later, but here is the table, with timings in minutes for soaked and non-soaked ingredients: in each case the weight of dried vegetables is 175 g (6 oz) – enough for four servings.

Vegetable	Dried (mins)	Pre-soaked (mins)	Instructions
CHICK PEAS (Garbanzos)	80	30	Use 750 ml (1½ pts) water. It is much better to soak, preferably for 24 hours. If used for thickening – grind up beans in pestle or coffee grinder while still dry. Cooking time is then 5 minutes.
HARICOTS (Butter, Blackeye, Kidney, Red)	60	20–30	Use 500 ml (1 pt) water. Larger specimens need the longer time.

Vegetable	Dried (mins)	Pre-soaked (mins)	Instructions
LENTILS (Green or Red)	45	20	Use 750 *ml* (1½ *pts*) water. Red lentils don't keep their form and go mushy fairly easily – neglect to pre-soak and they will certainly do so. Use them as thickener for soup and 'meat' loaf. Green (or brown) lentils retain their shape more readily and taste nicer.
LIMAS (and NAVY)	45–55	30–45	Use 750–1000 *ml* (1½–2 *pts*) water. These are the beans sometimes used for baking. Big, hard specimens may need longer cooking periods. Un-soaked beans tend to have a mealy texture.
MUSHROOMS (Chinese, Polish)	15–25	5	Pre-soaking is strongly recommended unless you are merely adding a few mushrooms to a whole mix of things to make a casserole. Chinese dried mushrooms are expensive but so strongly flavoured that a few will go a long way. You'll need 500 *ml* (1 *pt*) water for every 125 *g* (4 *oz*) of mushrooms but 25 *g* (1 *oz*) of mushrooms may be enough!
SPLIT PEAS (Yellow and Green)	15–20	To pressure	Some split peas require no soaking. You'll need only 125 *ml* (¼ *pt*) water.
SOYA BEANS	45	30	Use 750 *ml* (1½ *pts*) water. Note that this refers to the actual dried bean, not to the textured meat substitute.
TAPIOCA	15	5	Tapioca is used in desserts and it is better to use fruit juice instead of water. Use water plus milk if wished. Remember to boil any liquid first before adding the tapioca. You'll need 750 *ml* (1½ *pts*).

Use this table with less familiar pulses – match them up with the ones listed here. Aduki beans are mung peas and are treated like chick peas.

DEHYDRATED VEGETABLES

It is usually not worth cooking these freeze-dried vegetables by themselves in a pressure cooker as they already take so little time to cook. However, if you are adding them, as I do, to other ingredients, as in a soup or casserole, you need to know that the notional pressure-cooking time is 3 *to* 4 *minutes*. I always keep a small stock of dehydrated vegetables in my cupboard to provide instant variety and interest to whatever I may be cooking. If you are trying to produce a meal quickly (and that after all is one of the reasons for running a pressure cooker) then you may not worry about the low food value every now and then.

TINNED VEGETABLES

Tinned vegetables are cooked before canning and so only require reheating. Judging by the shelves in grocery stores and supermarkets people still believe in buying canned vegetables, though with a pressure cooker they are hardly necessary. Do not try to use tinned vegetables in a pressure cooker unless you want them to turn to puree. If, in the interests of speed, you want to add a tin of vegetables to a dish you are cooking by pressure, wait until the main period of cooking is over, depressurize, remove the lid, heat the food lightly in the open pan and pour in the contents of the can to heat rapidly.

THE RECIPES

Baked Beans   **55–60 minutes dried**
                                       20–30 minutes pre-soaked

200 g (7 oz) *dried beans (haricot or navy)*, $\frac{3}{4}$ *l* (1$\frac{1}{2}$ *pts*) *water or lager-type beer, 1 small chopped onion, 1 tablespoon of mustard, 50 ml (2 fl oz) molasses or 28 g (1 oz) brown sugar,*

120 g ($\frac{1}{4}$ *lb*) *cubed salt pork or chopped bacon*, 1–2 *tablespoons flour for thickening, seasoning, curry powder, Worcestershire sauce.*

1. Soak beans overnight in water or beer. Retain bean water and use for the basis of sauce. If you don't soak, pressure-cooking time is about 55 to 60 minutes, but you may find the beans look slightly wrinkled and prune-like and their texture a little too floury. You'll need 750 *ml* (1$\frac{1}{2}$–2 *pts*) water in the cooker. If beans are pre-soaked cook for 20 to 30 minutes in 400 *ml* ($\frac{3}{4}$ *pt*) water.

2. Remove trivet and sauté cubed pork or chopped bacon with the onions until golden brown. Add the beans, seasoning and the water (as above). Cook and reduce pressure at room temperature.

3. Place beans in uncovered ovenproof dish and brown in a hot oven for 10 to 15 minutes (205 °C, 400 °F, GM 6).

4. Prepare the bean sauce using 1 to 2 tablespoons of flour and bean water. Stir well and heat gently. Bring to boil and stir for a further 2 minutes. Adjust seasoning. Pour over beans. Keep hot until served.

5. Variation *à la française*: Add 1 or 2 cloves of crushed garlic to sauté mix. Season with thyme and dried parsley. If bean sauce is water-base (*not* beer) add 3 tablespoons cognac and 6 tablespoons dry red wine to ingredients just before pressurizing.

Mustard Lentils   **30 minutes**

230 g ($\frac{1}{2}$ *lb*) *dried red lentils*, 2 *onions*, 3 *tablespoons butter*, $\frac{1}{2}$ *teaspoon strong mustard powder*, 280 *ml* ($\frac{1}{2}$ *pt*) *stock or potato water*, 1 *teaspoon parsley flakes*, 120 g (4 *oz*) *ham*, 1 *tablespoon flour, salt and pepper.*

1. Pre-cook dried lentils for 25 minutes in 1 *l* (2 *pts*) water. If you use brown lentils, pre-cooking period is 40 minutes.

2. While lentils are cooking: In a frying pan or saucepan, melt butter and gently fry onions until brown, and add diced ham (or green bacon). Sprinkle on flour and stir in. Add the stock slowly. Season the mixture with salt and pepper and then sprinkle on mustard powder which should give off a delicate but not too violent aroma.

3. Drain pre-cooked lentils and add to the mustard sauce. Garnish with chives or parsley.

Just before serving you can add sesame oil or *miso* to taste.

Spiced Lentils   30 minutes

230 g (½ lb) dried red lentils, 280 ml (½ pt) stock or potato water, 4 cloves crushed garlic, ½ teaspoon curry powder, ⅛ teaspoon cayenne, ¼ teaspoon ginger, nutmeg or coriander or cardamom.

1. This is a variation that requires the same preparation and cooking time as above.

2. The spices are added immediately before pressure cooking. When cooked, salt to taste. Add water if necessary.

Savoury Chick Peas   30 minutes

230 g (½ lb) soaked chick peas, 3 plump tomatoes, 1 green pepper, 1 onion, 2 tablespoons olive oil, minced clove of garlic, basil, tarragon.

1. If chick peas are dry, pressure cook in 750 ml (1½ pt) water for 50 minutes – 1 hour by themselves. Otherwise . . .

2. Remove skins from tomatoes by dropping in hot water briefly and then peeling them (or use canned tomatoes). Cut into largish chunks.

3. Heat olive oil in cooker and sauté chopped onion with the pepper and minced garlic until onion is just turning brown. Add tomatoes and cook briefly. Add basil and tarragon.

4. Drain chick peas soaked or partly cooked, and add to the sauté mix. Cook in 400 *ml* (¾ *pt*) water or stock, for 30 minutes. Remove lid and adjust seasoning. Add water if too dry or reduce water on high heat if too much.

5. Just before serving add more fresh herbs and sesame oil, Worcestershire sauce or tabasco to taste.

Indian Lentils with Spinach   30 minutes

170 *g* (6 *oz*) *dried brown or red lentils*, 450 *g* (1 *lb*) *spinach*, ½ *teaspoon turmeric*, 1 *teaspoon salt*, ½ *teaspoon paprika or chili powder*, 2 *tablespoons ghee* (*Indian clarified butter or oil*), 1 *small chopped onion*, 1 *teaspoon mustard seeds*, ½ *teaspoon cumin seeds*, 1 *teaspoon garam masala*.

1. Wash and pre-cook lentils for 25 minutes in 1 *l* (2 *pts*) water with the turmeric, salt and paprika (40 minutes if brown lentils).

2. While lentils are cooking, wash spinach and remove any tough stalks. Chop finely.

3. Reduce pressure. Remove lid and add spinach. Reseal and bring to pressure only.

4. In a separate pan melt ghee (or butter or oil) and fry chopped onion, mustard and cumin seeds till golden. Stir this mixture into the lentils and spinach adding the garam masala at the same time.

5. Reduce excess liquid until quite dry. Stir continuously. Do not allow to burn. Serve with hot rice.

Soybean Casserole   30–45 minutes

230 *g* (½ *lb*) *soybeans*, 280 *ml* (½ *pt*) *bean water*, 1 *small onion*, 3 *medium tomatoes*, 2 *large courgettes* (*or* 1 *small marrow approximately* 340 *g* (¾ *lb*)), 50 *g* (2 *oz*) *Parmesan cheese*, 3 *tablespoons butter*, ½ *teaspoon thyme*, 1 *tablespoon dried parsley*, 2 *cloves garlic*, *crushed*, ½ *teaspoon dill*, *pepper*.

1. Wash and soak beans overnight. Pre-cook in 750 *ml* (1½ *pts*) water for 30 minutes if pre-soaked or 45 minutes if dried.

2. Remove beans from pressure cooker, reserving any liquid that might remain. Melt butter in open pressure cooker and sauté the onion and garlic for a few minutes. Add all the herbs. Sauté and mix again. Add beans and the 280 *ml* (½ *pt*) of bean water. Allow liquid to simmer and reduce (approximately 10 minutes).

3. Meanwhile, grease a casserole dish. Wash and slice tomatoes and courgettes thinly. Do not peel.

4. Add grated Parmesan to bean sauce and stir in well.

5. Pour a layer of beans into the base of casserole dish, followed by a layer of tomatoes and a layer of courgettes. Repeat. Put knobs of butter on top. Sprinkle with black pepper. Cover and bake for 2 hours at 180 °C (300 °F, GM 2).

6. *Variation with nutbutter and spices*

Omit: tomatoes, courgettes, onions and cheese.
Substitute: herbs with spices – chili, cumin, cardamom, coriander and butter with sesame oil or tahini, or if you can get it cashew, almond or walnut butter.
Add: 120 *g* (4 *oz*) peanut butter to beans before simmering and reducing.

7. *Japanese variation*

Cook soybeans alone and when cooked flavour with sugar, honey or molasses, and salt. If eaten as a main dish, season lightly. As a side dish be generous with the sweetening.

Soybean Croquettes   **45 minutes dried**
                                          30 minutes pre-soaked

230 *g* (½ *lb*) *cooked soybeans, 1 small onion, 1–2 cloves garlic, 4 cloves shallots, 4 tablespoons butter, 240 ml (½ pt) milk, 4 tablespoons flour, ½ teaspoon crushed rosemary, ½ teaspoon thyme, 1 tablespoon dried parsley, 4 tablespoons wheat germ, salt and pepper, 1 beaten egg, crushed cereal or breadcrumbs.*

1. Mash cooked soybeans in a mill or grinder. Melt 2 tablespoons of butter in bottom of pressure cooker and sauté the minced garlic, onion and shallots till onion is transparent.

2. Make a *roux* with the flour and remaining butter and the milk in another pan. Add it to the sauté onion mix. Crush the herbs.

3. In a large bowl combine the mashed soybeans, the onion sauce, the herbs and the wheat germ. Season to taste.

4. In a separate dish beat egg with a little milk. In another shallow dish spread out the breadcrumbs or crushed cereal.

5. Shape the soybean mix into croquettes, ovals or balls. Dip them alternately into egg mix and breadcrumbs until thoroughly coated.

6. Place croquettes in a shallow, greased, baking dish and bake in a fairly hot oven for 20 to 30 minutes (205 °C, 400 °F, GM 6). Serve with cranberry-Cumberland sauce, apple sauce or sour cream.

Chili Beans   **60 minutes dried**
                                    20–30 minutes pre-soaked

230 g ($\frac{1}{2}$ *lb*) *cooked kidney beans* (*or soybeans, pinto or blackeye*), 280 ml ($\frac{1}{2}$ *pt*) *bean water*, 1 *onion*, 1 *green pepper*, 2 *tomatoes*, 1 *small tin tomato puree*, $\frac{1}{2}$ *teaspoon chili powder*, *salt*, *pepper*, 1 *clove garlic*, $\frac{1}{2}$ *teaspoon grated root ginger or ginger powder*.

1. Cook the beans (see table pp. 104–5, 294–5). Dice the onions and green peppers and sauté them in the bottom of the pressure cooker for a few minutes. Add the chunks of tomato, tomato puree and some of the cooking liquid.

2. Add cooked beans and seasoning to taste. Garlic and ginger give an added bite to the dish. Simmer for 30 minutes.

3. For a milder version season tomato sauce with salt and pepper, and basil, tarragon or thyme. Serve.

Dried-Bean Patties (Burgers, Rissoles)
(see tables for timing)

150 g (6 oz) cooked beans (soya, lima, navy), 2 chopped onions, 30 g (1 oz) fresh chopped parsley, 2 egg yolks, 2 tablespoons cream or evaporated milk, salt and pepper, thyme or sage, 1 clove crushed garlic, flour, butter, barbecue sauce;
optional: grated raw potato, carrot or celery.

1. Grind and mash cooked beans. Add the chopped onion, crushed garlic and chopped parsley (and optional grated vegetables). Beat 2 egg yolks and add to the mix. Stir well. Add milk or cream, and seasonings.
2. Shape mix into balls and flatten. Dip them in flour. Chill for 1 hour. Sauté and brown them in butter or oil until evenly cooked.
3. Serve with tomato sauce, white sauce, barbecue sauce or any other.

Samosa
(see tables for timing)

170 g (6 oz) mixed soaked beans, 2 medium potatoes, 1 minced onion, pinch of ginger, 120 g (4 oz) mixed fresh vegetables, flaky pastry (which can be bought deep-frozen from grocers' shops), curry spices such as coriander, cumin, garam masala, oil.

This is a European version of a standard Indian snack.

1. Use pressure cooker to cook beans, vegetables and potatoes (see tables pp. 66–72, 104–5, 286–92 294–5,). Drain and mix.
2. Lightly fry curry spices in oil (you can use curry powder or a blend of your own choosing). Add cooked mixed beans, potatoes and vegetables.
3. Stir-fry briefly then remove from heat and add garam masala.
4. Roll out flaky pastry very thinly and cut into largish

triangles. Place dollops of the mixture in the middle of the triangles, wrap up carefully from the corners by moistening the edges of the pastry. You'll end up with 20 samosas.

5. Then: (*a*) either drop in deep fat until golden or crispy (2 to 3 minutes) or (*b*) heat in oven till pastry is fluffy and light brown (about 7 to 8 minutes at 220 °C, 425 °F, GM 7). Serve plain or with yoghurt sauce.

VEGETARIAN SPECIALITIES

The following recipes are not intended for vegetarians alone, but they are some of my favourites. As it happens, I am no vegetarian but I have grown to like their special dishes. The pressure cooker is at its best when cooking vegetables and these recipes should give plenty of scope for ideas.

Vegetable Casseroles

170 g (6 oz) ingredients (*other than liquid*) per person.

Grains: rice, cracked or bulghar wheat, barley, noodles, spaghetti.

Beans: soya, lentils, kidney, white, red, blackeye.

Vegetables: potatoes, onions, carrots, aubergines, cabbage, green beans, asparagus.

Extra flavour: mushrooms, celery, tomato, green pepper, nuts, dried fruits.

Liquids: water, stock, tomato sauce, milk, yoghurt, sour cream, white or brown sauce, egg and milk.

Seasoning: salt, pepper, herbs, garlic, spices.

Garnish: grated cheese, breadcrumbs, ricotta chesse, chopped nuts.

1. Cook the ingredients at the same time in separators in the pressure cooker according to the tables and 'build up' a

casserole in a suitable dish using hot, just-cooked ingredients.

2. Adjust the seasoning. Garnish with cheese or mashed potatoes, etc.

3. Heat in the oven at 180 °C (350 °F, GM 4) for 20 to 30 minutes.

4. The casserole can be layered with the different ingredients alternately or mixed together. Complement with seasoning and add a moistener.

5. Brown under grill if wished. This casserole method reduces normal cooking time to a quarter to one third and preserves more of the goodness!

Vegetable Spaghetti   8–10 minutes

This is a vegetable in its own right – a member of the squash/marrow family; it is often grown by gardeners though it rarely appears in shops.

1. Cook whole. Pressure-steaming time is 8 to 10 minutes.

2. Cut vegetable in half and the inside comes away like spaghetti strings.

3. Season with salt, pepper or tomato sauce.

4. *OR* chill and serve with salads and mayonnaise.

Bubble and Squeak

50 g (1½ oz) dripping or fat, 2 rashers streaky bacon, 1 onion, 1 small cabbage, 680 g (1½ lb) potatoes, salt and pepper, 1 tablespoon chopped parsley; optional: 4 eggs, fried or poached.

1. Peel potatoes. Shred cabbage. Pressure cook in separators for 8 minutes. Drain well.

2. Mash potatoes till smooth. Mix the cabbage with the mashed potato and season with salt and pepper.

3. Remove rinds from bacon and chop finely. Peel and chop onion. Cook rindless bacon and onion over a low heat till onion is clear. Mix in the potatoes and cabbage. Press down firmly to cover pan evenly.

4. Fry over a high heat for 10 minutes till the underneath is a crisp golden brown.

5. To serve: invert on to a serving dish. Garnish with chopped parsley and (optional) place 4 cooked eggs (fried or poached) on top.

Parsnips and Onions   5 minutes

680 g (1½ *lb*) *parsnips, juice of* ½ *lemon,* 2 *large onions,* 60 *g* (2 *oz*) *butter,* 280 *ml* (½ *pt*) *milk, salt and pepper,* 1 *tablespoon chopped parsley,* 140 *ml* (¼ *pt*) *water for cooker.*

1. Peel parsnips and cut lengthways in thin strips. Put into cold water and lemon juice. Peel and thinly slice the onions. Place both vegetables in separators. Add 140 *ml* (¼ *pt*) water to pressure cooker and pressure steam vegetables for 5 minutes in the usual way. Do not season.

2. Grease a baking dish. Arrange parsnips and onions in layers, seasoning each layer with salt and pepper. Pour over milk and dot with butter. Bake in pre-heated oven for 10 to 15 minutes at 220 °C (425 °F, GM 7). Baste with liquid. Garnish with chopped parsley.

Pease Pudding   12 minutes

230 g (½ *lb*) *pre-soaked green peas (see tables pp. 105, 295),* 570 *ml* (1 *pt*) *ham or bacon stock,* 1 *large or* 2 *small eggs, butter, seasoning, water for cooker.*

1. Remove trivet. Cook peas in the usual way (see p. 104) for 8 minutes. Cook with a ham or bacon bone if necessary to give extra flavour.

2. Remove bones if used. Mash the peas. Stir in the well-beaten egg(s). Add a large knob of butter. Adjust seasoning.

3. Put mash into a greased bowl or solid container and cover with greaseproof paper. For the second cooking period the pease pudding can be cooked on its own or with a selection of other vegetables to be served at the same time.

4. Seal pan containing water for cooker, trivet and bowl of pease pudding and bring to pressure in the usual way. Cook for 4 minutes.

Glazed Sweet Potatoes   **15 minutes**

4 *large sweet potatoes*, 120 g (4 oz) *sugar*, ½ *teaspoon salt*, 30 g (1 oz) *butter*, *water for cooker*.

1. Pre-cook sweet potatoes whole in jackets for 15 minutes (see tables pp. 172, 292). Then peel.

2. Throw away water. Melt butter and sugar in the pressure cooker and brown the potatoes.

Alternatively, arrange the potatoes in a baking tray, sprinkle over the sugar, dot with butter and place in a pre-heated oven till sugar and butter are melted (10 minutes at 180 °C, 350 °F, GM 4).

Sweet Potatoes and Apple   **15 minutes**

3 *large sweet potatoes*, 2 *large cooking apples*, 90 g (3 oz) *brown sugar*, 30 g (1 oz) *butter*.

1. Wash potatoes and leave in jackets. Place them on the trivet in the pressure cooker. Place washed, cored apples in wet parchment paper on top of potatoes.

2. Add water. Cover, seal, bring to pressure and cook for 15 minutes.

3. Lift out apples and potatoes, peel and slice. Arrange in alternate layers with sugar and butter in casserole and bake for $\frac{1}{2}$ hour in oven (180 °C, 350 °F, GM 4).

Yam Fritters   8–10 minutes

500 g (1 lb) small sliced yams, 4 tablespoons butter, 6 tablespoons flour, $\frac{1}{2}$ teaspoon salt, 2 tablespoons single cream, 1 egg, 2 teaspoons sugar, oil.

1. Pressure cook yams in usual way for 10 minutes.
2. Mash yams or put through mouli. Add butter, cream, flour, beaten egg, salt and sugar. Mix thoroughly. Leave for 15 minutes.
3. Heat oil in large saucepan. Drop spoonfuls of mix in hot fat and turn until nicely browned.
4. Serve with honey or golden syrup.

Steamed Yams   6–8 minutes (depending on size)

Can be fried whole to crisp up the outside or baked by dotting with butter, sugar and cinnamon.

Plantain   6–8 minutes

23–30 cm (9–12 in) green plantains, butter.

1. Remove fibrous strings before cooking. Peel green plantains under running water to keep from staining the hands.
2. Pressure boil in water for 6 to 8 minutes.

3. Season and serve with butter or finely dice and add to omelettes, soups or stews.

N.B. Over-cooking makes them bitter.

Spiked Steamed Potatoes   6–10 minutes

1 kg (2 *lb*) *small potatoes*, 1 *chopped onion*, 4 *cloves garlic*, 2·5 cm (1 *in*) *piece of ginger*, ½ *teaspoon paprika or chili powder*, *juice of* 1 *lemon*, 1 *teaspoon salt*, 850 ml (1½ *pts*) *milk*, 2·5 cm (1 *in*) *piece of broken cinnamon*, 4 *green cardamoms*, 6 *cloves*, 4 *tablespoons ghee or butter*, *turmeric*.

1. Peel potatoes and prick all over with a fork till they become spongy. Leave to soak in cold water.
2. Grind onion, garlic, ginger, turmeric and paprika to a paste. Mix paste with lemon juice, salt and milk. Stir well and pour over drained potatoes.
3. Remove trivet. Heat ghee or butter in pressure cooker and fry cinnamon, cardamom and cloves. Add the potato mixture. Seal, bring to pressure in the usual way and cook for 6 to 10 minutes (depending on size of potatoes). Serve like a hot curry.

Variant with spiced yoghurt   3–5 minutes

1 kg (2 *lb*) *potatoes*, 280 ml (½ *pt*) *yoghurt*, 1 *teaspoon turmeric*, 1 *teaspoon garam masala*, 1 *teaspoon salt*, 2 *tablespoons ghee or butter*, 3 *crushed bay leaves*, ½ *teaspoon paprika or chili powder*, ½ *teaspoon brown sugar*, 2 *tablespoons chopped coriander leaves*.

1. Pressure cook potatoes for half their cooking time (approximately 3 to 5 minutes). Drain and throw away water. Peel and prick all over with a fork.
2. Beat the yoghurt into the turmeric, garam masala and salt until smooth.
3. Heat the ghee or butter and fry bay leaves and paprika

for 2 minutes. Add the sugar and stir till it begins to brown. Stir in yoghurt.

4. In a casserole dish cover potatoes with yoghurt paste and sprinkle with chopped coriander leaves. Cover and bake in a moderate oven till potatoes are tender and encrusted with paste (15 to 20 minutes at 205 °C, 400 °F, GM 6). Serve hot.

Steamed Masala Cauliflower   4 minutes

For cauliflower: 1 *cauliflower cut into sprigs*, 6 *cloves garlic*, 2·5 *cm* (1 *in*) *piece ginger*, ½ *teaspoon paprika or chili powder*, 1 *teaspoon turmeric*, ½ *teaspoon garam masala*, 1 *teaspoon salt*, *juice of* ½ *lemon*, 430 *ml* (¾ *pt*) *water for cooker*.
For masala paste: 1 *tablespoon ghee or butter*, 1 *finely chopped onion*, 4 *cloves chopped garlic*, 2·5 *cm* (1 *in*) *piece ginger*, 1 *teaspoon coriander seeds*, ½ *teaspoon cumin seeds*, 6 *cloves*, 8 *black peppercorns*, 2·5 *cm* (1 *in*) *piece broken cinnamon*, 4 *skinned green cardamoms*, 10 *blanched almonds*, 2 *chopped tomatoes*.

1. Wash and cut up cauliflower into small sprigs. Remove trivet and place in pressure cooker with the water.
2. Grind the remaining ingredients for the cauliflower adding the lemon juice to make a paste. Pour over the cauliflower. Cover, seal, bring to pressure in the usual way and cook for 4 minutes.
3. Meanwhile make the curd masala paste. Heat ghee or butter and lightly fry onion and garlic. Grind the ginger, spices and almonds. Add to the fried onions the tomatoes and salt. Fry for a few minutes and stir in yoghurt slowly.
4. Pour over the cauliflower. Cover but do not seal pressure cooker and simmer for a few minutes until the ingredients are tender.

Green, Orange, White   3 minutes

This is a recipe where green vegetables are steamed on a *mire-poix* of carrots and onions.

Greens, carrots and onions for 4 servings, oil and salt, water for mire-poix.

1. Wash greens and cut into small pieces. Slice onion and carrot.
2. Remove trivet. Heat oil. Sauté onion then add carrot slices and continue to sauté. Add water to cover *mire-poix*. Place greens on top.
3. Seal, bring to pressure in the usual way and cook for 3 minutes.

Dried Mushrooms   5 minutes

10 to 12 *Chinese dried mushrooms, green onion, grated ginger root*, 1 *tablespoon corn starch*, 1 *tablespoon butter, margarine or oil, salt, sugar, soy sauce, sherry or sake*, 280 *ml* ($\frac{1}{2}$ *pt*) *mushroom liquid.*

1. Soak mushrooms in warm water till soft ($\frac{1}{2}$ to 3 hours), (or use pressure cooker to reconstitute rapidly – 10 to 12 minutes). Drain mushrooms and either leave whole or slice according to preference. Reserve liquid.
2. Season the mushroom liquid with salt, sugar, soy sauce, wine. Grate the ginger and chop up the onions.
3. Stir-fry the mushrooms in the bottom of the pressure cooker. Then add the onion and ginger.
4. Mix in the seasoned liquid. Seal and pressure cook in the usual way for 5 minutes.
5. In a separate pan melt the butter, margarine or oil and cook the corn starch carefully but do not allow to brown.

Add to pressure cooker at end of cooking period to thicken sauce. Adjust the taste with soy sauce or sugar if necessary.

This sauce can be served with many dishes, e.g. combinations of green and root vegetables.

5: FISH

Fish is a superb food – it is highly nutritious in proteins and vitamins – and the carbohydrates are in the form of oils that are very beneficial to health. It is quickly cooked and easily digested. A wide variety of different sorts of fish are available and over the next few years we can all, wherever we live, expect to see a wider variety still of unusual fish offered for sale. There are two reasons for this: first, meat has got steadily more and more expensive, and the public has found it worth while transferring their tastes to fish. Secondly, as a result of changing international laws regarding fishing rights, the types of fish we have been used to may not always be as readily available as the less familiar, though no less good, varieties.

The eating of fish has always been more subject to the vagaries of fashion than other types of food. Certainly in Britain a high premium has always been placed on 'white' fish like cod and plaice, at the expense of those with grey or pink flesh, like hus or rock salmon or coley. Other fish, like John Dory (also known as St Peter's Fish) look ugly – the head resembles a SciFi horror monster – but are very tasty and look good on the plate. Yet others – like seabream – are just unfashionable. I personally have never understood why mackerel are so under-valued – they are cheap, plentiful, tasty and nutritious. Herring too, probably the most nutritious of all fish, is usually eaten in Britain only in the smoked form – as kippers, or soused, when you buy it from the delicatessen. And any food historian has a field day when it comes to shellfish – how the humble Dublin Bay Prawn, a thoroughly proletarian food, became the commuter-belt delicacy, scampi; and how oysters were once sold as cheap snacks in the streets of London . . .

In other countries too, one finds conservatism in regard to the types of fish eaten and the ways in which they are prepared. We may soon see more freshwater fish, which may be farmed as they were in medieval times – carp, trout, roach and so on. Incidentally, fish farming is far more satisfactory in every way than battery chicken production.

For these reasons I have covered more fish than many readers may find familiar, though in fact methods of cooking and preparing don't vary all that much. Experimentation is very worth while, and not only out of budgetary necessity – all manner of cheap delicacies are there waiting to be discovered.

PRESSURE COOKING

Pressure cooking fish offers speed, control of cooking, and prevents the build-up of fishy smells in the kitchen. The standard method of pressure cooking fish is high-pressure steaming, and it is one of the best – and tastiest – ways of producing fish. The fish is laid on the trivet (sometimes on a bed of greaseproof or parchment paper to facilitate lifting off cleanly) over super-heated water (or a fumet – a light fish stock) and the juices inside the fish are heated up. The taste is like top-quality fried fish, but without the batter. Incidentally, when you deep-fry fish properly what happens is that the batter provides a seal against the oil and the fish is actually cooked by 'dry' heat – in other words, in its own juices. Steamed fish has a poor reputation because too many people confuse it with boiled or poached fish, which can be rather tasteless. The point to remember is that with steamed fish the meat does not sit in the cooking fluid, so there is no leaching away of juices.

Braising is a version of steaming – except that you use a bed of vegetables as a trivet on which to rest the fish. Water is poured on to pre-fried vegetables in the bottom of the pan so as to half cover them; the fish is clear of the water but is cooked in vegetable steam. The bed of vegetables is known as a *mire-poix* (see pp. 143, 154).

It is also possible to pressure poach, but this is a technique more easily applied to making thick fish stews than to cooking entire fish. A recipe for court bouillon is given on p. 130.

If you want a 'fried' effect, it is possible to sauté the fish lightly before pressure cooking, just to brown and flavour the outside. You do not have to deep fat fry, and the combination of frying the outside and pressure steaming the inside gives a superb balance of tasty exterior and juicy interior – an instance where the pressure cooker can offer techniques of cooking not available by any other means.

It is important to watch timings carefully – in each relevant case I have given them for both fresh and for frozen fish, though usually they are the same unless the fish is frozen into a very solid mass. Remember that many inland fishmongers receive their wares deep frozen and then defrost them for you on the marble display slab. If in doubt about timing, undercook and then finish off at normal temperature and pressure with the weight/valve off. Don't forget that you can always use your pressure cooker as a particularly effective steamer at ordinary temperatures and pressures – and for certain quick-cooking fish this may be the best thing to do. The flesh of cooked fish is thick and flaky – not transparent, and should not cling too much to the bone. The individual pieces of flesh are bound together by delicate layers of gelatine, which should not be allowed to melt. If you over-cook, the flesh starts to separate from the bone too readily and takes on a mushy, soggy texture. If you have a meat thermometer, the internal temperature of perfectly cooked fish (make sure the thermometer does not touch the bone) is 60 °C (140 °F).

All pressure-cooking times depend partly on the size of the individual pieces – remember that what counts is the rate of penetration of the heat.

BUYING FISH

As every good cook knows and every good cookbook keeps on stressing – good food starts with good ingredients. Buy your fish carefully, locate the best fishmonger in the area, cultivate him and stay loyal. We'll only prevent the sale of second-rate fish by refusing to patronize sloppy fishmongers. A fresh fish looks and feels firm – try poking the side gently, if a dent remains, the fish has been out of water a bit too long. The eyes should be transparent and slightly bulging – sunken and glazed eyes are a bad sign. The gills should be bright red inside and the scales shiny. Mackerel and herring in particular should be very fresh. If your fishmonger has obtained deep-frozen stock – and there is nothing wrong with this as fish is often frozen as soon as it is lifted out of the water – try and get a piece that is still icy rather than one which has defrosted completely. You can complete the defrosting in your cooker, fish being an exception to the general rule about the dangers of cooking partially thawed meats. Do not, however, try to refreeze defrosted fish.

If you ask a fishmonger to fillet or prepare a fish for you, save the heads and tails for soup or stock (see p. 41). The innards should be discarded.

To get rid of the smell of fish, boiling up a lump of sugar in a pan will counteract most kitchen smells; a slice of lemon will remove smells from the hands; a tablespoon of vinegar boiled up in the bottom of the pressure cooker will keep it smelling sweet.

THE TABLES

The tables give the basic cooking times, though allowance should be made for the size of individual pieces. Many fish are prepared in similar ways and you rely on the inherent difference in the flavour of the flesh and a wide assortment of sauces and garnishes to give variety.

In each case you need 140 *ml* ($\frac{1}{4}$ *pt*) of water for the cooker unless the pressure-cooking time is 15 minutes or more, when you should have 250 to 300 *ml* ($\frac{1}{2}$ *pt*) water. You can use fish stock instead of water but it is not really important if you are merely pressure steaming.

Fish	Type	Cooking time (mins)	Serving
BREAM	freshwater and sea	5–7	Sea-bream is the better, more delicate fish, the freshwater fish is rather coarse. Sold whole. Clean, open up and serve either simply or with a savoury stuffing (increase cooking time by 1 to 2 minutes for this).
BRILL	sea	4–6	Comes in steaks, tails or middle cut, or whole. Remove skin and bone after cooking. Serve with contrasting sauce.
CARP	freshwater	4–6 8 for large fish	Comes whole and is farmed. Remove heads, tails, fins and innards before cooking. Diced it can be used in Quenelles (or gefilte fish).
COD	sea	4–6	Comes in fillets and steaks. Remove skin and bone after cooking. Can be pre-fried or served with contrasting sauce.
COLEY	sea	4–6	A 'grey' fish, unattractive in the raw state. Usually sold filleted. Takes on a firm texture when cooked. Can be fried or served with contrasting sauce.
EEL	freshwater or sea	6–8	Eel is usually sold live or already cooked. The jellied form is a British working-class delicacy. It is best pressure poached or stewed.
FLOUNDER	sea	6–8	Sold either whole or filleted. Treat like cod, or can be pre-fried.
HADDOCK	sea	4–6	Comes in fillets, steaks or tails. Remove skin and bone

Fish	Type	Cooking time (mins)	Serving
			after cooking. Serve with contrasting sauce.
SMOKED HADDOCK (Haddie, Finnan)		4–6	Comes in fillets – best served simply with melted butter.
HAKE	sea	4–6	As for Cod and Halibut.
HALIBUT	sea	4–6	As for Cod, but steaks more usual.
HERRING	sea	5–8	Can be cooked whole, when it is best to begin by browning the outside in hot butter. Or should be opened up on the lower side, the bones (of which there are many) removed, and the fish flattened and then cooked, possibly with herbs. Herring are rather oily; lemon juice and fennel can counteract the taste.
HUS	sea	4–6	A 'grey' fish, unattractive in the raw state. Usually sold filleted. Takes on a firm texture when cooked. Can be 'fried' or served with contrasting sauce.
JOHN DORY (St Peter's Fish)	freshwater	6–8	Sold whole. Remove head and tail. Skin is quite attractive left on. Serve simply with butter and a slice of lemon or contrasting sauce.
KIPPER	smoked	5–8	Sold either as fillets or whole fish, opened out. Serve simply with melted butter. This can be a breakfast dish as well as one for supper!
MACKEREL	sea	6–8	Usually sold whole, sometimes filleted. The biggest mackerel may need 10 minutes. Can be cooked whole, deboned and flattened out, or can be filleted. Mackerel is rather oily and lemon juice, fennel or a tart

Fish		Cooking time (mins)	Serving
			contrasting sauce are the best accompaniments.
MULLET Grey Red	sea	6–8	Sold whole and cooked whole. The grey fish are larger, cheaper and less interesting than the red ones. May be cooked on or off the bone. Grey mullet usually needs a contrasting sauce, while red mullet is fine with melted butter and lemon juice.
PIKE	freshwater	6–8	Usually not sold much but often obtained from amateur anglers. Treat like John Dory.
PLAICE	sea	6–8	Sold either whole or filleted. Treat like Cod, or can be pre-fried.
ROACH	freshwater	6–8	Sold whole and now being farmed in Europe. Flesh sometimes turns reddish when cooked. Clean out, leaving head and tail on for decoration. Serve with a simple sauce.
ROCK SALMON	sea	6–8	Not related to salmon. Sold usually as boned fillets. Serve 'fried' or with contrasting sauce.
SALMON SALMON-TROUT	freshwater or sea	Steaks: 6–8. Tails or middle cut: 7 mins per 500 *g* (6 mins per *lb*)	Sold whole and in steaks. Can be steamed or poached. Serve simply, as this expensive, superb dish needs very little help. To serve cold: remove from cooker and wrap in muslin or parchment paper to keep moist.
SARDINES	sea	3–4	Sold whole. Should be browned in butter before pressure cooking, though it is doubtful whether pressure cooking is of much benefit.
SKATE	sea	6–8	Sold filleted. Treat like Cod.
SOLE FILLETS Lemon sole	sea	6–8	Treat like Plaice.

Fish	Type	Cooking time (mins)	Serving
SQUID/ OCTOPUS Calamari	sea	6–8	Cut up. Do not attempt to pressure steam, but serve in a stew.
SWORDFISH	sea; not usually available in Europe	4–6	Comes usually in steaks and has a closer, meatier texture than most fish. Pressure steam and then finish in a pan of melted butter for a classic treatment.
TUNA	sea	25–30	Tuna fish is difficult to obtain fresh but is best used in stews.
Tinned		3–4	Tinned tuna fish is already cooked and is usually preserved in olive oil. Serve with vegetables and herbs to make a tasty instant fish stew.
TURBOT	sea	6–8	Superlative and expensive white fish sold in steaks or large pieces. Should be steamed plainly and served with simple sauce. Or can be browned in butter before pressure cooking.
WHITEBAIT	sea	—	Too small to be worth pressure cooking – grill or fry in butter instead.
WHITING	sea	6–8	Treat like Herring.
SHELLFISH Lobster Crab Crawfish	sea	10	These shellfish are best cooked when just killed – drive a sharp skewer through the brain! Or just drop alive into boiling water if you are not squeamish. Remove trivet and separators. Bring $1\frac{1}{2}$ *l* ($2\frac{1}{2}$ *pts*) of water to boil. Plunge shellfish in. The pressure-cooking time is 10 minutes.
Mussels Prawns Shrimps Fresh Scampi		—	Cooking time is so short I do not recommend pressure cooking – use your pan open. 3 to 4 minutes is usually enough, 5 minutes for the larger ones.

THE RECIPES

Court Bouillon   10 minutes

1 *glass white wine*, 140 *ml* ($\frac{1}{4}$ *pt*) *water*, 1 *small onion*, 1 *clove garlic*, 1 *bay leaf*, *seasoning*, *lemon peel*.

1. Bring all ingredients to boil in a small saucepan.
2. Simmer for 10 minutes.
3. Cover and allow to cool.

Court Bouillon is used when cold and strained, or not, according to the recipe.

Browned Cod   8 minutes

This recipe for fresh cod can also be applied to a wide range of white sea and freshwater fish.

750 *g* (1$\frac{1}{2}$ *lb*) *fresh cod*, 4 *tablespoons butter*, 120 *ml* (4 *fl oz*) *dry white wine*, 1 *teaspoon dried parsley*, 50 *g* (2 *oz*) *diced celery*, 140 *ml* ($\frac{1}{4}$ *pt*) *water*, 1$\frac{1}{4}$ *kg* (2 *lb*) *potatoes*, *salt and pepper*.

1. Peel potatoes and cut into 2$\frac{1}{2}$ *cm* (1 *in*) cubes.
2. Slice cod into 4 large pieces and tie it in cheesecloth.
3. Remove trivet. Melt butter in open pressure cooker. Brown fish over a low heat – a few minutes on each side. Place potato cubes around fish and brown them too.
4. Add wine, water, seasoning, parsley and celery.
5. Pressure cook for 8 minutes. Serve.

Cod Creole   5 minutes

500 *g* (1 *lb*) *fresh or frozen cod whole or in steaks*, 140 *ml* ($\frac{1}{4}$ *pt*) *water or fish stock*, 1 *teaspoon lemon juice or vinegar*,

*seasoning, bouquet garni, 50 g (2 oz) butter, 4 medium peeled
tomatoes, 4 medium onions, chopped parsley or green pepper.*

1. Pre-heat oven to 180 °C (350 °F, GM 4).
2. The fish is pressure poached in this recipe. Remove
trivet. Pour water or stock, lemon juice or vinegar into
pressure cooker. Add seasoning, bouquet garni and fish
covered with buttered paper. Pressure cook for 5 minutes.
Allow pressure to reduce at room temperature. Lift out
fish and allow to drain.
3. Fry the thinly sliced onions and tomatoes separately in
melted butter.
4. Flake the fish and season lightly with pepper. Spread
the tomatoes over the bottom of an ovenproof dish. Spread
the fish on top and then cover completely with the onions.
Decorate with strips of green pepper or chopped parsley.
Bake for 10 minutes.

Fillets of Sole   **4–5 minutes**

*750 g (1½ lb) sole fillets, 1 teaspoon salt, 2 teaspoons parsley
flakes, ½ sliced lemon.*

1. Use trivet with 140 *ml* (¼ *pt*) water beneath. Cover
trivet with greaseproof paper (buttered to prevent fish
sticking).
2. Lay fillets across the paper. Sprinkle over salt and
parsley flakes.
3. Bring to pressure in the usual way and cook for 4
minutes. This timing does not vary if you have more or
fewer fillets. However, if the fillets are very small cook for
only 3 minutes. If they are very large cook for 5 minutes.
4. Depressurize and lift fillets from trivet. (If you don't
use greaseproof paper the fish may stick to the trivet.)
5. Place on a serving dish with sliced lemon.

This is the basic recipe; it will also work for plaice, cod and
many other white fish or for smoked haddock.

Fish Cakes   **5 minutes**

125 g (5 oz) *white fish*, 125 g (5 oz) *potatoes*, 1 *tablespoon butter*, 1 *anchovy*, *salt and pepper*, *chives*, *parsley*, *egg*, *breadcrumbs*, *flour*.

1. Cook fish fillets and thin sliced potatoes in separators for 5 minutes.
2. Mash together in bowl with one sliver of anchovy, salt and pepper, and chives.
3. Make into eight patties or cakes. Have a plate of flour, a bowl of beaten egg and a plate of breadcrumbs in a line and toss each patty through the production line so that you end up with a coated fish cake.
4. Fry or grill cake for 2 minutes in shallow fat or grill for 2 minutes on each side.
5. Serve with parsley sauce.

Fried Fish   **6–10 minutes (depending on size of fish fillets)**

Whole fish fillets, flour or cornmeal, oil or butter for frying.

This recipe gives some easy variety to usual pressure-cooking methods. At the same time it does not require a deep fat fryer and the attendant mess and smell. The flesh is juicy and the outside tasty.

1. Place flour in a bag and shake fillets inside to coat them. Shallow-fry individually in oil or butter till well browned. Oil should be hot, but not smoking.
2. Place fish in cooker on greaseproof paper laid over trivet. Pressure steam in the usual way for 6 to 10 minutes depending on size. Small whole fish may take 10 minutes.
3. Serve.

Poached Salmon   **6 minutes**

1 *steak of salmon per person, seasoning, lemon juice, fresh green peas, Hollandaise sauce* (see p. 76), *knobs of butter,* 240 *ml* ($\frac{1}{2}$ *pt*) *water or light chicken or vegetable stock, cucumber slices and fresh mint.*

1. Put water or stock and trivet into pressure cooker. Place salmon steaks – well seasoned and sprinkled with lemon juice – on to trivet and cover with buttered greaseproof paper. Pressure cook for 6 minutes. Reduce pressure with cold water.

2. Prepare Hollandaise sauce and cook green peas. Toss peas with butter and sprinkle with fresh chopped mint.

3. Serve salmon on a flat dish arranged in a circle around the edge. Place a row of cucumber slices on each steak and pile the green peas in the centre and between the steaks. Hollandaise sauce is passed round in a separate container.

Salmon in White Wine   **12 minutes**

4 *salmon steaks,* 140 *ml* ($\frac{1}{4}$ *pt*) *dry white wine,* 1 *large onion,* 1 *tablespoon oil, salt and pepper, thyme,* $\frac{1}{2}$ *lemon, rosemary.*

1. Place trivet in the cooker, turned upside down to act as a tray *or* use a saucer the size of the base of the cooker.

2. Layer the bottom of the tray with onion slices. Place the salmon steaks on top.

3. Mix together the wine, oil, pepper, rosemary and thyme. Pour it over the steaks. Lay thin lemon slices on the steaks. The wine will produce steam that will penetrate the salmon.

4. Pressure cook for 12 minutes. Serve.

Trout au Bleu   **5 minutes**

1 *trout per person, Court Bouillon* (see p. 130), *melted butter, chopped parsley;* optional: *white or Hollandaise sauce.*

1. Prepare Court Bouillon in advance.

2. The fish should not be washed or scaled and should be handled as little as possible. De-gut carefully without disturbing the natural slime on the outside which is what causes the fish to 'blue'. *Buy the fish as fresh as possible –* alive even. To help the blue process even more you can sprinkle boiling hot vinegar all over the fish.

3. Remove trivet. Add cold and strained Court Bouillon and trout covered with greaseproof paper.

4. Pressure cook for 5 minutes. Reduce pressure with cold water. Lift fish out and place them on a dish laying them alternately head to tail.

5. For a hot dish serve at once. To serve cold leave the fish to cool in the Court Bouillon and then drain well before serving. Delicious with mayonnaise.

Gefilte Fish   20 minutes

This is a classic Eastern European and Jewish dish. Serve either hot or cold with a cooked carrot slice for garnish.

230 g (½ lb) fish per person (carp or salmon), 1 egg, 150 ml (6 fl oz) water, 4 large onions, salt, 25 g (1 oz) white breadcrumbs, pepper, 2 thinly sliced carrots.

1. Remove skin and bone from fish. Chop fish and 3 large onions finely. Put in a bowl.

2. Add 1 well-beaten egg, water, salt and pepper and breadcrumbs. Mix together well.

3. Remove trivet. Put skin and bone in pressure cooker. Add water to cover, 1 sliced onion, 2 thinly sliced carrots, salt and pepper. Bring to boil.

4. Wet hands to facilitate handling of mixture. Make small balls from the fish mixture and drop them into the boiling stock. Pressure cook for 20 minutes.

5. Reduce pressure. Remove fish balls. Liquid may be strained and thickened with egg yolks to make a sauce (see p. 44).

Fisherman's Pie   **4–6 minutes + baking**

450 g (1 *lb*) *fresh cod, haddock or coley filleted,* 75 g (3 *oz*)
butter, juice of ½ *lemon,* 2 *hard-boiled eggs,* 120 g (4 *oz*)
frozen peas, 50 g (2 *oz*) *button mushrooms,* 2 *tablespoons
chopped parsley,* 450 g (1 *lb*) *potatoes,* 3 *tablespoons double
cream,* 40 g (1½ *oz*) *grated Cheddar cheese,* 1 *small onion,
salt and pepper, bouquet garni,* 6 *peppercorns.*

1. Pressure cook fish and potato chunks in different
separators for 4 to 6 minutes, depending on size. Remove
skin and bone from fish and then flake, reserving any
juices.
2. Drain and mash potatoes. Cream with 15 g (½ *oz*)
butter and season. Cook peas in boiling salted water until
just tender.
3. Combine milk, peeled onion, bouquet garni and
peppercorns in a saucepan. Bring to boil and simmer
gently for 2 minutes. Strain.
4. Melt 15 g (½ *oz*) butter in a pan, add flour and mix well.
Gradually blend in milk and stir continuously until sauce
comes to the boil and is thick and smooth. Blend in 30 g
(1 *oz*) of grated cheese and season with salt and pepper.
5. Chop hard-boiled eggs. Fold the fish, juice, parsley,
eggs and peas into sauce and transfer to a lightly greased
pie dish.
6. Spread mashed potato over the top. Sprinkle with
cheese. Heat in hot oven until cheese is golden brown and
bubbling. (220 °C, 425 °F, GM 7.)

Jellied Eels   **8 minutes**

500 g (1 *lb*) *eels; fish scraps, onion, carrot, dillweed to make
Court Bouillon* (see p. 130), *chives, parsley.*

1. The eel heads and tails can form part of the Court
Bouillon. Wine is not necessary. Strain.

2. Cut eels, with the skin still intact if they are young, into 2 to 5 *cm* (1 to 2 *in*) pieces. Place in pressure cooker and pour Court Bouillon over adding a pinch each of parsley and chives. Pressure cook for 8 minutes. Pour into individual cups.

3. Allow to cool. The eels will jellify without assistance.

Eel Stew   **10 minutes**

1 *large eel*, 150 *ml* (6 *fl oz*) *red or dry white wine*, 3 *tablespoons butter*, 3 *onions*, 1 *clove garlic*, 1 *carrot*, *bouquet garni*, 50 *ml* (1 *fl oz*) *cognac*, 120 *g* (4½ *oz*) *mushrooms*, 1 *tablespoon flour*, *salt and pepper*.

1. Cut skinned eel into 5 *cm* (2 *in*) lengths. Remove trivet. Melt butter in bottom of pressure cooker and fry the sliced carrot, chopped onion and garlic. Add eel, bouquet garni, salt and pepper. Sprinkle the cognac into the cooker and set it alight. Pour on the wine. Pressure cook for 10 minutes.

2. Remove bouquet garni. Remove mushroom stems and wash caps. Cut caps into thin strips and fry in butter. Add them to the stew immediately before serving.

3. Make stew thick to taste by adding a mix of flour and melted butter. Allow it to boil and blend for a minute or two. Help it by stirring gently.

Tuna Fish Stew   **10 minutes**

¾ *kg* (1¾ *lb*) *tinned tuna fish*, 280 *ml* (½ *pt*) *red wine*, 4 *tablespoons butter*, 4 *tomatoes* or 1 *tablespoon tomato paste*, 2 *onions*, 1 *clove garlic*, 1 *tablespoon flour*, *bouquet garni*, *salt and pepper*, *chopped parsley*.

1. Remove trivet. In base of pressure cooker brown fish and chopped onions in melted butter. Sprinkle with flour and mix well. Pour on red wine. Add skinned and sectioned

tomatoes (or paste), garlic, bouquet garni, salt and pepper. If necessary add water to cover ⅓ of fish.

2. Pressure cook for 10 minutes. Remove bouquet garni. Serve garnished with chopped parsley.

Kedgeree   5 minutes

230 g (½ lb) smoked haddock, 170 g (6 oz) long-grain rice, 1 egg for hard boiling, 2 tablespoons butter, 240 ml (½ pt) water with lemon juice or vinegar, pepper, chopped parsley.

1. Remove trivet. Add water, egg and a separator filled with rice and 350 ml (12 *fl oz*) salted water covered with greaseproof paper. *Place trivet on top* with the haddock dotted with butter and covered with greaseproof paper. Pressure cook for 5 minutes. Reduce pressure at room temperature.

2. Lift out fish and trivet. Drop egg in cold water. Turn rice into another saucepan and heat till dry. Do not burn. Add butter to the dry rice and stir. Then add the flaked fish and correct seasoning. Keep hot.

3. Chop egg white and sieve yolk. Pile kedgeree on to a hot dish and sprinkle with the egg and chopped parsley. Serve.

N.B. You can vary this by using brown rice (see pp. 228ff.) or by soaking 2 strands of saffron in the water to be added to the rice prior to cooking. Kedgeree is often improved by adding garam masala sprinkled on top of the finished dish.

Lobster   10 minutes

1 live lobster to fit pressure cooker, 1 l (2 pts) boiling water.

1. Remove trivet. Bring water to boil in cooker. Plunge lobster into cooker when water boils. Pressure cook for 10 minutes. Reduce pressure with cold water.

2. Plunge lobster into cold water and, when cool, dress for serving cold with salad or for hot dish.

Lobster Thermidor

1 *cooked lobster* (for 2 people), 240 *ml* ($\frac{1}{2}$ *pt*) *cheese sauce made with* 140 *ml* ($\frac{1}{4}$ *pt*) *Court Bouillon* (see p. 130) *and* 140 *ml* ($\frac{1}{4}$ *pt*) *milk*, 2 *tablespoons chopped parsley, mustard, grated cheese.*

1. Cut lobster in half lengthways. Remove the meat and cut roughly.
2. Add parsley to the hot cheese sauce and use just enough sauce to bind meat.
3. Spread empty lobster shells with mustard and fill them with the lobster mixture. Then coat with remainder of cheese sauce.
4. Sprinkle shells with grated cheese and brown under the grill.

Sweet and Sour Shrimp   2 minutes (4 minutes if frozen)

340 *g* (12 *oz*) *shrimps, peeled and cleaned*, 120 *g* (4 *oz*) *Chinese pea pods*, 3 *tablespoons soy sauce*, 2 *tablespoons vinegar*, 120 *ml* ($\frac{1}{4}$ *pt*) *pineapple juice*, 3 *tablespoons sugar*, 240 *ml* ($\frac{1}{2}$ *pt*) *chicken stock*.

1. Remove trivet. Combine all ingredients in pressure cooker and cook for 2 or 4 minutes (depending on whether fresh or frozen shrimps are used).
2. Thicken sauce if necessary. Serve on hot rice.

Chinese Steamed Fish   4–10 minutes (depending on size)

Fillets or whole fish (almost any kind); marinade: salt, fresh ground ginger, sugar, white wine, wine vinegar, soy sauce. Ham or bacon strips, dried shrimps, mushrooms, spring onions.

1. Rub fish inside and out with salt and fresh ginger. Make up marinade using white wine and wine vinegar in equal proportions with a touch of soy sauce and 2 table-spoons of sugar. Marinade fish for 1 hour.

2. Place fish on trivet in usual way but with garnishes – bacon, shrimps, mushroom, green onions, etc. Use the marinade thinned out with a little water as the steaming fluid – to make 280 *ml* ($\frac{1}{2}$ *pt*).

3. Pressure steam for the usual time for each fish and its size (see tables pp. 126ff, 296ff). This is one of the finest ways to cook and eat fish!

Salmon Loaf   12 minutes

1 *medium salmon*, 2 *tablespoons breadcrumbs*, 2 *tablespoons butter*, 2 *tablespoons parsley*, 1 *tablespoon minced onion*, *chives*, *salt and pepper*, 2 *eggs*, *cucumber slices for garnish*, 250 *ml* ($\frac{1}{2}$ *pt*) *water for cooker*.

1. Mix salmon (approximately 125 *g* (4 *oz*)) with bread-crumbs, butter, parsley, onion and seasoning. Place mixture in a buttered boilproof bowl or shape into a loaf and secure with buttered greaseproof paper.

2. Place on trivet and pressure cook for 12 minutes (long cooking time is necessary because bowl or paper prevents steam penetration).

3. Heat oven to 190 °C (375 °F, GM 5).

4. Cover loaf with breadcrumbs and bake for about 10 minutes.

Soused Mackerel   6–8 minutes

4 *mackerel*, 140 *ml* ($\frac{1}{4}$ *pt*) *each of vinegar and water*, 1 *sliced onion*, 6 *peppercorns*, 4 *cloves*, *bay leaf*, *slice of lemon peel*, *clove of garlic*, *chopped capers or chives or parsley*.

1. Wash fish and scale. Cut off heads. Remove trivet. Add liquid to cooker and lay fish on trivet, head to tail.

2. Sprinkle over the remaining ingredients. Cover fish with greaseproof paper. Seal, bring to pressure in usual way and cook for 6 to 8 minutes according to size.

3. *To serve hot:* Lift out fish and keep hot on a serving dish. Boil liquid in cooker and reduce by half. Strain and then pour over fish. Garnish with chopped capers or chives or parsley.

4. *To serve cold:* Allow pressure to reduce at room temperature. Leave fish in cooker till completely cold, then lift out and drain. Boil liquid in cooker till reduced by half. Allow it to cool. Strain it over the fish which can either be left whole or filleted. Serve with finely diced raw onion rings and chopped parsley.

6: MEAT

For the vast majority of families, meat is the heart of any main meal. Of all foods, meat alone contains the concentration of essential proteins and trace elements necessary to good health. The sight of a large roast joint or a simmering meat stew is regarded as the high point of a lunch, supper or dinner.

Yet, of all the ingredients available to the cook, meat has been the least successful mixer with pressure cooking, and if people tell you that pressure cooking has cost them expensive failures, the chances are that the meat has been the cause of the disappointment. Meat which has been miscooked can lack taste and texture.

However, successful pressure cooking of meat is not difficult – it is possible to create meals that are not only acceptable but memorable. In addition the pressure-cooking technique offers you speed and the chance to use those cheaper cuts of meat that are economical and often ignored. As it happens, the poorer cuts of meat are *better* for pressure cooking than the expensive tender cuts – and, in the end, they offer more flavour and probably more nutritional value as well! However, pressure cooking appears to break some of the so-called hallowed rules of good meat cooking, and that is where the confusion sometimes lies. The over-eagerness of manufacturers' instruction booklets too has persuaded cooks that certain results are obtainable when they are not.

A pressure cooker can either pot roast or braise (the pressure steam technique) or produce a stew or ragout or 'boiled' effect (the pressure boil technique). Every recipe is a variant on these two basics, no matter what name you give it. A pressure cooker cannot produce a true roast,* or grill,

---

* Some makes of pressure cooker can be used for roasting. I do not recommend this method – see Appendix 3 p. 280–1.

broil or fry. However, once you learn what the pressure cooker can do, and how it achieves its results, there is a vast variety of wonderful, tasty and by and large economical dishes that can be prepared within a few minutes.

Here are four basic recipes in their simplest form:

Pot-Roasted Beef　　　**13–16 mins/500 g (12–15 mins/lb)**

A joint no more than 1·4 kg (3 lb) of rump, topside, or brisket rolled into a 'round', salt, pepper, hot water (with a little stock or gravy cube), 1–1½ tablespoons flour, 1 tablespoon oil.

1. Choose a piece of meat with little marbling in it and trim off excess fat. Fix into a round shape with skewer. Heat oil in open cooker and brown joint all over.

2. Drain off excess fat, place trivet in bottom and load up with water plus stock to make sufficient fluid for cooking time. Solid joints of meat are timed by weight at the rate of 13–16 mins/500 g (12–13 mins/*lb*). You will need a minimum of 140 *ml* (1¼ *pt*) plus 140 *ml* (¼ *pt*) for each 15-minute period of cooking time. A 1 *kg* (2 *lb*) joint will take about 30 minutes to cook and will thus need 400–450 *ml* (*3 pt*) of fluid if it is not to boil dry.

3. Dust joint with salt and pepper. Close pan. Bring to pressure and cook for appropriate period. Reduce pressure under cold water tap. Open cooker and lift out joint.

4. Use the fluid at the bottom of the pan to make gravy (this is important if you are to get the most out of the piece of meat you have bought). Take a small portion of the hot fluid and place it in a jam jar with the tablespoon or so of flour. Seal jam jar and shake vigorously so that it is a limp paste – then transfer the whole to the remainder of the liquid in the base of the pressure cooker. Heat strongly in an open pan so that the flour is cooked and you get a full-flavoured gravy. The flour will brown anyway, but if you

want a stronger colour, drop in a well-fried onion. Adjust seasoning.

Braising

The technique of *braising* is very similar, except that, instead of using the trivet, the joint of meat is rested on a bed of solid vegetables (the French name for which is *mire-poix*) which, together with some stock, provides the steaming fluid. The *mire-poix*, or gunge flavours the meat while it is cooking and provides an extra-interesting gravy at the end. Usually, if you want to have vegetables as a side dish with a braised joint, you would cook them separately, perhaps by opening the cooker 5 or 6 minutes before the end and letting them cook with the joint of beef for the normal length of time. The recipes below give several variants on this theme.

Boiled Beef   13–16 mins/500 g (12–15 mins/lb)

Use a joint of silverside or brisket weighing no more than 1·4 kg (3 lb). Water to half-fill the cooker.

1. Trim the meat, removing excess fat and weigh. You can then calculate the cooking time as before.
2. Leaving out the trivet, fill the cooker with the joint and with water so that it comes up to the half-way mark. All but the top-most regions of the joint should be covered. Season according to the recipe: meat already brined by the butcher will require very little extra salt.
3. Bring to pressure and cook for pressure-cooking period. Vegetables may be added 5 minutes or so before the end of the cooking time according to the period normally specified for cooking them (see Chapter 4 and pp. 66ff, 286ff). For preference the trivet should be rested on top of the joint and

the vegetables laid across the trivet – in this way they will be properly steamed.

4. The boiling fluid does not lend itself easily to making gravy (which would be a little unusual with a boiled-meat dish anyway), but it could be saved and used as a thin stock or perhaps reserved for the basis of a soup later on.

There are plenty of variants on boiled meat dishes; recipes below give some of them.

Stewed Beef   **15–20 minutes**

750 g (1½ lb) stewing steak (skirt, shin, flank, chuck), mixed root vegetables (onions, carrots, turnips, swedes, parsnips), plus items like celery, as available; dripping or fat or oil for frying, 500 ml (1 pt) meat stock.

1. The meat is cut up into bite-size chunks, so the timing does not depend on the amount of meat you use.

2. Melt dripping/fat/oil in the bottom of the pan and fry and brown the onion in it. Add meat and fry all over. Then add stock and the chopped root vegetables.

3. Seal pan, bring to pressure and cook for 15 to 20 minutes. Depressurize carefully, open lid, test and adjust seasoning. Add, if you wish, a few leaf vegetables (seasonal greens as available) and seal pan and bring to pressure rapidly – then immediately depressurize so that the green leaves are just cooked. Serve.

Again there are many variants on this formula – you can add wine to the stock, other vegetables to the mix, and bulk the whole thing out with dumplings if you wish. You can give the dish a milk or cream base, or put in a great deal of a distinctive spicing like paprika and end up with a goulash. It is also possible to get various curried effects, though of course traditional Indian dishes are not cooked with a pressure cooker – so don't hope to achieve authenticity!

MEAT FOR PRESSURE COOKING

If it is all so easy, why then does pressure-cooked meat have such a poor reputation? Good cooks know the virtue of slow cooking methods and most conventional cookbooks either warn against the pressure cooker specifically or advise against letting the temperature of fluid used for pressure cooking rise much above 85 °C (185 °F).

In fact, when you cook meat by the pressure method some quite different things happen to your raw ingredient – and what is normally regarded as 'good' meat for ordinary cooking purposes turns out to be unsuitable for pressure cooking. The sort of meat you do need, by contrast, is tough, fatless, and normally rather inexpensive.

THE SECRET OF GOOD MEAT PRESSURE COOKERY IS TO BUY THE RIGHT KIND OF MEAT

Alas, while some butchers and supermarkets will label cuts of meat as being suited to roasting or frying or stewing and so on, none that I know of will help you when it comes to pressure cooking, so you'll have to learn to select yourself.

Meat consists of four separate substances – the fibres of flesh that in the raw meat usually look red and then turn brown after heat has been applied (or nearly always), streaks of fat that can look anything from a clear opaque white to a yellowy almost pasty consistency, sheets of connecting tissue which are largely made of gelatine, and, of course, bone. The strength of the flesh fibres depends partly on the age of the animal and partly on the function of the part of the body from which it has come – 'meat' does after all correspond to muscle tissue. The colour of the fat also depends on age – the yellower the appearance, by and large, the older the animal.

Under usual cooking conditions all the ingredients of meat (sometimes excepting the bone) contribute to the over-all taste of the finished dish. In the classic roast, the application of heat to the outside causes the flesh fibres to darken and cook while the gelatine starts dissolving and permeating the flesh with flavoursome juices. A little later on, the fat starts to melt and as it too has a considerable flavour when cooked, the fatty juices add to the gelatinous juices and interact. The outside of the meat cooks well before the inside so that the flesh fibres and outer fat may turn quite brown. The juices that run out are collected in the roasting tray and may then be used partly to baste the meat (not always actually a very good idea) and partly to make gravy.

Conventional cookbooks point out that the texture and toughness of meat depend on the flesh fibres which are made largely from protein. Above 85 °C (185 °F) protein hardens very rapidly – egg albumen turning white is an easy example – and it is only meat that starts out with a very tender flesh that can be used for grilling. If you subject meat to *very* prolonged cooking times the hardness of the fibres can be broken down, largely by melting all the inter-connecting gelatine that holds it together. That is what you do to make meat soup, stock or *pot-au-feu*. Alas, if you don't cook for quite long enough the meat turns out simultaneously mushy *and* stringy – and that is precisely the sort of result that has given pressure-cooked meat a bad name. If you cook meat for too long you cease to produce a joint or a stew and start making stock!

Pressure cooking works, however, by subjecting meat to high temperatures and pressures only for a short time – the fleshy protein pieces cook rapidly and the interconnecting gelatine starts to dissolve and flavour the flesh. However, the fat does not have time to dissolve and make its own contribution. The moistness of pressure-cooked meat comes from the injection of pressurized steam, something which does not normally happen to meat. What it means, in fact, is that the meat you need to buy should have very few veins of fat running through it.

THE SECOND SECRET OF GOOD MEAT PRESSURE COOKERY IS TO AVOID 'WELL-MARBLED' FAT MEATS

As an animal gets older, fat is deposited in the muscle fibre – and in top quality meat veins or streaks of fat appear like marble tracings in the red flesh. For a steak or roasting joint this usually means that it will be easy to cook. However, for pressure cooking you want older, less good meat, where the fat has been deposited round the outside – where it can be trimmed off. The flesh will be tougher, but the steam injection will take care of that; the flesh will also be more flavoursome – something very much to your advantage. If you attempt to pressure cook meat that is too young, although the texture may be fine, you will find the taste watery and any fragments of fat may appear rather obtrusive.

If you are pressure cooking chicken avoid small battery-farmed deep-frozen ones – they cook very rapidly but it is difficult to get them to taste of anything. You want an old boiling fowl that has been around a while.

This method of cooking means you are denied the pleasures of the flavouring that fat gives to meat – and in some cases you may want to replace it. Pressure cooked meat, even if its texture is superbly velvety, sometimes appears to be missing something. You can change this by making greater use of braising methods so that you are, in effect, injecting vegetable steam into your joint. Or you can experiment with browning the outside of the joint carefully – instead of merely searing and sealing (as in the pot roast recipe above on p. 142) you can use molasses, brown sugar or wheat germ with astonishingly good results.

The other things that affect the taste of meat are the food on which the animal has been fed and how well the animal has been butchered. Corn-fed free range animals inevitably taste better than ones fed on concentrates. A side of meat also needs hanging properly after slaughter – unfortunately this is sometimes regarded as expensive by butchers and you find yourself buying pieces of meat before they are well and truly ready. If you haven't done so already, learn which butcher in your neighbourhood to trust! None of this should inhibit you from buying a joint of meat at the last moment when unexpected visitors show up and producing a first-class result within a few minutes – that is what pressure cooking is really all about.

NEVER BUY A JOINT LARGER THAN 1·4 g (3 *lb*) unless you have an extra large cooker – the steam will not have room to circulate and penetrate if the joint takes up too much room. Again, remember that the outside of a joint gets cooked first and then the heat and moisture move inside; so, within limits, the smaller the joint the more chance you have of even cooking throughout. Do not attempt to cook meat that is only partly defrosted – you won't get good results and the end product may actually be dangerous. If you are buying for immediate cooking, buy fresh meat.

The aim in all meat cooking is to get the centre of any joint of meat up to a certain degree of 'doneness', which means a certain temperature. A meat thermometer is an excellent investment – the metal probe is inserted into the joint (avoiding any bone) at about the time the meat is expected to be finished. *As with all pressure cooking, you can undertime for safety, open up, inspect the results, and finish off without the weight/valve, so that you are cooking more slowly at ordinary temperatures and pressures* – the whole dish is always under your control.

TABLES, TEMPERATURES, TERMS, TECHNIQUES

Most cooking is simply juggling around with a handful of techniques and possible ingredients; recipes are simply 'ideal' workings-out of particular combinations. Rather than being endlessly repetitive I have arranged the material for ease of cross-reference: a few recipes are given in full, but after a while the implications for other meats should be fairly obvious. Where particular combinations work together especially well I have detailed them.

MEAT TABLES

You need a minimum of 140 *ml* ($\frac{1}{4}$ *pt*) plus 140 *ml* ($\frac{1}{4}$ *pt*) for each 15 minutes of cooking time for pressure steaming – more if pressure boiling. Do not use joints weighing more than 1·4 *kg* (3 *lb*).   Only large pieces are timed by weight.

By type of meat

Meat	Method	Preparation	Time mins/ 500 g	mins/ lb
BEEF:				
Topside, brisket, rolled rib, flank	Pot-roast (pressure steam)	Use trivet/pannier. Trim, remove fat. Weigh. Brown in hot fat in open pan. Season.	13–16	12–15
Brisket, silverside	Boiling (pressure boiling)	No trivet. Trim, remove fat. Weigh. Fill cooker with water to half-way mark.	16	15
Chuck, rump	Braise (pressure steam)	No trivet. Trim, weigh. Brown in hot fat. Cook over *mire-poix*. Add liquid to cover vegs.	11	10
Oxtail	Braise (pressure steam)	No trivet. Fry onions in hot fat – then fry joints – half cover joints with stock, approx. 750 *ml* (1$\frac{1}{2}$ *pts*).	40	
	Stew (pressure boil)	No trivet. See recipe p. 188.	40	
Stewing steak (fillets or pieces)	Braise (pressure steam)	No trivet. Season and cover with flour. Brown in hot fat on both sides. Lay on *mire-poix* and use water and tomato juice according to length of cooking time.	20 25 30	2$\frac{1}{2}$ cm (1 *in*) 5 cm (2 *in*) 7$\frac{1}{2}$ cm (3 *in*)

Meat	Method	Preparation	Time mins/ 500 g	mins/ lb
BEEF (cont.):				
Mince	Stew (pressure boil)	Mince can be stir-fried: cooking will take 3 to 4 mins in hot oil. Cook further in stock with other ingredients.	3–4	
Meat loaf	Pot-roast or braise (pressure steam)	See recipe p. 185.	20–25	
Salt beef (corned beef)	Boil (pressure boil)	Leave in clear water overnight. Drain most off. Weigh. Cover with water. Add potatoes, turnips, carrots and pepper. No salt needed.	27	25
Tripe	Boil (pressure boil)	Add minced macaroni. Cover with water.	15	
VEAL:				
Stuffed shoulder, loin	Pot-roast (pressure steam)	Brown in hot fat. Drain. Place on trivet with required amount of liquid.	13–15	12–14
Knuckle	Boil (pressure boil)	Half-fill cooker with water. No trivet.	11	10
Rolled, stuffed breast	Braise (pressure steam)	Roll tightly round stuffing and cook over *mire-poix* plus liquid.	13	12
Pieces, stew	Stew (pressure boil)	Fry lightly in butter but do not brown. Add vegs 5 mins before end.	15	
LAMB AND MUTTON:				
Stuffed, rolled breast	Pot-roast (pressure steam)	Standard method.	11–13	10–12
Chops, cutlets	Braise (pressure steam)	Standard method.	10	

Meat	Method	Preparation	Time mins/ 500 g	mins/ lb
LAMB AND MUTTON (cont.):				
Best end of neck	Stew (pressure steam)	Cut into pieces.	10–12	
Shoulder, stuffed breast	Braise (pressure steam)	Remove fat and skin. Rub with garlic clove. Season, brown and braise with standard method.	10–12	
Leg	Boil (pressure boil)	Standard boiling method.	17	15
Hearts	Stew (pressure boil)	Clean out and fill with stuffing – then standard stew method.	30	
Liver	Stew (pressure boil)	Standard stew method.	5	
Kidneys	Stew (pressure boil)	Brown in bacon fat – use only 280 *ml* ($\frac{1}{2}$ *pt*) liquid.	7	
PORK:				
Chops	Braise (pressure steam)	Standard braising method.	10–12	
Pickled leg, hand, belly	Boil (pressure boil)	Standard boiling method.	20	18
Pig's trotters	Boil (pressure boil)	Use 200 *ml* ($\frac{1}{4}$–$\frac{1}{3}$ *pt*) each of cider or wine vinegar and water.	30	

By cooking method

Method	Meats
Pot-roasting (with trivet) Pressure steaming	Beef: topside, brisket, rolled rib. Veal: stuffed shoulder, loin. Lamb/Mutton: stuffed, rolled breast.
Braising (without trivet but using *mire-poix* of vegetables) Pressure steaming	Beef: chuck, rump, Swiss steak, oxtail, rolled rib roast. Veal: rolled, stuffed breast. Mutton/Lamb: chops, cutlets, neck, shoulder, hearts, liver, kidneys. Pork: chops, stuffed, gammon slices.

Method	Meats
Boiling (without trivet) Pressure boiling	Beef: brisket, silverside, salt beef. Veal: knuckle. Mutton: leg, breast, neck. Pork: pickled leg, hand, belly. Ham: gammon, hock, collar, flank. Heads: pig, sheep, calf. Pig's trotters.
Stew (without trivet) Pressure boiling in stock	Beef: pieces, mince, oxtail, tripe. Veal: pieces. Mutton/Lamb: best end of neck, scrag end.
Stuffing	Beef: rolls. Veal: rolls, shoulder, breast, chops. Lamb/Mutton: shoulder, breast. Pork.

Meat Temperatures

If you have a meat thermometer, use it to check the degree of 'doneness' according to this table. Most meat thermometers do not like being immersed in water, so do not leave the instrument in the pan while you are cooking.

	°C	°F
Beef: rare	60	140
medium	70	160
well-done	77	170
Cured Pork, Bacon, Gammon etc.	77	170
Veal	77	170
Lamb, Mutton	82	180
Rabbit, and small game	82	180
Fresh Pork	88	190
Poultry	88	190

TERMS

The names by which the various dishes are described in the recipes are the traditional ones. Purist cooks trained in haute-cuisine methods will probably point out that each one of the names has a precious meaning – thus braising is carried out at below boiling point, that so-called 'boiled beef' is only simmered, that a ragout (gentle stew), navarin (lamb stew), daube (stew with wine), carbonnade (stew with beer), blanquette (meat with cream sauce), and so on can only be produced under certain very special conditions which the pressure cooker by its very nature excludes.

In a sense they are right, but in compiling recipes this leaves me with the choice either of being slightly dishonest but giving the reader some idea of what the finished dish will approximate to, or of inventing completely new names – which no one will recognize.

TECHNIQUES

Certain techniques occur in recipe after recipe with meat after meat – for simplicity, here are explanations of how to make *mire-poix*, marinade, stuffing, dumplings and gravy. And finally, a reminder on degreasing, and a word on multi-processing.

A *mire-poix* is used in braising: it is a bed of vegetables on which the food to be braised is placed. The solid vegetables act like a trivet and keep the meat out of the boiling fluid and the vegetables add considerable flavour. At the end of cooking time you can make the *mire-poix* or gunge into a gravy. If you want vegetables as a side dish to accompany the meat, do not rely upon the *mire-poix* to provide them, but prepare them separately by opening up the pressure cooker in the usual way 5 minutes or so before the end of cooking time and add the vegetables to be pressure steamed in the usual way – you can either rest them on the trivet on top of the joint of meat or around the sides of the joint itself. The vegetable tables (pp. 66, 286) will give you the timings.

Recipe for *mire-poix*

1. Fry a *slice of streaky bacon* in a *little oil* till the fat runs clear and transparent. Add some *root vegetables* (*carrots, turnips, etc.*) and some *large onions* and roughly cut up *celery stalks*.
2. Drain off fat and arrange in bottom of pressure cooker without trivet. Remember the vegetables will support the meat. Add meat or vegetable stock to come half-way up bed of vegetables, but do not allow to cover.
3. Make sure you have enough liquid for the cooking time (140 *ml* plus 140 *ml* ($\frac{1}{4}$ *pt* plus $\frac{1}{4}$ *pt*) for each 15-minute period). Place meat on top and proceed with recipe.

A *mire-poix* can also be used in vegetarian cooking – wherever in fact you wish to braise and steam with some flavour.

A *marinade* is used to soften the fibres of meat prior to cooking. A mildly acidic and flavoured juice is poured over the meat 12 to 24 hours before cooking. It may seem a little odd to advise the use of a technique which demands forethought in a basically 'instant' method of cooking, but there are plenty of occasions when you may have time to do a little preparation but still not have much time just before the occasion when you eat – if you have been out all day, for example.

Recipes for Marinade

1. 2 *tablespoons lemon juice*, 4 *tablespoons oil*, 1 *tablespoon salt*, *pinch of pepper* (*for lamb*).
2. 1 *tablespoon curry powder*, 1 *crushed garlic clove*, 2 *tablespoons lemon juice*.

3. 60 *ml* (2 *fl oz*) *wine*, 30 *ml* (1 *fl oz*) *vinegar*, 30 *ml* (1 *fl oz*) *olive oil*, 1 *garlic clove*, *assorted bouquet garni herbs*, 1 *tablespoon sugar*, *salt*, *pepper*, *tabasco*.

4. *wine*, *vinegar*, *olive oil as before*, *curry spices*, *mustard powder*, *chopped onion*, *garlic*, *nutmeg*, *mixed herbs*.

5. *wine*, *vinegar*, *olive oil as before*, *dash soy sauce*, 8 *to* 10 *cloves*, 1 *onion*, *grated ginger* (*for a Chinese effect*).

6. 300 *ml* (12 *fl oz*) *beer*, 60 *ml* (2 *fl oz*) *oil*, 2 *tablespoons lemon juice*, 1 *tablespoon sugar*, 1 *tablespoon salt*, *cloves;* optional: *bouquet garni herbs*. (This is a good one for beef.)

Some people add all sorts of things: paprika, chilis, even marmalade!

A stuffing is used partly to bulk out a dish and partly to provide a flavour which enhances the good qualities of the ingredient being cooked or to offset the disagreeable ones. In meat cookery, stuffing is sometimes used to counteract the greasy aspects of very fat meats. The French name is *farce*, and a stuffed dish, whether meat or vegetable, is called a *farcie*.

Stuffing for Meat

Breadcrumbs, *sausage meat*, *shallots or minced onion*, *sage*, *thyme*, *salt*, *pepper*, *bacon or ham scraps*. Optional: *beaten egg for binding*, *garlic*, *nutmeg*. You can put together and mix well almost any selection of the above ingredients with success; miss out the ones you don't like.

Dumplings are a good way to stretch out a meal and provide a starchy contrast to the meat and vegetables. When potatoes become more expensive in the shops these make an excellent substitute or variant.

60 g (2 oz) *each of self-raising flour and breadcrumbs* or 120 g
(4 oz) *self-raising flour* or *ordinary flour with a pinch of
baking powder.* 60 g (2 oz) *minced or chopped suet,* 1 *egg for
binding, salt, pepper* (optional: *herbs*). Mix all the dry
ingredients together, add in beaten egg and form mixture
into little balls which will then swell up in the cooking
process. If you wish to economize, use water or water-with-
milk for the binding instead of the egg.

To make gravy: pour away the fat from your *cooking fluid*
carefully, leaving the other juices behind. If you wish, add a
browned onion and *a smidgin of tomato puree* for colour.
Thicken slightly with *flour, cornflour (corn starch),* or *arrowroot* and cook for a few minutes. Season with *salt and
pepper* and, if wished, a *little brown sugar.*

Degreasing is sometimes necessary with the fattier pieces of
meat, like oxtail, breast of lamb, pork and so on. If you are
in a hurry, the best thing to do is to let the cooking fluid
simmer down and then mop the top with a rolled-up
absorbent kitchen towel. Snip off the end when it becomes
soaked and start again. If you have the time to cook your
meal in two stages with an interval between, strain off meat
and put to one side and pour liquid into glass or bowl. Cool
rapidly: the fat will float to the top, where it can be removed
with a flat spoon.

Multi-processing. This is the awful word I use to signify a
cooking method which uses pressure cooking as only part
of the operation necessary to produce the finished dish.
Thus, a pot-roast is first sautéed and then pressure steamed.
A ham is first pressure boiled (or pressure steamed) and
then baked. It is often quite a good idea to take certain
dishes and finish them off either by frying or crisping-up in
the oven – we have got used to meat which is well done and

crisp on the outside and as pressure cooking doesn't always give us this, we have to add it on. The recipes will show how.

BEEF RECIPES

Beef should be open-grained and a good red colour; not too dark. For pressure cooking you should avoid 'well-marbled' pieces.

Pot Roast Creole   13–16 mins/500 g (12–15 mins/lb)

1·4 kg (3 lb) rump, 2 tablespoons olive oil, 6 bacon slices, 6 cloves garlic, allspice, 570 ml (1 pt) tomato juice, 4 diced carrots, 1 head of celery (cut), 4 chopped onions, 60 ml (2 fl oz) vinegar, 1 crushed bay leaf, 2 teaspoons salt, ¼ teaspoon pepper.

1. Trim meat, removing surplus fat. Shape into a round and secure with a skewer. Weigh. Brown in bottom of pressure cooker and brush with olive oil.
2. Cut bacon slices and garlic cloves in half. Sprinkle bacon with allspice. Wrap bacon around the garlic and make 6 rolls. Make gashes in the roast and push rolls into meat around the whole surface of the joint.
3. Place trivet in base of pressure cooker. Place joint on top and surround with the other ingredients. Pour in the tomato juice
4. Pressure steam for the required amount of time. Add potatoes if wished 6 minutes before the end of cooking period. Make sauce out of tomato juice and vegetable mixture.

Savoury Beef Stew   **40 minutes**

800 g (1¾ lb) stewing beef, 1 marrow bone, 3 leeks, 3 carrots, 1 onion with 4 cloves inserted in it, 1 clove garlic, 1 bouquet garni, 7 large potatoes, 1 turnip, 1 stalk celery, 1¾ l (3½ pts) water or to cover meat and vegetables, salt.

1. Put all herbs and vegetables (except potatoes) in the salted water and bring to boil in pressure cooker. When boiling, plunge in meat and seal. Pressure boil for 30 minutes, calculated by weight of joint. After cooking time reduce pressure, open lid and add potatoes. Pressure cook for another 8 minutes. Reduce pressure and remove bouquet garni.
2. Lift out meat and serve with vegetables, salt and gherkins. The broth can be served as it is or can be thickened with 1 tablespoon of tapioca or pearl barley per person.

Stewed Steak   **20–30 minutes**

4 slices steak, 4 tablespoons butter, 2 tablespoons tomato paste, 1 bouquet garni, 280 ml (½ pt) dry white wine, 2 large diced onions, 4 diced carrots, salt and pepper.

1. Lightly fry the steak in butter. Remove steak and fry the carrots and onions. When browned, replace meat. Pour on enough wine to cover everything. Add tomato paste, seasoning and bouquet garni.
2. Cook for 20 to 30 minutes depending on size. Reduce pressure and remove bouquet garni. Adjust seasoning and serve.

Merchant's Beef Stew   **15–20 minutes**

700 g (1½ lb) beef – topside or stewing steak, 2 tablespoons dripping or fat, 12 button onions, 3 tablespoons flour, 1 glass

*red wine, 1 bouquet garni, 1 crushed garlic clove, 500 ml
(1 pt) vegetable or meat stock, salt and pepper, 30 g (1 oz)
shelled walnuts, 1 head of celery, 1 tablespoon shredded and
blanched orange peel, butter.*

1. Cut meat into bite-sized chunks. Brown the onion in
dripping in open pressure cooker. Add crushed garlic clove
and fry in for one minute. Add meat chunks and brown all
over. Add stock and pressure cook for 15 to 20 minutes.
Remove bouquet garni.
2. Meanwhile cut celery head into chunks. In a separate
pan melt butter and throw in walnuts – toss, fry and salt
them till crisp. Add celery and toss.
3. Place contents of pressure cooker in casserole for
serving. Top with walnuts and celery from separate pan.
Adjust seasoning. Serve casserole sprinkled with orange
rind.

Boiled Brisket   **16 mins/500 g (15 mins/lb)**

800 g (1¾ lb) beef brisket, water, salt and pepper.

1. Pressure boil meat in water for required time (see
tables pp. 149ff., 300ff.).
2. Season liberally. Serve garnished with cress.

Braised Steak   **10 minutes**

*4 pieces of chuck or other braising steak, 1 tablespoon dripping
or fat, 1 slice streaky bacon, 1 large onion, carrot and turnip,
1 stick celery, bouquet garni, seasoning, mire-poix: potatoes,
carrots (and other vegetables), stock, chopped parsley, sauce.*

1. Slice the onion and roughly cut the other vegetables for
the *mire-poix*. Keep separate from the vegetables you might
be cooking in the separators at the end of the cooking period.
2. Heat fat in open pressure cooker and fry the meat

quickly till well browned. Lift out. Add bacon and onions and brown too.

3. Add the stock to cover vegetables and stir. Add remainder of vegetables for *mire-poix* and place meat on top.

4. Pressure cook for the required time. Serve the vegetables garnished with chopped parsley.

5. To make a sauce remove the bouquet garni and bacon slice from stock and mash the *mire-poix* vegetables, or make a gravy (see p. 156).

Boeuf en Daube   11 mins/500 g (10 mins/lb)

1·4 *kg (3 lb) top rump or buttock of beef, 2 large onions, 7 tablespoons butter, 500 ml (1 pt) red or dry white wine, 280 ml (½ pt) cognac, strips of bacon rind, 2 tablespoons tomato puree, 4 potatoes, 2 carrots, 2 cloves garlic, 100 g (3 oz) turnip, bouquet garni, salt and pepper.*

1. Prepare marinade (see pp. 154–5) and soak meat overnight in the wine and cognac with 1 large chopped onion, 2 sliced carrots, pepper, garlic and herbs.

2. To cook, drain the meat and fry in butter. Lay bacon in base of cooker. Put meat on top and pour in marinade. Add seasoning and tomato puree.

3. Pressure cook by weight (see timing tables pp. 149ff, 300ff.) Meanwhile fry the remaining onions in butter.

4. Empty the contents of the cooker and strain liquid at end of cooking time.

5. Return the liquid, meat and vegetables to the cooker and cook for another 10 minutes under pressure.

Italian Braised Beef   11 mins/500 g (10 mins/lb)

1 *kg (2 lb) top rump of beef, 1 tablespoon olive oil, 60 g (2 oz) minced onion, 60 g (2 oz) quartered button mushrooms, 15 g*

($\frac{1}{2}$ *oz*) *flour*, 120 g (4 oz) *chopped, peeled and gutted tomatoes*, 1 *teaspoon tomato puree*, 2 *cloves crushed garlic*, *bouquet garni*, 2 *glasses red wine*, 430 ml ($\frac{3}{4}$ *pt*) *stock*, *marinade* (see p. 154ff), *salt and pepper, gnocchi paste* or *polenta* or *semolina* (see p. 235).

1. Marinade meat overnight. Drain and dry before cooking.
2. Brown beef in oil and remove it. Add onions and allow to become transparent then add mushrooms. Fry briskly, add flour and allow it to brown.
3. Remove from the heat. Add remaining ingredients and the meat. Pressure cook for required time.
4. Make gnocchi paste (see p. 235).
5. To serve slice the beef on to a dish and pour on gravy.

Swiss Steak   **30 minutes**

1·4 kg (3 lb) *round steak cut in pieces* 3 *to* 4 cm (1$\frac{1}{2}$ in) *thick, salt and pepper*, 3 *tablespoons flour*, 2 *tablespoons fat*, 1 *medium minced onion*, 280 ml ($\frac{1}{2}$ *pt*) *tomato juice* or 2 *large diced tomatoes*.

1. Brown the onion then the meat. Pour on tomato juice. Bring to pressure and cook for 30 minutes (see standard braising method p. 143).
2. Place whole carrots, potatoes and onions on top of meat towards end of cooking period if wished.

Boeuf Bourgignon   **10 minutes**

800 g (1$\frac{3}{4}$ *lb*) *braising beef or beef chuck*, 280 ml ($\frac{1}{2}$ *pt*) *red wine* or 140 ml ($\frac{1}{4}$ *pt*) *wine and* 140 ml ($\frac{1}{4}$ *pt*) *brown stock*, *bacon fat*, 3 *sliced onions*, 1 *clove crushed garlic*, *bouquet garni*, 170 g (6 oz) *button mushrooms*, *seasoning*, *chopped parsley*.

1. Cut meat into chunks. Brown onion in open pressure cooker. Add meat and brown. Add stock and seasonings (see standard stewing method p. 144). Pressure cook for 10 minutes.

2. Just before serving add the fried mushrooms to the meat. Sprinkle the dish with chopped parsley.

Carbonnade de Boeuf   20–30 minutes

680 g (1½ *lb*) *beef rump*, 6 *tablespoons butter*, 3 *medium onions*, 1 *l* (1¾ *pts*) *beer, bouquet garni*, 7 *potatoes, salt and pepper.*

1. Cut beef into thin slices. Follow the standard stewing method (see p. 144) and pressure cook for 20 minutes.

2. Add the potatoes towards the end of the cooking period. Seal and re-cook for 10 more minutes.

Goulash   30–40 minutes

450 g (1 *lb*) *cubed stewing beef*, 4 *tablespoons butter*, 2 *medium chopped onions*, 220 *ml* (8 *fl oz*) *tomato juice*, 170 g (6 *oz*) *carrot chunks*, 170 g (6 *oz*) *diced turnip*, 340 g (12 *oz*) *diced potatoes, salt, paprika;* optional: *fresh cream to taste.*

1. Brown meat and onions. Follow the standard stewing method (see p. —) and pressure cook for 30 minutes.

2. Add mixed vegetables after the initial 30 minutes. Reseal cooker and cook for a further 7 minutes.

3. To thicken the stew make a flour paste and stir into stew with the mixed vegetables.

4. Serve with potatoes and fresh cream to taste.

Stroganoff   **15–20 minutes**

This is a stewing method, with sour cream used to thicken
and flavour the liquid.

Basic ingredients: 1 *kg* (2 *lb*) *fillet of beef or beef chuck,*
3 *medium onions,* 230 *g* (8 *oz*) *button mushrooms,* 60 *g*
(2 *oz*) *butter,* 140 *ml* ($\frac{1}{4}$ *pt*) *sour cream, salt and pepper;*
optional: 340 *g* (12 *oz*) *egg noodles;* optional vegetables
additions: 3 *medium green peppers,* 5 *stalks celery,* 2 *medium
tomatoes,* 3 *medium carrots;* optional herb additions:
1 *teaspoon dried chives,* 1 *teaspoon dried parsley,* 2 *bay
leaves,* 1 *teaspoon basil,* 1 *teaspoon oregano,* 1 *teaspoon
rosemary;* optional spice additions: 1 *tablespoon paprika,*
$\frac{1}{4}$ *teaspoon celery salt,* $\frac{1}{4}$ *teaspoon garlic salt,* $\frac{1}{4}$ *teaspoon
onion powder,* 1 *teaspoon Worcestershire sauce.*

1. Cut meat into 2 *cm* (1 *in*) cubes or into thinnish strips.
Slice onions finely. Wash mushrooms, cut stems level with
caps and slice finely.
2. Melt half the butter in the pressure cooker. Fry the
onions, and add mushrooms (and more butter if necessary).
Remove the onions and mushrooms.
3. Add the remaining butter and allow it to get hot. Fry
the beef quickly for 3 to 4 minutes. Return the onions and
mushrooms to the pressure pan and add plenty of seasoning.
4. Pressure cook for 8 minutes. Add the cream and cook
unsealed carefully for another minute. Serve at once.

Variant using the optional ingredients as above:

1. Clean the vegetables. Dice the peppers, finely chop the
carrots and celery. Slice the mushrooms and tomato.
2. Fry mushrooms and set them aside. Brown the meat
with half the green peppers. Add the celery and seasonings.
Cover the meat with sliced tomatoes. Pressure cook for
12 minutes.

3. Depressurize and add the carrots and mushrooms. Lay the noodles over the mixture and the remaining green peppers on the noodles. Pour over the vegetable and tomato juices. *Do not stir.*

4. Pressure cook for a further 6 minutes.

5. Depressurize and stir in the sour cream and chives. Let stand for 5 minutes before serving. Garnish with parsley.

Paprikash Beef or Pork   15 minutes

1 g (2 *lb*) *pork roast or beef chuck* (or 450 g (1 *lb*) *of each*), 4 *tablespoons butter*, 1 *onion*, 5 *stalks celery*, 2 *medium green peppers*, 2 *potatoes*, 3 *large carrots*, 2 *tablespoons paprika*, 1 *teaspoon basil*, 2 *bay leaves*, 1 *teaspoon oregano*, $\frac{1}{4}$ *teaspoon marjoram*, $\frac{1}{4}$ *teaspoon curry powder*, 1 *teaspoon rosemary*, $\frac{1}{4}$ *teaspoon celery salt*, $\frac{1}{4}$ *teaspoon garlic powder*, $\frac{1}{4}$ *teaspoon onion powder*, 1 *teaspoon dried parsley*, *salt and pepper*.

1. Brown meat with the onion, celery and half the green peppers in butter. Add seasonings. Pressure cook for 6 minutes.

2. Depressurize and add the potatoes, stirring them in. Layer the carrots and green peppers on top of the meat. Season each layer lightly.

3. Seal and cook for another 10 minutes (for pork or $\frac{1}{2}$ pork/$\frac{1}{2}$ beef) or 8 minutes (for beef).

4. Serve garnished with parsley.

Short Ribs Barbecue   30 minutes

1·4 *kg* (3 *lb*) *short ribs*, 3 *tablespoons fat*, 1 *small minced onion*, 1 *tablespoon honey*, 280 *ml* ($\frac{1}{2}$ *pt*) *tomato juice*, 1 *teaspoon mustard*, *salt and pepper*, 1 *clove garlic*.

1. Rub meat with the seasonings, rubbing cut clove of garlic on the ribs where there is skin but no meat.

2. Brown ribs in hot fat in the pressure cooker, and brown onion. Add honey and tomato juice.

3. Seal and pressure cook for 30 minutes.

Alternative method:

1. Brown ribs thoroughly in fat with diced onions and pressure steam in usual way for 10 to 12 minutes.

2. Remove from cooker. Cover with barbecue sauce – honey, tomato juice, garlic, cinnamon – and place on rack in roasting tray in medium oven 220 °C (425 °F, GM 7) for 15 to 20 minutes until thoroughly brown.

Beef Olives   **10 minutes**

450 g (1 *lb*) *rump or lean stewing steak* ½ *cm* (¼ *in*) *thick, salt and pepper, stuffing* (see p. 155), *mire-poix* (see p. 153), 280 *ml* (½ *pt*) *gravy or tomato juice.*

1. Cut meat into strips about 7 to 8 *cm* (3 *in*) wide. Sprinkle each with salt and pepper. Spread meat with the stuffing. Roll and secure with cocktail sticks.

2. Cook by braising method (see p. 143) and serve.

Variant:

Instead of stuffing, use streaky bacon with a stoned half prune.

Stuffed Flank Steak   **approx. 40 minutes**

Variant with vegetable stuffing:

1 *kg* (2 *lb*) *flank steak,* 2 *tablespoons fat or butter,* 3 *stalks chopped celery,* 1 *tablespoon minced onion,* 1 *tablespoon*

minced parsley, 1 *large grated carrot*, ½ *minced green pepper*,
1 *teaspoon salt*, 3 *tablespoons French dressing*.

1. Score meat on both sides cutting across fibres. Mix the
vegetables together and spread over the steak. Sprinkle with
French dressing.
2. Proceed to follow the standard method for cooking
stuffed meat (see above and on p. 153).
3. Other vegetables may be cooked in with the steak
towards the end of the cooking period.
4. Brush the meat with a kitchen bouquet just before
serving to give a 'roasted' look.

Variant with wine and sausage stuffing:

1 *kg* (2 *lb*) *flank steak*, 2 *tablespoons fat or butter*, 5 *large
onions*, 3 *stalks chopped celery*, 5 *carrots*, 1 *clove garlic*,
¼ *teaspoon marjoram*, 230 *g* (½ *lb*) *pork sausage*, 1 *beaten egg*,
2 *teaspoons dried parsley*, 140 *ml* (¾ *pt*) *dry white wine*, *salt
and pepper*.

1. Brown the sausage. Prepare stuffing by crumbling
sausage meat. Dice ½ onion and garlic finely. Add this to the
beaten egg, dried parsley and sausage.
2. Score steak on both sides as above and continue to
prepare the meat in the same way.
3. Mix together the wine, herbs and spices. Dice ½ onion,
celery, 1 carrot and add them to the wine. Pour the mixture
over the meat and pressure cook for 18 minutes.
4. Towards end of cooking time place the remaining
whole onions and carrots in a separator above the meat and
cook.
5. While dish is cooking make a brown sauce base (see
pp. 38, 76) using the stock from the cooker. Season to taste.

Stuffed Beef   **16 mins/500 g (15 mins/lb)**

Not more than 1·4 kg (3 lb) round or topside in long roll,
3 medium onions, 3 slices streaky bacon, 2 tablespoons
chopped parsley, mixed meat herbs, 1 beaten egg, seasoning,
liquid to cover trivet not less than 280 ml (½ pt).

1. Trim and wipe meat. Make deep cuts through it
lengthways about 1·5 *cm* (½ *in*) apart and ¾ of the way
through.
2. Heat chopped bacon in pan until fat runs out and
bacon is crisp, then fry the chopped onion till golden
brown. Mix with the rest of the stuffing ingredients and add
enough beaten egg to bind.
3. Press the stuffing into the cuts in the meat. Tie, secure
and weigh.
4. Cook as for pot roast (see p. 142). When cooked, lift
joint into an oven-proof dish and baste it with hot fat as for
a roast joint. Heat it in an oven at 190 °C (375 °F, GM 5).

Salt Beef

The classic English way of serving this dish is with dumplings. The French equivalent is called *Pot-au-feu* and uses
unsalted beef. Suitable cuts for both dishes are round,
silverside, aitchbone. Salted brisket has a larger proportion
of fat and is used for cold pressed beef. Salted silverside is
leaner and more suitable for boiled beef and dumplings.
Both thin and thick salted flank are used for pressed beef.

Boiled Salt Beef and Dumplings   **27 mins/500 g (25 mins/lb)**

1·4 *kg* (3 *lb*) *salt silverside or topside, bouquet garni, 6 pepper-*
corns, 1 medium onion stuck with clove, 4 medium onions,
4 medium carrots, quartered, 2 turnips, quartered, dumplings
(see recipe pp. 155–6).

1. If meat is very salty leave it soaking in unsalted water overnight. Pour away water and put fresh unsalted water into pressure cooker to cover meat for cooking.

2. Bring water to boil. Add bouquet garni, peppercorns and onion with clove, skimming frequently. Simmer under pressure for the time required by weight.

3. After cooking time remove bouquet garni, onion and skim again. Add the vegetables and pressure cook for a further 3 minutes. Add dumplings and cook for a further 3 minutes.

4. Serve on a large dish with dumplings and carrots. Horseradish is all right but not traditional as a relish with this dish. To serve cold: allow the joint to cool in its own cooking liquid. The meat should cut like butter. Serve with grated raw red cabbage and grated onion with a sharp French dressing.

Pot-au-Feu   50 minutes

1·4 *kg (3 lb) shoulder, brisket or topside*, 1 *carrot*, 1 *turnip*, *parsley*, *bay leaf*, 1 *onion*, 1 *leek*, *celery seeds*, *pepper and salt*, 2 *parsnips*, 1 *small white cabbage*.

1. Make like a stock (see pp. 36ff) only keep the meat pieces.
2. If you add chicken you get PETITE MARMITE HENRI IV.
3. Ladle fat off before serving.
4. Serve with mustard or horseradish sauce.

VEAL RECIPES

Veal is young calf. Under three months it is described as milk-fed; once the animal moves on to eating grass the flesh darkens. Veal has very little fat, which is good for pressure cooking, but very little taste, which is not. It benefits from strong sauces, as in *blanquette*, stuffings and strong-tasting accompaniments.

Pot-Roast Veal   **13–15 mins/500 g (12–14 mins/lb)**

1·4 *kg (3 lb) veal neck, loin or shoulder, 4 tablespoons butter or fat, 1 onion, salt and pepper, thyme, 140 ml (¼ pt) water.*

1. Season and brown meat and onions in butter.
2. Place meat on trivet. Add thyme and water.
3. Seal and cook for required time.
4. If wished, cook other vegetables and potatoes in separators towards end of cooking period.

Veal Cutlets Lucullus   **5 minutes**

4 *veal cutlets, 3 tablespoons butter, 4 slices bacon, 4 slices Gruyère cheese, pepper.*

1. Melt butter in pressure cooker. Put in cutlets. Lay bacon then cheese on top. Cook with lid off for 5 minutes.
2. Seal and cook for a further 5 minutes. Serve cutlets bathed in their own juice.

Veal Blanquette   **12 minutes**

450 *g (1 lb) veal pieces, 1 small onion, a slice of lemon peel, seasoning, 280 ml (½ pt) white sauce (see p. 76), 2 table-spoons cream, 1 egg yolk, 280 ml (½ pt) white stock or water, chopped parsley, lemon quarters, crisp-fried bacon rolls for garnish*

1. Season meat. Remove trivet and place meat and sliced onion in cooker. Pour in the stock or water.
2. Seal and pressure cook for 12 minutes.

3. Make a thick white sauce using half the amount of milk usually required.

4. Lift meat into deep serving dish and keep hot. Strain stock and make up sauce with stock to give it a good coating consistency. Reheat sauce, adjust seasoning, add cream and egg yolk. Cook for a minute or so without boiling or curdling it.

5. Pour sauce over veal and garnish dish with chopped parsley, bacon rolls and lemon slices.

Veal Niçoise   13–15 mins/500 g (12–14 mins/lb)

1·4 *kg (3 lb) piece of roasting veal – fillet, loin or shoulder, 2 tablespoons olive oil or dripping, 1 kg (2 lb) peeled tomatoes, 450 g (1 lb) small onions, clove garlic, thyme, rosemary, herbs as available, seasoning, white vegetable or chicken stock.*

1. Rub garlic, salt and pepper into the meat. Melt fat and brown meat thoroughly. Remove meat and drain fat. Add required amount of liquid. Replace meat and trivet. Pressure cook for required time.

2. 4 minutes before end of cooking time reduce pressure with cold water. Remove meat and trivet. Leave enough water to cover bottom of cooker. Put in whole onions, seasonings, then meat on top. Place tomatoes around the joint. Finish pressure cooking time and allow pressure to reduce at room temperature.

3. Make a thin sauce from the cooking liquid and pour around meat when serving.

Veal Fricassee   12 minutes

450 *g (1 lb) veal pieces, 2 tablespoons butter, 4 small sweet carrots, 8 spring onions, 2 young turnips, 12 new potatoes, 1 teaspoon sugar, bouquet garni, seasoning, 280 ml (½ pt)*

white stock, 280 ml (½ pt) white sauce, 2 tablespoons cream, chopped parsley.

1. Season and brown meat till sealed. Add stock and seasoning. Seal and pressure cook for 8 minutes. Reduce pressure with cold water.
2. Cut carrots, onions, potatoes and turnips into small uniform pieces. Mix butter with sugar in a saucepan. Add vegetables and cook them gently, shaking the pan now and again until they are glazed. Add vegetables to pressure cooker and re-seal and cook for a further 4 minutes. Reduce pressure with cold water.
3. Make white sauce using half milk and half stock from pressure cooker sufficient to give a good pouring consistency. Place meat and vegetables in a deep serving dish and keep hot. Reboil sauce, adjust seasoning and pour over meat. Garnish with chopped parsley.

Veal Sauté – method 1   15 minutes

800 g (1¾ lb) shoulder of veal, 4 tablespoons butter, 280 ml (½ pt) dry white wine, 1 clove garlic, 2 shallots, 1 teaspoon paprika, 1 tablespoon tomato paste, 1 tablespoon flour, salt and pepper, thyme, 2 bay leaves.

1. Dice and brown meat and shallots in butter. Sprinkle with the flour and paprika. Allow to brown.
2. Pour on wine. Add herbs, seasoning and tomato paste and garlic. Pressure cook for 15 minutes.
3. Serve with rice.

Veal Sauté – method 2   20 minutes

800 g (1¾ lb) veal flank or shoulder, 5 tablespoons butter, 7 medium tomatoes, 230 g (8 oz) pimentos, 1 large onion, 2 cloves garlic, 1 tablespoon flour, 280 ml (½ pt) dry white wine, salt and pepper.

1. Melt butter and brown the slices of veal and onions. Sprinkle on flour and stir. Add wine and crushed garlic.

2. Peel tomatoes. Remove pips from pimentos. Cut into chunks. Add them to cooker. Season. Pressure cook for 20 minutes.

Stuffed Breast of Veal   13 mins/500 g (12 mins/lb)

1 *boned veal breast, salt and pepper, ginger, 2 tablespoons flour, 2 tablespoons butter* or *fat, kitchen bouquet, bread stuffing (see pp. 155, 193).*

1. Weigh meat. Season with salt and pepper. Spread bread stuffing over meat. Roll, tie and secure with skewer. Brush outside with a kitchen bouquet. Sprinkle with ginger and dredge with flour.

2. Melt butter and brown meat in pressure cooker. Put in trivet and place meat on top. Add 140 *ml* ($\frac{1}{4}$ *pt*) water to pan. Seal and pressure cook for required period.

3. Potatoes and other vegetables can be placed around meat and cooked at the end of the cooking period.

Stuffed Veal Rolls   12 minutes

450 *g* (1 *lb*) *veal cut in thin slices*, 120 *g* ($\frac{1}{4}$ *lb*) *sliced bacon*, 2 *tablespoons butter*, 1 *medium sliced onion, thin slice of lemon peel, bouquet garni*, 140 *ml* ($\frac{1}{4}$ *pt*) *water, glass of white wine* or 280 *ml* ($\frac{1}{2}$ *pt*) *white, vegetable* or *chicken stock, chopped parsley, salt and pepper*.

1. Follow the basic method for stuffed beef recipes (see p. 167).

2. Cut veal into 5 *cm* by 12 *cm* (2 *in* by 5 *in*) strips and season with lemon juice, salt and pepper. Lay a bacon piece on each strip then roll, tie and secure with sticks.

3. Follow stuffed beef method as above.
4. Vary the sauce by adding tomato puree to taste.

LAMB AND MUTTON RECIPES

Lamb and mutton have more fat than beef, both around the
joints and embedded in the flesh. Choose joints where it
will be easy to trim off their fat. Lamb is killed before it is a
year old (or 18 months in some countries); after that it
becomes mutton. Milk-fed lamb is killed before it is weaned.
It is not normally a good idea to pressure cook milk-fed
lamb – it cooks so quickly by ordinary methods. Lamb and
mutton should be well cooked. Breast of lamb is the joint
with the most fat. Sage stuffings and apple-and-onion
sauces can be used to offset grease.

Braised Lamb Chops   **10 minutes**

*Lamb chop per person, 2 tablespoons fat or dripping, mire-
poix (see p. 153), seasoning, vegetables to choice (potatoes,
carrots, greens), brown stock, gravy colouring, chopped-
parsley, bouquet garni.*

1. This recipe follows the standard braising method
(see p. 143). Brown meat, prepare a *mire-poix* and add stock
to cover.
2. Cook vegetables in a separator after 3 minutes of
pressure cooking the meat alone. Cook for a further 4
minutes.
3. Mash and sieve *mire-poix* and pour over the chops
before serving.

Fricassee of Mutton   **35 minutes**

570 g (1¼ *lb*) *mutton neck*, 6 *tablespoons butter*, 3 *small sliced carrots*, 3 *onions stuck with* 1 *clove each*, 2 *chopped stalks of celery*, 1 *tablespoon flour*, 140 *ml* (¼ *pt*) *water*, *bouquet garni*, 2 *heads of celery, broccoli or cauliflower, salt and pepper*.

1. Melt butter in cooker and brown meat. Sprinkle with flour. Stir and brown. Add water. Stir until it boils.

2. Add vegetables (except the head of celery, broccoli or cauliflower), herbs and seasoning. Pressure cook for 30 minutes.

3. Wash head of celery, broccoli or cauliflower. Depressurize cooker after 30 minutes and add separator containing celery and broccoli, or cauliflower and cook for a further 5 minutes.

4. Remove meat and place on a serving dish. Remove bouquet garni. Mash liquid and strain over meat. Garnish with vegetables.

Lamb Stew   **40 minutes**

1·4 *kg* (3 *lb*) *lamb shank, middle neck or breast, cut in* 2 *cm* (1 *in*) *pieces*, 450 g (1 *lb*) *peeled new potatoes*, 8 *small young carrots*, 2 *to* 3 *young turnips*, 450 g (1 *lb*) *shelled peas*, 2 *chopped onions*, 3 *teaspoons fresh chopped mint, bay leaf, salt and pepper*, 3 *tablespoons butter or fat*, 1 *l* (2 *pts*) *brown stock;* optional: *dumplings (see p. 155) instead of potatoes*.

1. Dredge meat with seasoned flour. Brown meat and onions. Add hot stock to cover. Seal and cook by weight (see tables p. 150, 302). Depressurize, remove meat from cooker and strain liquid. This removes any splinters of bone. Skim and degrease fat from gravy. Wash out cooker and return meat and gravy.

2. Prepare vegetables. Add root vegetables to the cooker and cook for 5 minutes. Depressurize and add peas. Cook for 2 minutes.

3. If making dumplings add them at this point. Depressurize and drop them into the boiling stew. Cover but do not seal and cook for 17 minutes.

4. Taste and correct seasoning. Remove meat and vegetables from cooker. Skim sauce again. Pile meat and vegetables into a deep dish. Boil up gravy, thicken with blended flour if necessary and pour over stew.

Blanquette of Lamb   **25 minutes**

800 g (1¾ lb) *lamb top rib or neck*, 4 *tablespoons butter*, 1 *carrot*, 1 *onion inserted with* 2 *cloves*, 1 *clove garlic*, 7 *potatoes, bouquet garni*, 1 *tablespoon flour*, 1 *egg yolk*, 1 *l* (1¾ *pts) stock or water, salt and pepper*.

1. Bring stock to boil in pressure cooker along with onions, cloves, herbs, garlic, salt and pepper. Add meat and pressure cook for 15 minutes.

2. Drain meat. Set aside a large dish of stock. Empty and clean cooker.

3. Melt butter in cooker. Brown meat. Sprinkle on flour. Pour on reserved stock. Add peeled potatoes and seasoning. Pressure cook for 10 minutes.

4. Beat egg yolk and add successive small amounts of stock to it. Whisk continuously. Add this mixture to the remaining hot sauce. Stir but do not boil. Serve the meat covered with sauce and surrounded by potatoes or rice.

Leg of Lamb   **17 mins/500 g (15 mins/lb)**

1·4 *kg* (3 *lb) leg of lamb*, 5 *carrots*, ½ *celery stalk*, 2 *onions*, 2 *cloves*, 2 *bay leaves*, ¼ *teaspoon thyme*, ¼ *teaspoon dill*,

1 *teaspoon dried parsley, salt and pepper* (optional: 1 *crushed garlic clove*), *water for cooker, mint jelly.*

1. Wipe, trim and weigh meat. Peel vegetables and leave whole. Remove trivet. Add lamb, vegetables and seasonings. Half fill cooker with water. Pressure cook for required time.
2. Put meat on a serving dish. Garnish with vegetables. Strain stock and make sufficient sauce to give good pouring consistency.
3. Serve with mint jelly.

Marinaded variant:

1. Rub leg of lamb in as much olive oil as it will absorb. Mix together the following ingredients for marinade: 280 *ml* ($\frac{1}{2}$ *pt*) *red wine, salt and pepper, crushed thyme and bay leaf, allspice, onion with* 2 *cloves inserted, thinly sliced celery stalk.*
2. Place leg in a dish and pour marinade over. Marinade for 1 to 3 days. Refrigerate and turn leg in marinade about twice a day.
3. Strain marinade through a sieve and use as cooking liquid. Proceed to cook as above.

Stuffed Shoulder of Mutton   **10–12 mins/500 g/lb**

1 *kg* (2 *lb*) *boned shoulder of mutton,* 4 *tablespoons butter,* 280 *ml* ($\frac{1}{2}$ *pt*) *dry white wine or water, bouquet garni, stuffing from a packet* or 120 *g* (4 *oz*) *pig's throat/gore,* 120 *g* (4 *oz*) *veal* or 250 *g* (8 *oz*) *sausage meat,* 2 *teaspoons dried parsley,* 1 *clove garlic,* 1 *tablespoon cognac, salt and pepper.*

1. Prepare stuffing in usual way (see p. 155) and make it into a sausage and insert into the boned shoulder. Secure meat with a skewer. Weigh.

2. Follow the usual method for preparing and cooking stuffed meat (see p. 167). Calculate cooking time by weight.

Barbecue Spare Ribs

1·4 *kg* (3 *lb*) *spare ribs*, 1 *small minced onion*, 430 *ml* (16 *fl oz*) *tomato juice*, 1 *tablespoon fat*, *salt and pepper;* optional: 1 *teaspoon mustard*, 2 *tablespoons honey*, *sauerkraut*.

1. Follow the usual method for cooking spare ribs which is a multi-process combining pressure steaming initially and roasting or baking to finish in the oven (see pp. 156, 162).
2. To vary the sauce add mustard and honey *or* sauerkraut in tomato juice.

Mutton and Bean Stew   30–35 minutes

120 *g* (4 *oz*) *beans* (*haricot*, *kidney*, *blackeye*), 1 *small sliced onion*, 280 *ml* (½ *pt*) *water*, *seasoning*, 680 *g* (1½ *lb*) *best end of neck of mutton or small leg*, 1 *onion*, 2 *tablespoons dripping or fat*, 1 *carrot*, 1 *turnip*, *bouquet garni*, 430 *ml* (¾ *pt*) *brown stock*, *flour*, *grilled tomato slices*.

1. Prepare and cook beans for 10 minutes (see p. 103ff).
2. Prepare meat in usual way (see p. 150) and season well.
3. Peel and slice vegetables. Proceed to cook as for lamb stew (see p. 174) for 20 to 25 minutes. Meanwhile grill the tomato slices for garnishing the dish.
4. After cooking, strain vegetables and place in a deep serving dish with the meat. Adjust seasoning in stock and thicken with blended flour if necessary. Pour over stew and garnish with tomato slices.

Crisped Breast of Lamb   11–13 mins/500 g (10–12 mins/lb)

1 *kg* (2 *lb*) *breast of lamb,* 2 *sprigs parsley, sprig of thyme,* 2 *bay leaves,* 1 *onion,* 2 *large carrots, salt and pepper,* 1 *beaten egg,* 60 *g* (2 *oz*) *breadcrumbs,* 30 *g* (1 *oz*) *butter.*

1. Peel and chop onions and carrots. Place meat, herbs, vegetables, salt and pepper in pressure cooker and cover with boiling water. (N.B. No trivet.)
2. Seal and cook for required time. The bones should slip easily from the meat, when the meat has cooled. Place deboned meat in refrigerator for 4 hours pressed down with another plate on top. Reserve liquid for stock base.
3. Cut the meat into finger-size pieces and dip into the beaten egg and then roll in the breadcrumbs and season with salt and pepper.
4. Melt butter and fry meat pieces until golden brown. Drain and then serve accompanied with a spicy (tomato) sauce.

PORK RECIPES

Pork has a pale-pink flesh, white fat and a thin rind. The flesh should be quite smooth and free from smell. As much fat as possible should be removed prior to cooking. Pork stews can be difficult because of the degreasing problem. Normally pork is accompanied by a sweet or sharp sauce or herbed stuffing to counteract the greasiness.

Roast Pork with Apple Sauce   30 minutes

1 *kg* (2 *lb*) *boneless pork,* 4 *tablespoons butter,* 7 *apples, salt and pepper.*

1. Melt butter and brown pork. Season with salt and pepper.

2. Remove trivet. Seal and pressure cook for 20 minutes.

3. Peel and pip apples. Depressurize at end of cooking time and place apples around the meat. Re-seal and cook for a further 10 minutes.

Pork, Bacon and Cabbage   50 minutes

450 g (1 *lb*) *salted fresh pork*, 200 g (7 *oz*) *smoked bacon*, 1 *cabbage*, 2 *medium carrots*, 230 g ($\frac{1}{2}$ *lb*) *leeks*, 2 *cloves garlic*, 6 *potatoes*, *bouquet garni*, 4 *chipolata sausages*.

1. Half fill pressure cooker with water and bring to boil. Add pork and bacon. Skim as necessary. Add all the vegetables (except potatoes and the cabbage). Season with pepper only. Seal and pressure cook for 40 minutes.

2. Depressurize and add potatoes. Cook for a further 10 minutes.

3. Wash and quarter cabbage. Remove any discoloured leaves. Pressure boil for 5 minutes (see tables p. 68, 287).

4. Fry or grill the potatoes separately before serving and place them around the side of the serving dish.

Braised Pork Chops   10–12 minutes

4 *pork chops about* 2 *cm* ($\frac{3}{4}$ *in*) *thick*, 1 *large eating apple*, 2 *tablespoons butter*, *mire-poix* (see p. 154), *stock*, *seasoning*, *gravy colouring*, *small packet of frozen or dehydrated peas*.

1. Peel and core apple. Cut into 4 thick rings. Brown chops in butter. Fry apple rings.

2. Prepare *mire-poix* in pressure cooker and cover with stock. Place chops on top with an apple ring on each chop. Seal and pressure cook for 10 minutes.

3. Cook peas in a separate saucepan.

4. After cooking time, keep chops hot. Mash and sieve

mire-poix into gravy (if necessary thicken with blended flour), adjust seasoning and pour around chops. Put peas in centre of apple rings for garnish

Pork Fillets   **8–10 minutes**

4 *pork fillets*, 1–2 cm ($\frac{1}{2}$–$\frac{3}{4}$ *in*) *thick*, 2 *tablespoons butter*, 1 *small onion*, 230 g (8 *oz*) *button mushrooms*, 140 ml ($\frac{1}{4}$ *pt*) *stock or water*, 140 ml ($\frac{1}{4}$ *pt*) *sour cream, seasoning, chopped parsley or chives.*

1. Wipe and trim fillets. Peel and dice onion. Wash and dry mushrooms. Melt butter and fry onion and fillets thoroughly. Pour in cream. Seal and pressure cook for 6 minutes. Reduce pressure with cold water.

2. Pile mushrooms on chops, seal and cook for a further 2 minutes. Reduce pressure with cold water.

3. Keep chops and mushrooms hot in serving dish. Boil sauce rapidly until thick and whisk well. Pour over the chops. Garnish with chopped parsley or chives.

HAM RECIPES

Ham is the hind leg of pork, salted and dry cured, or smoked. There are a number of treatments carried out by the food trade. Gammon is the hind quarter of a cured side of bacon and in its entirety can weigh 5$\frac{1}{2}$ *kg* (12 *lb*), though a more commonly sold piece is a corner weighing 1$\frac{1}{2}$ *kg* (3 to 4 *lb*). Choose pieces where the fat is not too impregnated in the flesh. Use the pressure cooker for the first stage in cooking and then finish off by sweet-baking in an oven.

Ham Hocks   **14 mins/500 g (12 mins/lb)**

1·4 *kg* (3 *lb*) *ham hocks,* 6 *medium potatoes,* 6 *medium onions,* 6 *medium carrots,* 1 *medium cabbage,* 450 *ml* (¾ *pt*) *water, salt.*

1. Wash ham hocks and weigh. Place on trivet in pressure cooker. Add boiling water and 1 teaspoon salt if the hocks are fresh. Seal and cook for the required time.
2. Prepare the vegetables and add towards the end of cooking time. Whole potatoes and onions take approximately 10 minutes. Later add the carrots and cabbage (approximately 5 minutes' cooking time).

Salt Ham   **14 mins/500 g (12 mins/lb)**

1·4 *kg* (3 *lb*) *ham,* 1 *l* (2 *pts*) *water,* 450 *ml* (¾ *pt*) *dry white wine or cider,* 2 *carrots,* 1 *onion, bouquet garni,* 2 *cloves, pepper.*

1. Soak ham overnight in water. Change water 2 to 3 times during soaking. Then drain, dry and weigh.
2. Put wine/cider and water into the pressure cooker. Add carrots, onion, cloves, bouquet garni and pepper and ham.
3. Seal and cook for required time calculated by weight.

Hawaii Ham Slices   **10 minutes**

2½ *cm* (1 *in*) *thick slice of lean uncooked ham,* 2 *tablespoons butter, small tin of pineapple slices, medium potatoes for* 4 *servings,* 250 *g* (½ *lb*) *shelled peas or frozen equivalent,* 280 *ml* (½ *pt*) *parsley sauce (see p. 76), salt and pepper,* 2 *to* 3 *cloves, made-up mustard.*

1. Trim any fat off ham and cut into 4 pieces. Peel potatoes. Strain pineapple and reserve juice.

2. Melt butter and brown ham. Remove and spread with mustard and pepper. Make up pineapple juice to 140 *ml* ($\frac{1}{4}$ *pt*) with water and pour into cooker. Place trivet with ham slices topped with pineapple slices into cooker. Put salted potatoes to the side of ham.

3. Seal and cook for 6 minutes. Put peas in a separator and add to pressure cooker for 4 minutes. Remove meat and vegetables. Keep hot.

4. Make parsley sauce using half quantity of milk and using stock to give a sufficient coating consistency. Reheat, adjust seasoning. Pour around ham. Garnish ham with peas.

Boiled and Baked Hams   **14 mins/500 g (12 mins/lb)**

Boiled:

1. Fresh ham – cook in open cooker without trivet. Cover with water, bring to boil and throw away water.

2. Smoked ham – soak for 2 hours and then prepare as for fresh ham.

3. Lean ham – to preserve moisture, cook without trivet with water to cover but not more than half full.

4. Fat ham – cook on trivet with water for cooking time but not less than 280 *ml* ($\frac{1}{2}$ *pt*).

5. Pre-packed ham – follow instructions on packet.

6. Vegetables – onions, carrots, celery, herbs, bouquet garni. For sweetness use diluted peach, pineapple or orange juice.

7. To serve hot – coat with golden crumbs on fat side while still hot.

8. To serve cold – serve with green or mixed salad, new potatoes or potatoes in their jackets. Allow ham to cool in its own liquid then skim off fat and remove joint.

Baked:

1. Pressure-cooking time reduced to 12 mins/500 *g* or 10 mins/*lb*. Pre-heat oven to 205 °C (400 °F, GM 6) and bake ham until golden brown (approx. 15 to 20 minutes).

2. Rub the fat with mustard and sweetening, stick with cloves. Baste while baking to produce a glaze.

3. To serve, the fat can be stuck with chunks of pineapple, apricot or peach in a variety of decorative patterns (stars, diamonds, circles, triangles) and especially effective is the use of cloves in this pattern making. Cloves add a special flavour.

4. The following combinations are merely suggestions for what is known as *sweet-baked* ham:

    honey
    brown sugar
    cloves and honey or sugar or molasses
    cloves and mustard and honey or sugar or molasses

MINCE RECIPES

Savoury Mince   **7 minutes**

450 *g* (1 *lb*) *fresh minced beef*, 2 *tablespoons dripping or fat*, 1 *large onion*, 1 *large carrot*, 2 *medium tomatoes*, *seasoning*, 280 *ml* (½ *pt*) *thin gravy or stock*, *flour*, 2 *slices of toast*, *chopped parsley*.

1. Season meat. Slice onion. Dice carrot. Slice tomato. Brown meat in fat and remove. Fry vegetables and remove. Drain off fat.

2. Add liquid and boil. Put in meat and vegetables. Seal and cook for 7 minutes.

3. Make toast and cut into shapes. Put to one side.

4. Add blended flour to mince to thicken and gravy

colouring if necessary. Stir and boil for a few minutes. Serve garnished with toast and chopped parsley.

Collops with Poached Egg   7 minutes

450 g (1 *lb*) *fresh minced beef*, 1 *large onion*, 1 *tablespoon oatmeal*, 280 ml ($\frac{1}{2}$ *pt*) *stock, salt and pepper, butter or fat, chopped parsley*, 680 g (1$\frac{1}{2}$ *lb*) *mashed potatoes, poached eggs*.

1. Prepare meat and vegetables as above and follow same cooking method with the addition of the chopped parsley and oatmeal to the pressure cooker before sealing and cooking.

2. To serve – put the mince in the centre of the dish with the poached eggs on top and garnish with parsley. Arrange the mashed potatoes around the edge of the dish.

Meat Balls   16 minutes

340 g (12 *oz*) *lean minced beef*, 4 *tablespoons rice*, 1 *finely chopped medium onion*, 1 *egg, seasoning*, 1 *tablespoon chopped parsley*, 280 ml ($\frac{1}{2}$ *pt*) *tomato puree or soup or water*, 280 ml ($\frac{1}{2}$ *pt*) *sauce, bay leaf, spaghetti*.

1. Mix all the ingredients (except liquid and spaghetti) to make approximately 8 meat balls. Roll each ball in some rice to give more solidity.

2. Add liquid, sauce and bay leaf to pressure cooker and bring to boil. Add meat balls. Seal and cook for 10 minutes.

3. Pre-heat oven to 180 °C (300 °F, GM 2). Remove meat balls from cooker and keep hot. If necessary add water to sauce in cooker and boil spaghetti under pressure for 6 minutes.

4. To serve, place spaghetti around meat balls in a dish. Reheat sauce, adjust seasoning and pour over meat balls.

Savoury Meat Loaf   25 minutes

450 g (1 lb) minced beef, 120 g (¼ lb) fat salt pork or 230 g (½ lb) each of minced beef, veal and pork, 170 g (6 oz) bread-crumbs, 1 finely diced green pepper, 1 finely chopped medium onion, 2 teaspoons chopped mixed herbs (either chives, chervil, fennel and tarragon or mace, thyme and bay leaves), 2 tablespoons red wine, 2 tablespoons dripping or fat, 2 tea-spoons French mustard, 2 eggs, 280 ml (½ pt) tomato sauce or brown gravy, salt, celery salt, pepper, 1 crushed garlic clove.

1. Mix all ingredients together (except fat/dripping and sauce/gravy). Bind with beaten eggs. Pack mixture into a greased tin. Chill for an hour or so.
2. Melt dripping and brown meat loaf thoroughly. Wrap loaf in several thicknesses of greaseproof paper and allow for expansion. Put loaf on the trivet and add water for cooking time (see p. 150). Seal and cook for 25 minutes.
3. If served hot, heat up tomato sauce with bouquet garni. If served cold, roll the loaf in golden crumbs while still hot. Chill and serve with garnishes such as tomato slices, cucumber slices, egg slices, cress, parsley.
4. If wished, the outside can be crisped-up by placing in hot oven 230 °C (450 °F, GM 8) for 10 minutes or so.

Chili con Carne   7 minutes

450 g (1 lb) minced beef, 1 chopped medium onion, 1 crushed garlic clove, 340 g (12 oz) cooked kidney beans (see p. 105), 120 g (4 oz) Parmesan cheese, 2 tablespoons dripping or fat, 430 ml (15 fl oz) tomato puree, salt and pepper, 1 teaspoon chili powder.

1. Melt fat and brown meat. Add and brown onion and garlic. Add remaining ingredients except cheese. Seal and cook for 7 minutes.

2. Serve in bowls with a cheese garnish.

Irish Stew   12 minutes

700 g (1½ lb) *mutton neck or breast or chops,* 1 kg (2 lb) *large potatoes,* 4 *large onions,* 4 *small carrots;* optional: 2 *cloves crushed garlic, bouquet garni, chopped parsley or chives, salt and pepper,* 140 ml (¼ pt) *hot water.*

1. Ask butcher to cut meat into small chunks. Season well. Peel potatoes and onions and cut them into thick chunks or slices. Leave carrots whole.

2. Remove trivet. Add hot water and chops to cooker. Make layers alternately with the onions, potatoes and carrots and, if wished, garlic. Seal and cook for 12 minutes. Serve garnished with parsley.

Lancashire Hot-Pot   12 minutes

450 g (1 lb) *lean stewing steak or scrag of mutton,* 450 g (1 lb) *potatoes,* 2 *large carrots,* 2 *medium turnips,* 1 *stalk of celery,* 2 *onions, bouquet garni,* 2 *tablespoons dripping or fat,* 280 ml (½ pt) *brown or vegetable stock, salt and pepper.*

1. Chop meat into small chunks and brown in melted fat. Sprinkle with flour and stir. Add stock. Peel and slice vegetables and add them to the cooker in layers. Season each layer well and finish with a sliced potato layer on top.

2. Seal and cook for 12 minutes. Transfer the hot-pot to a casserole dish keeping the potato layer on top.

3. Add thickening to the stock and stir. Adjust seasoning. Boil and then pour it down the side of the casserole. Butter

the top and grill until golden brown. Garnish with chopped parsley.

Steak and Kidney Pudding   15 minutes plus 55 minutes

450 g (1 lb) stewing steak, 2 ox kidneys, 140 ml ($\frac{1}{4}$ pt) brown stock or red wine, 2 tablespoons seasoned flour, Worcestershire sauce, 850 ml (1$\frac{1}{2}$ pts) water (with lemon juice or vinegar) for cooker; optional: 230 g (8 oz) button mushrooms. Pastry: 230 g (8 oz) self-raising flour, 120 g (4 oz) shredded suet, salt and water.

1. Use a boilproof plastic, metal or glass bowl for pudding which should be covered with double greaseproof paper, foil or pudding cloth for the cooking period.

2. Cut meat into 2$\frac{1}{2}$ cm (1 in) strips. Skin kidney, halve and remove all tubes and membrane. Cut into small pieces. Toss all the meat in seasoned flour. Roll up steak strips with pieces of kidney.

3. Make pastry (see p. 262). Line the pudding bowl with it, pressing firmly against the sides. Put in meat and vegetables and half the liquid. Moisten the edges of the pastry with water. Form a lid of pastry on top. Pinch pastry edges together all round the bowl. Tie on the cloth or paper (see note 1) and if necessary make a simple handle to facilitate lifting out the pudding.

4. Place the trivet in the cooker with the pudding on top. Pour in the boiling water for the cooker. Close lid but do not seal and steam the pudding at ordinary pressure for 15 minutes. Then raise heat, seal the cooker and pressure cook in usual way for 55 minutes.

5. Remove covering from pudding bowl and slit the pastry crust a little. Fill the pudding with the other half of the stock.

N.B. This recipe is for raw meat. If you use pre-cooked meat you braise the meat first (see p. 143) and then continue as above except steaming time is reduced to 15 minutes and pressure cooking time is only to 25 minutes.

If you use individual serving bowls of aluminium or plastic the time is reduced again to 10 minutes steaming and 35 minutes pressure cooking.

General information on puddings is given on p. 257ff.

OFFAL

There is a whole range of bits and pieces of animal that are often ignored by cooks – the tails, feet, heads and various items of the innards. Very few of them lend themselves to easy cooking by conventional methods, which is why they have fallen out of fashion. Yet, precisely because no one appears to want them, they are very cheap. With a pressure cooker preparation times are much shortened and the considerable nutritional value, to say nothing of the splendid taste, can be appreciated. Further, since so many of these offals are basically very muscular and lacking in fat, they are ideal for treating with the moisture-injection advantages that pressure cooking can offer. These items of food are usually also very high in gelatine, so that the gravies you get from them are particularly nutritious and strong-tasting. If you allow a well-cooked oxtail, pig's trotter or calf's foot to cool, part of the juice will form a strong and nutritious jelly. If you are fond of meat jellies of this sort, you should cook for a slightly longer period than that indicated in the recipes that follow.

Braised Oxtail   **40 minutes**

1 *oxtail approximately* 1 *to* 1·4 *kg* (2 *to* 3 *lb*), *salt and pepper*, 1 *l* (2 *pts*) *stock*, 2 *tablespoons dripping or fat, bouquet garni, chopped parsley*, 3 *large sliced carrots*, 3 *large sliced onions*, 1 *glass red wine or port*, 1 *tablespoon redcurrant jelly*.

1. If you prefer, get the butcher to clean and cut the oxtail for you before you start. Otherwise soak the oxtail overnight in water. Then blanch it slowly by bringing water to boil and skimming off the scum regularly. Allow to simmer 10 to 15 minutes then drain and dry thoroughly. Cut oxtail through at the joints. Season with salt and pepper.

2. Remove trivet. Melt fat and brown sliced onions. Lift out and brown oxtail. Strain off any fat. Add the stock, onions, carrots and bouquet garni. Seal and pressure cook for 40 minutes.

3. Remove oxtail and vegetables from stock and keep hot. Degrease the stock (see p. 156). Strain the stock and add blended flour. Stir for 2 to 3 minutes. If the sauce is not thick enough reduce it by boiling and then thicken. Add the wine and redcurrant jelly. Adjust seasoning.

4. Pour sauce over meat and garnish with carrots and chopped parsley. If the oxtail is properly cooked the meat practically falls off the bones and melts in the mouth.

Additional ingredients:

1. Vegetables for braising (onions, carrots, celery) can be used in larger quantity.

2. Vegetables for garnish (small carrots, and turnips, pickling onions, small cabbage hearts) can be cooked separately or added towards end of cooking time and served with the main dish.

3. Plain boiled potatoes are a good accompaniment and a good contrast.

4. Haricot beans can be prepared (see p. 104) and added in a small quantity (about 120 *g*, 4 *oz*) after 20 minutes.

SWEETBREADS

They must always be pre-cooked.

Pre-cook method

1. Wash sweetbreads and place in a pan with water to cover. Bring slowly to boil.
2. Plunge immediately into cold salted water and add some lemon juice.
3. Trim carefully. Remove all membrane and tubes. Press between two plates until cool.

Creamed Sweetbreads   6 minutes

2 *pre-cooked sweetbreads, 140 ml ($\frac{1}{4}$ pt) white stock, 1 small onion, 3 small carrots, lemon rind, peppercorns, mace, seasoning, 570 ml (1 pt) white sauce (see p. 176), 2 tablespoons cream, lemon juice, 2 tablespoons chopped cooked ham, fried bread and lemon slices for garnish.*

1. Add stock to pressure cooker then the sliced sweetbreads, vegetables and seasoning. Seal and cook for 6 minutes.
2. Prepare white sauce using half quantity of milk (supplemented later by stock). Fry bread and cut into decorative shapes.
3. Place sweetbreads in a dish and place chopped ham around. Keep hot.
4. Strain stock and add to sauce to make it thick and coating. Reheat, add lemon juice and cream, and adjust seasoning.
5. Pour sauce over sweetbreads and decorate with lemon and fried bread pieces.

Braised Sweetbreads   **8 minutes**

2 *pre-cooked sweetbreads, 4 medium onions, 2 tablespoons
butter, 60 g (2 oz) mushrooms, 280 ml (½ pt) brown stock or
water, seasoning, 4 slices bread, flour, sherry or red wine,
chopped parsley.*

1. Cut each sweetbread into 8 pieces and dredge in
seasoned flour. Slice onions and mushrooms finely.
2. Melt butter and brown onions and mushrooms.
Remove and brown the sweetbreads. Remove. Add stock
and stir well. Return sweetbreads and vegetables to cooker
and season. Seal and cook for 8 minutes.
3. Fry the bread and line the base of the serving dish with
it. Place sweetbread and vegetables on top. Keep hot.
4. Thicken sauce with blended flour. Add red wine,
Reheat. Adjust seasoning. Pour into dish and garnish with
chopped parsley.

Kidneys   **7 minutes**

6 *lamb's kidneys, 4 slices streaky bacon, 2 tablespoons butter,
120 g (4 oz) button mushrooms, 140 ml (¼ pt) red wine, flour,
seasoning, chopped parsley.*

1. Prepare and trim kidneys. Cut into quarters and
season well. Make 12 bacon rolls and put them on to 2
skewers. Skin mushrooms if necessary, wash dry and slice
them.
2. Remove trivet. Fry bacon rolls. Take out of cooker and
remove skewers. Lightly brown kidneys, adding butter if
necessary.
3. Add the wine, stir well and add bacon and mushrooms.
Seal and pressure cook for 7 minutes.
4. Meanwhile make a *roux* (see p. 76). Strain liquid from
cooker and add some to the sauce to make it thick and

coating. Reheat sauce, adjust seasoning and pour over kidneys. Garnish with parsley.

Stuffed Hearts   30 minutes

4 *sheep's hearts, stuffing* (see p. 155) *or packet stuffing,* 2 *tablespoons dripping or fat,* 1 *carrot,* 1 *turnip,* 280 *ml* ($\frac{1}{2}$ *pt*) *brown stock, flour, seasoning, dash of sherry.*

1. Wash hearts. Remove all fat and tubes. Slice open half-way to make a pocket. Season inside with salt and pepper. Fill threequarters full with stuffing and secure loosely. Dredge hearts in seasoned flour.
2. Remove trivet. Melt fat and brown hearts. Remove and fry vegetables. Pour in hot stock, adjust seasoning, replace hearts. Seal and pressure cook for 30 minutes.
3. Lift hearts out and keep hot on a dish. Mash the vegetables into the gravy and add blended flour to thicken. Bring to boil. Adjust seasoning and pour over hearts. Add a dash of sherry to sauce at last moment if wished.

Jellied Spiced Pork   65 minutes

1 *large pork bone,* 1 *large onion, bay leaf,* 280 *ml* ($\frac{1}{2}$ *pt*) *chicken stock, salt,* 8 *peppercorns,* 450 *g* (1 *lb*) *pork fillet,* $\frac{1}{4}$ *teaspoon ground ginger,* $\frac{1}{4}$ *teaspoon ground cinnamon,* 1 *teaspoon paprika, salt and pepper, cooked chopped beetroot, watercress, pickles, fruit sauce.*

1. Have pork bone cut into 4 pieces. Combine bones, onion, bay leaf, chicken stock and peppercorns in the pressure cooker. Seal and pressure cook for 50 minutes. Strain stock through a sieve and then clean out pressure cooker.
2. Cut pork fillets into smallish chunks and put into the clean pressure cooker with the strained stock, spices and

generous seasoning. Bring to boil. Skim off any scum from surface. Seal and pressure cook for 12 to 15 minutes.

3. Transfer contents of cooker to a 1 *l* (2 *pt*) bowl and leave to cool. Cover with a plate and weigh down with a heavy object. Refrigerate for at least 4 hours until set firm.

4. To serve, turn out the pork and garnish with cooked chopped beetroot or watercress. Serve in slices with pickles and fruit sauce.

Brawn   35 minutes

½ salted pig's head (or cow's head or pig's cheek), small knuckle of veal, 2 small onions, 2 small carrots, ½ teaspoon nutmeg, 3 cloves, peppercorns, mixed herbs, seasoning, 570 ml (1 pt) cold water, 1 hard-boiled egg, and pickles or cucumber slices.

1. Remove trivet. Put in meats and water. Bring to boil. Skim thoroughly. Add remaining ingredients. Seal and pressure cook for 35 minutes.

2. Remove joints and meat. Chop meat into 1 *cm* (½ *in*) pieces.

3. Strain stock. Boil it till reduced to half a pint. Adjust seasoning.

4. Return meat and reboil. Turn the contents of the cooker into a small mould or basin so that it is full. Allow to set.

5. Turn out of mould by dipping quickly in and out of hot water. Serve garnished with egg and cucumber or pickle slices.

Pig's Trotter   40 minutes

4 pig's trotters, 4 small onions, carrots and turnips, potatoes for 4 servings, 140 ml (¼ pt) vinegar, 140 ml (¼ pt) water,

1 *tablespoon butter, allspice, flour, salt and pepper, bouquet garni, fried parsley.*

1. If pig's trotters are salted, soak them overnight in cold unsalted water. Then scrub trotters well, drain and dry. Season.
2. Remove trivet. Add liquid, seasoning and trotters. Seal and pressure cook for 25 minutes.
3. Meanwhile prepare vegetables. Leave carrots, onions and turnips whole. Cut potatoes small enough to cook in 5 minutes. Add vegetables to stock. Put trivet on top and then potatoes. Cook for 5 minutes.
4. Prepare and fry parsley. Serve potatoes, trotters and vegetables garnished with fried parsley. Degrease the stock (see p. 156).
5. Make a *roux* (see p. 76) and add the stock to it stirring well. Adjust seasoning. Reheat and cook for 2 to 3 minutes and serve separately.

Grilled Trotters

1. Pressure cook as above for 25 minutes. Add carrots, turnips and onions at beginning of cooking time.
2. Lift out trotters. Drain, halve and dip them first in melted butter then roll in breadcrumbs. Brown evenly under the grill. Garnish with fried parsley and serve with a sharp sauce like mustard or caper using ½ milk and ½ degreased, strained stock.

Osso Buco   30 minutes

800 *g* (1¾ *lb*) *veal knuckle slices, 4 tablespoons butter, 2 tablespoons flour, 2 tablespoons tomato paste, bouquet garni, 2 shallots or large onions, 1 clove garlic, 60 g (2 oz) grated Gruyère or Parmesan cheese, salt and pepper, 1 lemon, 570 ml (1 pt) water.*

1. Season veal slices. Dredge in flour. Brown veal slices and sliced onion in melted butter. Sprinkle on flour and stir.

2. Add water, tomato paste, herbs, garlic, salt and pepper. Seal and cook for 30 minutes.

3. To serve place meat on bed of spaghetti or rice (see pp. 227ff.). Pour on sauce and sprinkle with grated cheese. Heat in oven for a few minutes.

Jellied Veal   **30 minutes**

1 kg (2 lb) veal knuckle, 450 g (1 lb) veal bone, 200 g (7 oz) bacon rind, 4 large onions, 2 carrots, bouquet garni, 500 ml (¾ pt) dry white wine, 2 cloves, salt and pepper.

1. Remove trivet. Spread bacon rind over base of cooker. Place sliced carrots and onions on it then the meat above. Place bones around the side (broken up by butcher). Add herbs and seasoning. Pour on wine and bring to boil. Seal and cook for 30 minutes.

2. Wait for 10 minutes before taking off the lid – this tenderizes the meat. Place veal in a deep dish and pour over the cooking liquid. Add carrots. Leave until next day when jelly has formed. Serve with gherkins.

Tripe and Onions   **15 minutes**

700 g to 1 kg (1½ to 2 lb) blanched tripe prepared by butcher, 4 to 5 medium onions, seasoning, water, flour, 140 ml (¼ pt) milk, fried croutons, chopped parsley.

1. Cut tripe into 4 cm (1½ in) pieces. Remove trivet. Put in tripe with water to cover. Bring to boil in open cooker and throw away the water. Add whole onions, seasoning and water to cover. Seal and cook for 15 minutes.

2. Strain liquid. Blend flour with milk and a tablespoon of hot stock. Add to cooker and return to heat. Stir and boil

for 2 to 3 minutes. Add more stock to give sauce a pouring consistency. Adjust seasoning.

3. Serve hot, garnished with fried croutons dipped in chopped parsley.

Variants:

1. Add sliced carrots, mushrooms, stalks and crushed garlic for flavouring. This makes it TRIPE A LA BOURGEOISE.

2. Instead of using milk and water for sauce base use a combination of 280 *ml* ($\frac{1}{2}$ *pt*) *dry white wine*, 60 *ml* (2 *fl oz*) *cognac* and 2 *tablespoons tomato paste*.

3. Additional ingredients can be 120 *g* (4 *oz*) browned bacon and onions inserted with cloves, and a bouquet garni.

Calf's Liver   7 minutes

340 *g* (12 *oz*) *liver in large pieces, slices of lean bacon*, 340 *g* (12 *oz*) *baby carrots*, 140 *ml* ($\frac{1}{4}$ *pt*) *water or stock*, 140 *ml* ($\frac{1}{4}$ *pt*) *white wine, mire-poix (see p. 154), butter, seasoning*.

1. Wipe and season liver. Make small cuts in each piece. Cut bacon into strips lengthways and put one in each cut in the liver.

2. Remove trivet, prepare *mire-poix* in the base. Add sufficient liquid. Put in liver, trivet and carrots. Seal and cook for 7 minutes.

3. Remove meat, vegetables and keep hot in dish.

4. Degrease liquid (see p. 156). Boil until reduced by half. Pour over liver. Garnish with carrots and dots of butter.

Stewed Liver   **4 minutes**

340 g (12 oz) *liver*, 1 *tablespoon butter*, 2 *slices streaky bacon*, 3 *medium onions*, 140 ml ($\frac{1}{4}$ pt) *water*, 2 *tablespoons vinegar*, 1 *clove, sprig parsley, seasoning, vegetables (small potatoes, peas, mint), chopped parsley*.

1. If separate vegetables are required wash and prepare them and place in separator. Wash and dry liver. Cut into small strips and dredge in flour.

2. Remove trivet. Brown onions and bacon. Lift out and strain off fat. Add hot liquid to cooker, bacon, onions, seasonings and liver. Follow the standard stewing method (see p. 144) and pressure cook for 4 minutes. Garnish dish with chopped parsley.

Barbecue Liver   **10 minutes**

450 g (1 lb) *cubed beef liver*, 2 *tablespoons flour*, 1 *slice shredded bacon*, 2 *tablespoons ground suet*, 1 *chopped green pepper*, 1 *minced onion*, $\frac{1}{2}$ *teaspoon pepper*, $\frac{1}{2}$ *teaspoon curry powder*, 340 g (12 oz) *cooked tomatoes*.

1. Dredge liver cubes in seasoned flour. Heat bacon and suet in pan until crisp and brown. Add liver and fry lightly. Add pepper and onion and fry until brown. Add remaining ingredients. Seal and cook for 10 minutes.

2. Serve with boiled rice.

Braised Sheep's Tongue   **45 minutes**

4 *tongues*, 5 *slices bacon*, 2 *carrots*, 2 *onions*, 570 ml (1 pt) *water, bay leaf, peppercorns, parsley*.

1. Clean tongues. Scald by plunging into boiling water. Pressure cook for 3 to 4 minutes. Open lid and remove tongues. Drain and peel off their outer skins.

2. Empty cooker. Add bacon pieces, sliced onion and carrots, tongues on top and seasoning. Add water. Seal and cook for 40 minutes.

3. Serve with tomato sauce and beans or lentils prepared in advance.

Braised Ox Tongue

Use the same method as for sheep's tongue (see above). Omit the bacon from the ingredients. Additional vegetables such as turnip can be used.

Boiled Beef Tongue   60 minutes

1 *beef tongue*, 1½ *l* (3 *pts*) *water*, 1 *carrot and onion*, 1 *onion with cloves inserted, bouquet garni*, 430 *ml* (15 *fl oz*) *cider vinegar, salt and pepper.*

1. Soak tongue for 10 hours in water and vinegar. Clean and scald as above.

2. Add remaining ingredients and cook as above (see p. 197) for 60 minutes.

3. Serve hot or cold. If hot – with tomato sauce. If cold – with sauce vinaigrette, chopped herbs and gherkins.

MEAT CURRIES

Authentic Indian dishes are not pressure cooked, but the ones that need long simmering can be pressure cooked with ease and to great effect. Obviously tandoori specialities which require baking in a very hot oven are ruled out, but the following six recipes give some idea of the possibilities. If you are contemplating adapting your own favourites remember that the preparation and spicing need plenty of care and subtlety if first-rate results are to be obtained. The pressure cooker makes the meat more tender more rapidly – you can cut the timing of that part of the recipe down to one-quarter or one-fifth. The meat tables should give guidance.

The first recipe is called English Beef Curry because it is produced in a style favoured by the English when they ruled India; the other five are the sort of North Indian cooking that has been made popular by the vast spread of Indian, Pakistani and Bangla Deshi restaurants. All the ingredients are easily obtained at specialist stores.

English Beef Curry   **15–20 minutes**

450 g (1 lb) steak, 170 g (6 oz) rice, 280 ml ($\frac{1}{2}$ pt) hot salted water. Basic curry sauce: 2 tablespoons coconut, 430 ml ($\frac{3}{4}$ pt) white stock, 2 tablespoons butter, 1 medium onion, 1 small hard apple, 2 teaspoons flour and curry powder, 1 tablespoon mango chutney, 1 teaspoon lemon juice, 1 teaspoon red jelly or jam, seasoning.

1. Infuse coconut in boiling stock for $\frac{1}{2}$ hour. Then strain off stock.
2. Cut meat into small cubes and fry in butter. Fry chopped apple and onion. Fry flour and curry powder. Remove heat. Add chutney and stock. Stir. Return to heat. Boil. Add meat. Seal and cook for 10 minutes.
3. Cook rice (see pp. 228ff.).
4. Pre-heat oven to 180 °C (350 °F, GM 4). Pile rice on to a serving dish and put in oven to dry off.
5. Stir curry. If too thick add extra stock. Add lemon juice and jelly. Correct seasoning. Serve.

Beef Korma   **10–12 minutes**

1 kg (2 lb) lean stewing beef, 2 large chopped onions, small sliced ginger root, 1 tablespoon cumin, 5 cloves, pinch saffron,

60 *ml* (2 *fl oz*) *yoghurt, 2 tablespoons ghee or oil, 8 cloves of garlic, 5 shelled cardamom seeds, cinnamon, salt, 250 ml* ($\frac{1}{2}$ *pt*) *water.*

1. Soak saffron for 30 minutes in $\frac{1}{2}$ cup of hot water.
2. Add all ingredients to bottom of pressure cooker (you don't use the trivet of course) and pressure cook 10 to 12 minutes.
3. The curry will be almost dry when you come to serve it; watch the cooker carefully as you approach the end of cooking time – if the valve stops hissing you may have run out of cooking liquid. You can always open up and add more if needed.
4. This recipe works equally well for lamb pieces or textured vegetable protein (TVP) chunks, or chicken. This is a mild, dry curry.

Lamb Dopiaza   **10 minutes**

500 *g* (1 *lb*) *stewing lamb, 500 ml* (1 *pt*) *yoghurt, fresh ginger root, 1 tablespoon tomato puree, 1 teaspoon ground cumin,* $\frac{1}{2}$ *teaspoon turmeric, 1 kg* (2 *lb*) *sliced onions, 2 tablespoons ghee or oil, 1 teaspoon garlic powder or 2 crushed cloves of garlic, 1 tablespoon coriander,* $\frac{1}{2}$ *teaspoon cayenne pepper.*

1. Combine meat, yoghurt, tomato puree, cumin, ginger, turmeric, garlic, coriander, cayenne and salt and fry gently in oil till all oil is absorbed. Add 140 *ml* ($\frac{1}{4}$ *pt*) water and simmer in open pan till that too is absorbed.
2. Now add a further 100 *ml* (under $\frac{1}{4}$ *pt*) water and lay sliced onion on top.
3. Pressure cook 10 minutes. Watch and listen carefully towards the end of cooking time. If valve stops hissing you have run out of cooking liquid.
4. Before serving, squeeze lemon juice and sprinkle garam masala.
Works equally well with beef and chicken.

Madras Beef Curry   **10–12 minutes**

500 g (1 lb) stewing beef, 1 teaspoon garlic powder or 2 cloves crushed garlic, 1 tablespoon curry powder, 3 green chillies, 1 diced onion, 2 tablespoons tomato puree, 1 tablespoon lemon juice, 2 tablespoons ghee or oil, garam masala.

1. Heat oil in bottom of pan and sauté onions till golden clear. Add garlic, curry powder and green chillies and fry gently for 5 minutes.
2. Add meat, tomato puree and 200 *ml* (just under ½ *pt*) water. Pressure cook 10 to 12 minutes.
3. To serve squeeze lemon juice over meat and sprinkle with garam masala. This can also be used with lamb, chicken or TVP.

Beef Vindaloo   **10 minutes**

500 g (1 lb) stewing beef, 1 teaspoon garlic powder or 2 minced garlic cloves, 1 tablespoon turmeric, 1 teaspoon ginger, pinch of fenugreek, white vinegar as needed, salt and pepper, 1 chopped onion, 2 tablespoons ground coriander, 1 teaspoon ground cumin, ½ teaspoon mustard powder, 2 tablespoons ghee or oil; optional: cayenne pepper, chili powder.

1. Take all ingredients except beef and oil and make thick paste with white vinegar.
2. Add meat and marinade for at least 12 hours.
3. Heat oil in bottom of pressure pan and add meat plus entire marinade. Add 150 *ml* (just over ¼ *pt*) water.
4. Seal and pressure cook for 7 to 10 minutes.
5. The cayenne and chili powder can be added at the end to suit individual taste.

This is one of the hotter Indian curries. Works equally well with lamb, chicken and TVP.

Meat Molee   **10 minutes**

Molee is a basic mild curry technique which can be used for a variety of meats. A recipe for chicken molee is given on p. 213. If you are using another meat, check in the meat tables for guidance as to timing (pp. 149ff., 300ff.).

7: CHICKEN, POULTRY AND GAME

By and large, deep-frozen battery-reared chicken do not work well with pressure cooking – they have very little taste and the cooking method does not give much opportunity for improving on the raw ingredient. It is far better to roast, grill or fry by conventional means, unless cooking for invalids.

The best thing to go for is a really old bird, preferably free range – the ones marked 'boiling' in butchers' shops. If you buy a deep-frozen one, make sure it defrosts slowly. Pressure cooking minimizes the health danger of trying to cook partly defrosted birds, but imperfect cooking and a spoilt texture and taste are still risks. If you have time, allow a defrosted bird to sit at room temperature for 24 hours before using – this gives some substitute for the hanging a really good butcher would give fresh chicken.

I recommend fairly spiced-up methods of pressure cooking chicken in order to overcome the initial blandness of taste. The recipes give a range of ideas. The following table gives the basic cooking times for chickens of all ages so that you should be able to adapt your own favourite recipes as well as the ones given below. Do not over-cook. If you are using a meat thermometer, the internal temperature of cooked chicken (make sure you are not touching the bone!) is 88 °C, 190 °F.

Age and Size	Preparation and Use	Pressure-Cooking Time
Baby (under 1 kg/2 lb)	Halved or jointed	4–7 mins depending on size
Roasting (1–1½ kg/2–3 lb)	Whole, stuffed or jointed	6 mins/500 g, 5 mins/lb 5–6 mins
Boiling (1½ kg+/3½ lb+)	Whole, stuffed	12 mins/500 g, 10 mins/lb
	Whole, marinated	10 mins/500 g, 8 mins/lb
	Halved	20 mins
	Jointed	12 mins

Frozen joints, even if defrosted, require less cooking time than fresh ones – take 10% to 15% off the timing above.

CHICKEN RECIPES

Roast Chicken   **6 mins/500 g (5 mins/lb)**

1 *roasting chicken 1·4–1·8 kg (3–4 lb), 3 slices thin streaky bacon, 2 tablespoons dripping or fat, flour, bacon rolls, bread sauce, watercress, 280 ml (½ pt) water for cooker, salt and pepper. For stuffing: 1 tablespoon breadcrumbs, 15 g (½ oz) chopped suet, pinch of mixed herbs, grated lemon rind, 1 tablespoon chopped parsley, giblets, seasoning, milk/egg or ready-made packet mix.*

1. Soak giblets for ½ hour in salted water and then rinse thoroughly. Make the stuffing (see p. 155).
2. Wipe the chicken inside and out and season with salt and pepper. Stuff the chicken and close it up. Weigh.
3. Remove trivet from pressure cooker. Melt fat and brown chicken. Drain fat into a roasting tin. Add water to the cooker with the remaining giblets (feet etc.). Lay bacon rashers over the chicken breast and wrap the chicken securely in greaseproof paper. Seal and pressure cook for required time.
4. Pre-heat oven to 190 °C (375 °F, GM 5). Make bread sauce. Pre-heat fat in the roasting tin.
5. Lift chicken from pressure cooker. Remove bacon rashers. Dust chicken breast with seasoned flour. Place chicken in roasting tin and baste. 'Roast' chicken in oven for 15 minutes and baste once more during that time.
6. Strain and degrease chicken stock (see p. 156). Make gravy in the roasting tin. To serve, garnish chicken with watercress and bacon rolls. Serve with bread sauce and gravy.

This gives a rapid, juicy version of the traditional English method of serving.

Braised Chicken   5–8 minutes

Boiling fowl (jointed) or frozen chicken portions, 230 g (½ lb) chipolata sausages, mire-poix (see p. 154), seasoned flour, 2 tablespoons dripping or fat, vegetables for 4 servings (potatoes, carrots, greens), flour, gravy colouring, sherry or cognac, bouquet garni.

1. Allow frozen chicken to thaw.
2. Skin chicken pieces and toss in seasoned flour.
3. Prepare *mire-poix* ingredients (see p. 154).
4. Remove trivet. Melt fat. Brown sausages and lift out. Brown chicken pieces and lift out.
5. Make *mire-poix* in cooker then add water to just below the surface of vegetables, and bouquet garni. Place chicken pieces and sausages on top, covered with greaseproof paper. Then place trivet on top with vegetables placed in separate piles. Bring water to boil. Seal and pressure cook for 5 minutes (if frozen) or 8 minutes (if fresh).
6. Mash *mire-poix* vegetables and use stock as basis for sauce, adjust seasoning and add a dash of wine, sherry or cognac.

Boiled Chicken   12 mins/500 g (10 mins/lb)

1 boiling fowl, 1·4–1·8 kg (3–4 lb), lemon juice and rind, butter, seasoning, 570 ml (1 pt) water, 1 large carrot, 1 onion with 2 cloves inserted, 2 stalks celery, 1 leak, bouquet garni, peppercorns, 170 g (6 oz) savoury rice, flour, chopped parsley; 1 egg and 4 tablespoons cream for cream sauce (optional); for stuffing: slices of stale bread, 230 g (8 oz) cooked ham, 1 clove garlic, chopped parsley, 2 eggs, salt and pepper, giblets.

1. Make stuffing (see p. 155) and stuff chicken. Add a bit of grated lemon rind. Seal the chicken carcase. Wipe and weigh chicken. Season with salt and pepper and rub with lemon juice.

2. Prepare vegetables.

3. Remove trivet. Add water and chicken to cooker and bring to boil in open pan. Skim. Add chopped vegetables, seasonings and herbs. Seal and bring to pressure. Cook for all but 5 minutes of the time.

4. Reduce pressure. Lift out chicken. Strain stock and make it up to 850 *ml* (1½ *pts*) with water if necessary. Put stock back in cooker and bring to boil. Throw in the rice and then add the chicken. Seal and cook for remaining 5 minutes.

5. Skin chicken and serve whole or portioned. Degrease and thicken stock for gravy (see p. 156). Make cream sauce by beating egg and cream in a small bowl with a squeeze of lemon juice. Add 1 tablespoon stock and then gently whisk in another 280 *ml* (½ *pt*) of boiling stock. Heat the sauce in a small saucepan without curdling cream. Pour over chicken and garnish with chopped parsley.

Chicken Pieces with Vegetable and Wine   15 minutes

12 *chicken pieces*, 4 *tablespoons butter*, 2 *tablespoons flour*, 1 *onion*, 1 *carrot*, 1 *chicken bouillon cube or chicken stock*, 280 *ml* (½ *pt*) *hot water*, 140 *ml* (¼ *pt*) *dry white wine*, ¼ *teaspoon thyme*, 1 *teaspoon dried parsley*, *salt and pepper*, *vegetables* (*potatoes, turnips, green beans, onions, carrots*).

1. Brown chicken pieces in butter. Place them on bottom of cooker.

2. Dice an onion, carrot, and turnips and potatoes. Dissolve bouillon cube in hot water. Add water, wine, herbs, seasoning and green beans to cooker.

3. Place remaining whole vegetables in separator or on trivet above the chicken. Seal and cook for 15 minutes.

Stuffed Chicken   4–7 mins/500 g/lb depending on size

1·4 *kg* (3 *lb*) *chicken, 4 tablespoons butter, 4 bacon rashers,
20 small onions, 4 potatoes, 60 ml (2 fl oz) cognac, salt and
pepper;* for stuffing: *giblets, 1 large onion, 4 tablespoons
butter, 150 g (5 oz) sausage meat, 2 slices of bread with no
crust.*

1. Prepare stuffing (see p. 155). Simmer the stuffing
ingredients for 10 minutes in the cognac. Stuff chicken and
truss. Brown chicken with diced bacon and small onions.
Add diced potatoes. Mix together and season.
2. Seal and cook for 4 to 7 minutes depending on size
(see p. 203).

Southern Fried Chicken   5–6 minutes

*Jointed chicken pieces, flour, minced onion, garlic, cinnamon,
nutmeg, paprika, chili powder, cumin powder, thyme, sage,
chives, lemon slices, salt, pepper, oil.*

This method is similar to one used by a world-famous
franchise chain of take-away food.

1. Use oldish chicken. Rub joints with minced onion,
garlic and lemon juice. Pressure steam for 5 to 6 minutes.
Pieces can either be used immediately or put on one
side.
2. Place flour and pinches of assorted spices and herbs to
choice and salt and pepper in bag and shake each joint
rapidly in it so as to cover all over.
3. Shallow fry 3 to 4 minutes browning all over or deep
fry for 2 minutes till brown and crisp.

This method gives you rapid plump fried chicken every time
and will guarantee that the inside is plump, juicy, and all
cooked through.

Alternative method:

1. Cover joints with seasoned flour as before and fry *prior* to pressure cooking.
2. Pressure steam 5 to 6 minutes.

There is little to choose between these two methods – the first will give you a crisper outside, the second may be more convenient. You can vary the herbs and spices quite a bit.

For a thicker coating of batter, whisk an *egg* and 250 *ml* ($\frac{1}{2}$ *pt*) *milk* in a bowl. Dip chicken pieces in egg-and-milk before flouring.

Chicken Supreme   5 minutes

4 *chicken pieces* (*wings and breast*), 4 *slices uncooked ham about* $\frac{1}{2}$ *cm* ($\frac{1}{4}$ *in*) *thick,* 140 *ml* ($\frac{1}{4}$ *pt*) *double cream, seasoned flour,* 4 *tablespoons butter,* 120 *g* (4 *oz*) *button mushrooms,* 280 *ml* ($\frac{1}{2}$ *pt*) *chicken stock, salt and pepper, parsley;* sauce: 140 *ml* ($\frac{1}{4}$ *pt*) *each of chicken stock and milk, some cream,* 1 *egg yolk, seasoning, dash of sherry.*

1. Thaw chicken if frozen. Skin and bone each chicken piece and use bones for chicken stock. Brush chicken lightly with cream and roll in seasoned flour. Wash and slice mushrooms.
2. Remove trivet. Melt butter and brown ham slices. Lift out. Brown chicken pieces till golden and lift out.
3. Add stock to cooker. Lay each chicken piece on a ham slice and place in cooker. Lay mushrooms on top and dot with butter. Cover with greaseproof paper. Seal and pressure cook for 5 minutes.
4. Meanwhile make sauce but omit cream and egg at this point.
5. Lift out the chicken and ham portions. Arrange on a dish with the mushrooms. Reheat sauce. Adjust seasoning.

Mix egg and cream together and add to sauce away from heat. Cook for 2 minutes but do not boil or the cream will curdle. Add a dash of sherry just before pouring sauce over chicken. Garnish with parsley.

Jellied Chicken   35 minutes

1·4–1·8 *kg (3–4 lb) chicken, 570 ml (1 pt) water, 1 tablespoon gelatine, 2 beaten egg yolks, 280 ml (½ pt) chicken stock, 120 g (4 oz) chopped almonds, 1 minced pimento, 30 g (1 oz) chopped olives, 140 ml (¼ pt) whipped cream, salt and pepper.*

1. Disjoint chicken and place on the trivet in pressure cooker. Add water, seal and cook for 35 minutes. Remove chicken. Degrease and strain broth. Mince the chicken meat.
2. Dissolve the gelatine in cold water and stir in the hot chicken broth. Pour hot stock on to beaten egg yolks, stir in salt and allow to cool until partially set.
3. Fold remaining ingredients into the jelly leaving whipped cream till last. Pour into loaf mould and chill. When set slice and serve on lettuce.

Chicken Chow Mein   5 minutes

340 *g (12 oz) chopped chicken meat, 4 tablespoons olive oil, 1 large sweet sliced onion, 170 g (6 oz) diced celery, 170 g (6 oz) bean sprouts, 230 g (½ lb) sliced mushrooms, 280 ml (½ pt) chicken stock or water, salt, 1 tablespoon honey, 4 tablespoons soy sauce.*

1. Heat oil in cooker and sauté chicken, salt, celery, onion. Add bean sprouts and mushrooms. Fry till light brown. Add remaining ingredients.
2. Seal and cook for 5 minutes. Serve on crisp fried Chinese noodles. Other meats can be used. Molasses can be added for colour.

Chinese Steamed Chicken 16–22 mins/500 g (15–20 mins/lb)

Whole or half boiling fowl, fresh chopped ginger, lemon, green onions, salt and pepper, garlic, soy sauce, sherry.

1. Chicken should be cut in halves and cooking time should be calculated from the weight of each half.
2. Rub chicken with garlic cloves.
3. Make fumet or boiling fluid from water and soy sauce and sherry, mixed to taste.
4. Lay chicken halves on trivet with minced ginger, green onions and very thin lemon slices. Pressure steam for appropriate period.
5. To serve, garnish with cooked green onions and fresh lemon slices. Serve with plain boiled rice to which a bit of the fumet has been added.

The skin will be a pale yellow and will taste marvellous.

Chicken Paprika　　　　　　　　　　　　7 minutes

1·4 kg (2½–3 lb) young roasting chicken, 4 tablespoons butter, 4 medium onions, 2 medium tomatoes, 1 tablespoon paprika, 140 ml (¼ pt) water, 1 tablespoon flour, 2 tablespoons sour cream, 750 g (1½ lb) potatoes, 2 cups water in solid container, paprika for garnish, salt and pepper.

1. Cut chicken into portions. Chop onions finely and slice the tomatoes.
2. Remove trivet. Melt butter and brown onions slightly. Add paprika and mix well. Add tomatoes, water and chicken portions. Place trivet on top and the container of diced potatoes. Seal and pressure cook for 7 minutes.
3. Meanwhile pre-heat the oven; blend flour and cream.
4. Mash the potatoes mixed with some lightly fried onion, salt, pepper and paprika and fry brown in butter.
5. Keep chicken and vegetables hot.

6. Add strained stock slowly to the flour and cream. Adjust seasoning. Reheat but do not boil or else cream will curdle. Pour over chicken. Serve with paprika potatoes.

Greek Lemon Chicken   25 minutes

1·4 kg (2½–3 lb) chicken, knobs of butter, 1 lemon, 1 onion with 2 cloves inserted, 1 stalk celery, bouquet garni, crushed garlic clove, 1 carrot, seasoning, 570 ml (1 pt) chicken stock, 170 g (6 oz) rice; for sauce: strained juice of 1 lemon, 2 egg yolks, 1 tablespoon cold water, some chicken stock; lemon quarters with chopped parsley.

1. Soak giblets for ½ hour in salted water. Wash thoroughly.
2. Wipe chicken. Put lemon peel, seasoning and butter inside the chicken. Rub the outside with lemon, salt, pepper and garlic.
3. Remove trivet. Add chicken stock, vegetables, giblets, seasoning and the chicken. Seal and cook for 20 minutes.
4. Depressurize and open lid. Bring stock to boil and then add the washed rice. Seal and cook for 5 more minutes.
5. Lift out chicken. Cut into portions and keep hot. Strain stock and remove bouquet garni, giblets and vegetables. Shake the rice dry and pile on serving dish with chicken on top. Keep hot.
6. In a separate bowl beat egg yolks, add lemon juice, water and 2 tablespoons hot chicken stock. Whisk and heat over low flame. Stir continuously. Do not boil in order to avoid curdling. Add more stock until sauce is thick and coating. Adjust seasoning. Pour over chicken. Garnish rice with lemon quarters and chopped parsley.

CHICKEN CURRIES

The general method of pressure cooking curries is given in the meat chapter pp. 198–202. For most purposes cooking time, in order to make the chicken tender, will be 5 to 7 minutes. A young chicken of course cooks more rapidly than an older one and chicken pieces marinated beforehand (as in quite a number of recipes) also require very little cooking time. If you are using really old unmarinated chicken pieces, cooking time is 10 minutes or so. Here is an English curry recipe followed by a more authentic version.

Curried Chicken   **35 minutes**

1·4 *kg (3 lb) chicken,* 280 *ml* ($\frac{1}{2}$ *pt*) *water,* 1 *large sweet minced onion,* 1 *large minced cooking apple,* 3 *stalks chopped celery,* 60 *ml (2 fl oz) olive oil,* 2 *tablespoons flour,* 2 *beaten egg yolks,* 140 *ml* ($\frac{1}{4}$ *pt*) *single cream,* 1 *teaspoon salt,* 2 *teaspoons curry powder,* $\frac{1}{2}$ *teaspoon ginger, Tabasco,* 2 *teaspoons Worcestershire sauce.*

1. Disjoint chicken. Place on trivet in pressure cooker. Add water. Seal and cook for 35 minutes. Remove chicken. Strain stock and degrease. Chop chicken into small pieces having removed bones.

2. Brown onion, apple and celery in pressure cooker. Stir in flour. Add seasoning, spices and chicken stock. Make liquid up with water to 570 *ml* (1 *pt*).

3. Return chicken meat to stock and bring to boil in open pan. Allow the dish to cool for as long as possible so that spices permeate the meat (about 3 hours).

4. Just before serving reheat and stir in mixed egg and cream. Serve with rice or noodles.

Chicken Molee   **5–7 minutes**

1·4 *kg* (3 *lb*) *chicken cut in pieces*, 2 *cloves minced garlic*, 1½ *teaspoons ground ginger*, 2 *tablespoons ghee or oil*, 1 *large chopped onion*, 1 *teaspoon turmeric*, 1 *teaspoon ground cardamom*, 1 *teaspoon cinnamon*, 125 *ml* (4 *fl oz*) *coconut milk* (*infusion of unsweetened grated coconut*), *salt and pepper*, *garam masala*.

1. Pressure steam chicken pieces for 5 to 6 minutes.
2. Heat oil and fry onions light golden brown. Add garlic, ginger, cloves, turmeric, cardamom, cinnamon, and salt and fry for 3 to 4 minutes.
3. Gradually add coconut milk and bring to a moderate boil.
4. Add chicken pieces and leave for just long enough to make pieces hot. The pan is left open in this final stage.

Molee is a basic mild curry technique which may be used with other meats – the pressure cooker enables you to pre-cook them quickly.

GAME

The smaller birds and animals can readily be pressure cooked. Since they already have a strong taste they present less problems than the domesticated chicken.

Animal	Preparation	Cooking Time
Duckling	Whole	13–16 mins/500 g
		12–15 mins/lb
	Jointed	12 mins
Duck and Goose	Whole	15–17 mins/500 g
		13–17 mins/lb
	Jointed	15 mins
Partridge Pheasant Guinea Fowl Pigeon	Whole, in casserole or braised	7–12 mins
Hare	Jointed	35–40 mins
Rabbit	Jointed	12–15 mins

GAME RECIPES

Duck with Fruit   15–17 mins/500 g (13–17 mins/lb)

1 *duck cleaned and trussed, seasoned flour, mire-poix,* 4 *slices streaky bacon,* 2 *medium sliced onions,* 2 *medium sliced carrots,* 1 *stalk celery,* 2–3 *turnip cubes, bay leaf,* 280 ml ($\frac{1}{2}$ *pt) brown stock, sliced oranges,* 1 *glass of red or white wine.*

1. Wipe and weigh duck. Remove trivet. Brown bacon allowing fat to run out. Brown breasts of duck only. Lift out and dust with seasoned flour. Brown stock is essential to the recipe so if necessary brown the onions too. Add to pressure cooker the stock, the duck and the vegetables. Pour in glass of wine. Seal and cook for required time. Reduce pressure by standing in cold water.
2. Pre-heat oven to 190 °C (375 °F, GM 5) and have a roasting tin with hot fat in it. Lift out duck, baste with hot fat and brown it in the oven.
3. When the contents of the pressure cooker are nearly cold skim off as much fat as possible. Then sieve and strain stock and return it to the gravy pan. Reheat, adjust seasoning and pour into deep casserole. Place duck in dish and sliced oranges on top.

Duck is a rather fatty bird which is why simple pressure steaming is unsatisfactory. You should crisp-up the fat either by roasting or frying. Orange, lemon, or other fruit helps offset the fattiness.

Goose Stew   30 minutes

1 *kg* (2 *lb) goose pieces,* 3 *tablespoons butter,* 1 *tablespoon flour,* 570 ml (1 *pt) white or red wine,* 60 ml (2 *fl oz) cognac,*

1 *carrot, onion, bouquet garni, salt and pepper, chopped parsley.*

1. Remove fat from goose pieces (goose fat not used here). Melt butter in pressure cooker and fry goose with sliced onion until brown. Sprinkle with flour and stir. Season. Pour on cognac and set it alight. Add wine, carrot and herbs. Seal and cook for 30 minutes.
2. Prepare accompanying vegetables and add to cooker towards end of cooking time in separator (e.g. potatoes – 10 minutes).

Ragout of Goose   30 minutes

1 *kg (2 lb) goose pieces, 4 tablespoons butter, 2 tablespoons flour, 7 potatoes, 2 medium carrots, 230 g (½ lb) turnips, 1 clove garlic, bouquet garni, salt and pepper, 570 ml (1 pt) water.*

1. Remove trivet. Melt butter and brown goose and diced vegetables. Sprinkle on 2 tablespoons flour and stir. Pour in water, seasoning, garlic and herbs.
2. Seal and cook for 30 minutes.

Jugged Hare   30–40 minutes

1 *hare, 2 tablespoons dripping or fat, seasoned flour, 2 chopped onions, 1 clove crushed garlic, blade of mace, 140 ml (¼ pt) brown stock, seasoning, 1 glass red wine, 3 mushrooms, 2 slices fried bread, redcurrant jelly;* optional: *blood of hare, vinegar.*

1. Joint the hare and clean thoroughly. Remove trivet. Melt fat and brown joints. Remove and toss them in seasoned flour.

2. Brown onions and drain fat. Add sliced mushrooms, stock, wine, seasonings and joints. Seal and cook for required time.

3. Meanwhile fry bread and cut into triangles.

4. Lift joints into casserole dish and keep hot. Boil stock until thickened. Add blood if wished, blended carefully with a little vinegar, but do *not* allow to boil. Adjust seasoning. Pour over joints. Dip fried-bread triangles into redcurrant jelly and use as garnish.

Partridge and Pheasant

Partridge and pheasant are prepared alike and recipes are applicable to both birds. The only difference is the cooking time (see tables p. 213).

4 *small partridges or pheasants* (or 2 *large ones*); for stuffing: 4 *tablespoons butter*, 450 g (1 *lb*) *shelled walnuts*, 170 g (6 *oz*) *raisins*, 280 *ml* ($\frac{1}{2}$ *pt*) *cooking oil*, 60 *ml* (2 *fl oz*) *cognac. Bouquet garni*, 1 *carrot*, 1 *onion*, 4 *slices bread*, *salt and pepper*, 450 g (1 *lb*) *bacon.*

1. Soften raisins in cognac and the nuts in oil for several hours. Then crush nuts with a pestle or rolling pin and fry quickly in butter on low heat.

2. Chop up giblets (hearts and livers) finely and add them to the drained raisins. Then mix the giblets and raisins with the nuts and season liberally. Stuff the birds.

3. Tie up each bird with the slices of bacon. Season outside. Brown well in the pressure cooker. Add chopped carrot and onion and herbs. Seal and pressure cook for 8 minutes.

4. Place thin strips of bread on a long dish. Remove birds from pressure cooker and place the bacon slices on to the bread. Degrease sauce in pressure cooker (see p. 156). Add cognac in which raisins were soaked to sauce and set alight.

Place birds on the dish and pour hot sauce over just before serving.

Rabbit   15 mins/500 g/lb

1 *rabbit*, 4 *sweet onions*, 250 *ml* (8 *fl oz*) *sour cream* (optional), 1 *l* (2 *pts*) *chicken, beef or vegetable stock*, 30 *g* (1 *oz*) *flour*, 4 *tablespoons dripping or fat*, 2 *teaspoons salt*, $\frac{1}{4}$ *teaspoon pepper*.

1. Clean rabbit and weigh. Cut into suitable pieces for serving. Dredge with seasoned flour. Melt fat and brown rabbit well. Stir in thick sliced onion and stock.
2. Seal and pressure cook for required time calculated by weight. Sour cream can be added at the very end of cooking time, otherwise it curdles. Adjust seasoning. Serve.

Rabbit or Hare and Prunes   rabbit 12–15 mins
                                                  hare 35–40 mins

1 *hare or rabbit*, 300 *ml* ($\frac{1}{2}$ *pt*) *red wine*, 4 *medium carrots*, 1 *large onion, bay leaf, salt and pepper*, 2 *tablespoons butter*, 2 *tablespoons olive oil*, 300 *g* ($\frac{3}{4}$ *lb*) *dried prunes*, 1–2 *tablespoons redcurrant jelly*.

1. Cut the carcase into serving portions. Marinate for 24 hours with sliced carrots, minced onion, bay leaf, salt and pepper, red wine. Soak prunes separately.
2. Dry the portions and sauté quickly in butter and oil (or just oil if you prefer). The meat should be allowed to turn brown.
3. Pour marinade juices into pressure cooker with the meat and soaked prunes and add water to cover.
4. Pressure cook for the appropriate time according to the animal you are using. Meat should be tender.

5. Lift out meat portions. Reduce sauce over a high heat. Blend in the redcurrant jelly and adjust seasoning.

This unusual combination works very well even if you discard the prunes on the serving dish.

8: MEAT SUBSTITUTES

Although meat substitutes, or textured vegetable protein (TVP) are still considered to be the province of health food fanatics or a dark secret of the cheap end of the catering trade, an increasing number of people are incorporating them into their regular diet and the big food manufacturers are making tentative efforts at marketing their 'TVP' products in attractive ways to the general public.

The creation of recipes using their products is still in its infancy, but that is no reason why the pressure cooker should not be used to good effect.

TEXTURED VEGETABLE PROTEIN

The meat substitutes start off as the bean of the soya plant which contains an unusual range of proteins. Nutrition experts say that the protein we need to exist on is made up of a number of amino acids. Meats contain all of the amino acids, but most plants lack a few essential ones. What is unusual about the soya bean, and one or two other vegetables, is that they contain quantities of the essential amino acids plants lack. It is much cheaper to grow soya plants and the lucerne (a leaf like a giant clover) than to raise cows, sheep and pigs. Unfortunately the soya bean has a bland floury taste which is why few people try to cook it, though some recipes are given in this book in the vegetable chapter pp. 71ff., 105ff., 109ff.

TVP has been developed as a way of overcoming public prejudice. The substitute meat is made by rendering the bean down into flour and then subjecting it to pressure and temperature. It gets its texture partly from the natural coagulation of protein (the way eggs harden) and partly through spinning. Manufacturers can produce a variety of sizes and textures. Taste is injected largely from yeasts and extracts of wheat, and barley grains, and from the essential oils of certain plants. Only a few manufacturers use flavour that is wholly created in the laboratory. The other advantage of TVP is that it is low on fat and there is no potentially dangerous cholesterol.

COOKING

The two most commonly marketed forms are 'mince' and 'chunky' though there is also a sausage meat substitute as well. Cooking is normally in two stages, though sometimes they can be combined – hydration and cooking proper.

The textured protein is sold in a dried form and the manufacturers give instructions for rehydration. A standard pack of 141 g (5 oz) makes 450 g (1 lb) when water is added and fully absorbed, or, to express it metrically, to produce 1 kg of reconstituted meat substitute takes about 320 g of dried chunks or mince.

Once the TVP has been rehydrated it is like using ready-cooked meat and a wide variety of stews, casseroles, rissoles, loaves and pies can be made using ordinary recipes. The TVP is by most standards under-flavoured, so heavy spicing and herbing is recommended. TVP appears to stand a fair amount of over-cooking – easily up to one hour in a stew cooked by conventional means, or 15 minutes in a pressure-cooked version. If you over-cook, the pieces tend to lose their texture and fall apart, so violent and prolonged boiling is not recommended. You can mix hydrated TVP with left-over cooked meats, and with minced TVP you can mix half-and-half with raw minced meat (to make hamburgers for example).

HYDRATION

Follow the manufacturers' instructions. For 'mince' styles you usually add twice the volume of hot water to dried particles and leave for 4 to 5 minutes. In some cases you can simmer the mix gently for about a minute. All the liquid should be absorbed. It is obviously not worth using a pressure cooker in this instance.

'Chunky' styles take longer and the pressure cooker can shorten this time drastically. You should divide the time suggested by the manufacturers by 4 to get an appropriate figure. Thus a product which needs 20 to 30 minutes simmering under normal circumstances will reconstitute in a pressure cooker in 5 minutes. Add a fraction more water – 30 *ml* or 1 *fl oz* more than that suggested by the manufacturer to prevent the cooker boiling dry. You can always drain afterwards.

RECIPES

Many of the meat and vegetable recipes throughout this book are suitable for adaptation to TVP. The ones given below are merely for guidance. In some cases you can add the dried TVP right at the beginning, but remember:

1. The TVP will absorb twice its volume in cooking fluid, so allow enough for that.
2. TVP chunks must pressure cook for at least 5 minutes to reconstitute.

If your total pressure cooking time is over 15 minutes, TVP chunks might start to disintegrate. TVP mince will be all right if it is packed into a shape, e.g. stuffed into a vegetable or made into a loaf or a pie.

You can increase the meaty taste by adding a yeast extract product (like Marmite or Yeastrel) at the beginning of cooking time or *miso* at the end of cooking time.

TVP Stew 5–6 minutes

140 g (5 oz) TVP chunks (which will make 450 g (1 lb) of reconstituted meat), 3 onions, 250 g (½ lb) carrots, 250 g (½ lb) mushrooms, 250 g (½ lb) green peppers, plus tomatoes, celery as available, salt and pepper, cooking oil, yeast extract or miso, bouquet garni, 1 l (2 pts) water or vegetable stock or brown stock.

1. Slice and chop half an onion and fry in oil till brown. Add sliced carrots, tomatoes, strips of green pepper and any other vegetables used except tomatoes.

2. Add stock or water, tomatoes, bouquet garni and dry chunks, salt and pepper. Bring to boil and seal pan. Pressure cook 5 to 6 minutes.

3. Depressurize and open cooker. Taste fluid. Adjust seasoning with salt and pepper, and yeast extract or *miso*. Remove bouquet garni and serve.

This basic recipe can be varied in a number of ways:

1. The liquid can be thickened by the addition of a small amount of flour, or a thick white sauce (butter and flour melted together in equal proportions and dissolved into a little milk).

2. Alternative thickeners would be red lentils, oatmeal, rice, or pearl barley.

3. The spicing can be made much stronger. If you hydrate the TVP before you add it to the stew, drain TVP chunks and fry gently till it darkens. You can fry in onion or garlic or curry spices at this stage. Then proceed as before, only you will need *less* water or stock – put in 430 *ml* (¾ *pt*) *less* than if the TVP is dry.

TVP Loaf 10–12 minutes (+ 10 in oven)

140 g (5 oz) TVP mince (which will make 450 g (1 lb) when reconstituted), 1 chopped onion, 2 tablespoons rolled oats, 2 medium mashed potatoes, 1 teaspoon celery or caraway or fenugreek seeds or curry powder, 2 large eggs, 1 clove garlic, minced, 1 large tomato, 2 tablespoons oil, salt and pepper.

1. Hydrate TVP mince using 280 *ml* (just under $\frac{1}{2}$ *pt*) water, or as directed.

2. Mix all ingredients together, using oatmeal to dry out wet ingredients like mashed potato and lightly whisked eggs to act as binder.

3. Form into a loaf and cover all over with greaseproof paper. Secure.

4. Place on trivet above 280 *ml* ($\frac{1}{2}$ *pt*) water. Seal and pressure cook 10 to 12 minutes.

5. Depressurize, open pan, and remove loaf (without greaseproof paper) to hot oven 230 °C (450 °F, GM 8) for 10 minutes or so to crisp up the outside.

If you want a more 'herby' effect, add chives, chopped bay leaf, tarragon, parsley, sage or thyme, or any suitable combination to the mixture prior to cooking.

TVP Stuffed Vegetables   5–12 minutes

Stuffing: *hydrated minced TVP, breadcrumbs or rolled oats, assorted herbs, smidgin of cooking oil, salt and pepper, yeast extract.* Mix to taste.

See vegetable chapter p. 92ff. for general instructions on preparing and cooking stuffed vegetables. The timing is determined by the size and type of the vegetable hull – you can regard the TVP as already cooked. The purpose of the cooking time is to ensure that the outer hull is cooked through and that the inside is heated. Peppers will take 5 minutes, as will large tomatoes; a stuffed marrow needs 12 minutes, and an aubergine 10 minutes.

TVP Meat Sauce   **5–7 minutes**

This gives you a 'meat' sauce suitable for covering rice or pasta.

30 g (1 oz) TVP mince (which will make 100 g (4 oz) reconstituted), 1 onion, 1 carrot, 2 tablespoons tomato puree, 1 minced garlic clove, 2 tablespoons oil, salt and pepper; optional: nutmeg, mustard, chili powder, curry powder; 280 ml (½ pt) water or stock.

1. Hydrate TVP mince.
2. Fry chopped onion till brown, add diced carrot, garlic clove, and such spices as you wish. The chili will give a hot Mexican effect; the curry powder will, of course, give an Indian cast to the dish.
3. Add hydrated TVP, tomato puree and water or stock to cover.
4. Seal and pressure cook for 5 to 7 minutes. Adjust seasoning with salt and pepper.
5. Serve over rice or pasta.

While to the potato-eaters of North Western Europe, the United States and certain parts of the 'old' Commonwealth, rice, grains, cereal and pasta merely provide alternative 'fillers' to their meals, or are relegated to breakfast and sweet dishes, the rest of the world eats them all the time. With a pressure cooker the full flavour of these sometimes difficult-to-cook items can be brought out and the taste made nuttier and juicier without any danger of over-cooking. Cooking under pressure forces moisture into grains, which is where the secret lies. Timings are about one-third of that required by conventional techniques, but the results are better – this is one of a number of categories of food where the pressure cooker has benefits beyond merely saving time.

You'll find yourself cooking grain in your pressure cooker for several reasons. First – using the separators you'll want to prepare your rice or pasta at the same time as you are cooking green and root vegetables and meat. Second – you'll have more opportunity to prepare 'two-stage' versions of cereal, particularly rice, where light frying after cooking brings a variety of benefits. Third – you'll discover a whole range of grains and cereals which you may have neglected as being too difficult, long and complicated to cook. Grains and cereals are cheap and wholesome, particularly if bought in their unprocessed form. Too many of us have forgotten that the flaked, fluffed, extruded, toasted and sugared contents of cereal boxes were once the living seeds of plants and that, by and large, the manufacturing process has added packaging, perhaps some convenience, but little food benefit. The pressure cooker can open a whole new world. Most of the grains mentioned in this chapter are available in supermarkets, though in some cases you may have to go to more specialist outlets like health food stores.

With the exception of pasta, which is of course fabricated

and is dealt with later, and buckwheat, which is technically related to dock and rhubarb, all grain and cereal are varieties of seed. The seed has a very tough husk, a starchy filler and a germ. Whole grains are normally fairly indigestible because the stomach can't break down the tough outer husk – and even prolonged cooking is not enough either. In fact, rice, millet, barley and buckwheat are the only whole grains that can be cooked. Otherwise some form of milling or processing is necessary. The husks can either be cracked (as in the case of wheat), rolled in a simple machine (like oats), cracked, steamed and roasted (which is what has happened to Bulgar wheat when you buy it in the shops), or it can be milled or polished to remove the husks altogether (which is how brown rice becomes white rice). Further stages of milling start removing and eroding the starchy filler and you get a cream (in the United States and sometimes elsewhere you can buy creams of wheat and of rice) or a meal (as in cornmeal from dried maize, or farina, which is a mixture of several meals, sometimes with dried ground roots in them).

Take the milling process still further and of course you get flour.

COOKING METHODS

People tend to shy away from cooking rice and other grains because of the twin dangers of lumpiness and burning. The pressure cooker makes life a great deal easier. Most of the difficulties arise because grains have an outer covering that can become gummy after a degree of cooking – resulting in stickiness. Using one of the three methods specified below all troubles can be averted. The only point to remember is not to cook too much at any one time. *Do not allow the cooker to be more than one-third full.* Most grains give off a scum while cooking and this scum can rise up and boil through the escape vent. Should this happen the pressure cooker will not function properly and eventually the emergency vent will blow. However, *a more than adequate portion of dried cereal is* 60 g (2 oz) *per person*, so that 5 or 6 large portions of most grains can easily be cooked in most cookers with perfect safety.

GRAIN COOKING METHOD 1: BOILING WATER

Have right amount of water in cooker (see tables), ready salted and boiling furiously. Drop grain slowly into water, not allowing it to go off boil. When all the grain is in, allow the pan to stay open for a few seconds and then seal up and bring to pressure in the usual way for the time specified.

GRAIN COOKING METHOD 2: SAUTÉ AND BOILING WATER

This is almost the same as method 1, except that the grain is lightly sautéed in oil or toasted, without oil, in a non-stick fry pan or saucepan. Stir the grain vigorously to prevent sticking and burning, but let the grain turn slightly brown, to taste. This gives a nuttier flavour. Then add slowly to the boiling water as before.

GRAIN COOKING METHOD 3: COLD WATER

Wash the grain in a colander or sieve under running water (there is no need to do this if you are using a processed rice) and then add grain to a small amount of water and stir gently, dispersing the grain. You should not allow the grains to break as that will release more of the stickiness to the water. Lightly grease the inside of the pressure cooker with a little oil smeared round with greaseproof paper (to prevent sticking) and then add dispersed grain to cooker together with remainder of salted water needed for recipe (see tables).

Points to remember

1. All cooking is in salted water – add to suit your taste, and use pepper as well if you wish.

2. You do not need the trivet. If you are cooking grain with other ingredients, use the solid separator or a thin boilproof bowl or cup.

3. During cooking, water is needed both to be absorbed into the grain (rice takes in a minimum of twice its own volume in water and some whole grains absorb over four times their own volume) and to keep the pressure cooker going. The quantities in the tables make allowance for both these factors.

4. Individual grains vary according to the amount of moisture already in them; it depends how old they are, how and where they have been stored – so precise quantities are difficult to give. The tables err on the side of generosity in indicating quantities of water.

5. If you are using a new type of grain and there are no instructions given here, a rough guide is that cooking times are cut to one-third of that specified on the packet.

6. After cooking, drain grains through a colander and then place them in a low oven – the grains will continue to absorb moisture for a while after cooking. Stir lightly before serving.

7. This may all sound formidable – really it's easy to make it all become a happy routine. Well-cooked grains are clean and separate, plump and slightly fluffy.

RICE

Rice is sold in a variety of forms. The 'purest' version is brown rice; white rice has had the hull milled off and polished. Ordinary white rice usually needs to be washed thoroughly to remove surface talc and flour before cooking. Long-grain rice (patna or the better basmati) are used for main dishes and for Indian and Chinese cookery, short-grain (*risotto*) is used for sweet dishes and for Italian risotto. It is a matter of preference which to use in Spanish *paella*. Pre-fluffed or parboiled or processed rice is usually sold in packets. They do not require washing and are less prone to gumminess. However, the cooking time is longer and more water is absorbed. You need less dry rice per portion when it has been processed. Wild rice is not a true rice at all and grows in the United States. Because of its expense it is usually mixed with other types of rice.

Rice type	Description	Weight	Water	PC time/ Normal time (minutes)
Basmati	Long grain Top quality polished	170 g/6 oz	570 ml/1 pt	5/15
Patna	Long grain	170 g/6 oz	570 ml/1 pt	5/15
Risotto	Short grain Pudding	170 g/6 oz	570 ml/1 pt	4–5/12–15
Brown	Unpolished nutritious	170 g/6 oz	650 ml/1¼ pts	20/45–55
Wild	Sold largely in U.S.A.	170 g/6 oz	650 ml/1¼ pts	20/45–55
Pre-fluffed	Parboiled to avoid stickiness	170 g/6 oz	1 l/1¾ pts	8–9/25
Pre-fluffed brown	Parboiled to avoid stickiness	140 g/5 oz	1 l/1¾ pts	16–18/50

N.B. 170 g or 6 oz of cereal is the amount that will go into a level Imperial cup measure (½ Imperial pint liquid measure). If you are using a US cup, you should heap the rice. 90 g or 3 oz of dry rice is enough for one portion.

RICE VARIANTS

Rice cooked by these methods will probably need draining. You can dry it off and fluff it up by standing in a low oven for 5 to 10 minutes.

1. *Toasted rice.* If you have not used grain cooking method 2 already you can also toast after pressure cooking. Put rice in non-stick pan and allow to brown at the edges.

2. *Herb rice.* After main cooking period, *partially* drain rice and sprinkle over the top and mix in parsley, chervil, tarragon, coriander leaves, ground cloves, pepper, curry plant (this is a separate herb), and fennel leaves to taste. Don't use too many different ones. Allow to steam gently dry in slow oven for 5 minutes or so.

3. *Spiced rice.* Cook rice from the beginning with several cloves. You could also add cardamom seeds and a pinch of powdered cinnamon as well as the usual salt and pepper.

4. *Nut rice.* After cooking in the normal way, sprinkle a few drops of sesame oil over rice and stir in. You could also add a few pinches of chopped, toasted nuts and pumpkin seeds.

5. *Fried rice.* Turn cooked rice over in hot oil until all is absorbed. Different oils give different flavours – you can use butter, olive oil, sunflower oil or ordinary cooking oil. Do not use the aromatic oils like sesame, as they spoil easily when heated.

6. *Chinese fried rice.* The Chinese often fry in eggs and peas and even shrimps while carrying out (5) above. You could add drops of soy sauce after.

7. *Pilau rice.* This is the yellow rice served in Indian restaurants and is usually basmati. Pressure cook with salt, pepper and a few cloves. In some hot oil fry a finely chopped onion till brown, some light curry spices (it is usually better not to use a cheap grade of curry powder as it tends to burn easily) and then add rice, turning all the time. Before serving sprinkle with the Indian condiment garam masala.

8. *Saffron rice.* Before beginning pressure cooking, soak a few strands of saffron in a cup of hot water for 15 minutes and then add to water and cook in the usual manner. If you are cooking *paella* (see p. 233) you can add the saffron afterwards.

9. *Arabian rice.* Cook with sultanas, raisins and

blanched almonds, added either before or after pressure cooking time.

These are only suggestions – you can also add paprika, chili powder, slivers of cooked mushroom, a cheese topping . . .

RICE RECIPES

Rice Pudding   **10 minutes**

170 g (6 oz) risotto rice, 430 ml (¾ pt) milk, 1 vanilla pod, 3 tablespoons sugar, 1 egg, salt.

1. Wash and drain rice. Remove trivet and place rice in pressure cooker. Pour in water to cover. Bring to boil and allow rice to absorb it. Then add the milk, vanilla pod and a pinch of salt.
2. Seal and cook for 10 minutes. Add sugar and egg. Stir well. Allow to cool before serving.

Risotto   **6 minutes**

Always use Italian or round grain rice. Long-grain rice is *not* absorbent enough to give the desired result.

2 tablespoons olive oil, 1 diced medium onion, 1 clove garlic, 170 g (6 oz) rice, 1 l (2 pts) boiling, well-seasoned chicken stock, 4 heaped tablespoons Parmesan cheese.

1. Remove trivet. Heat oil and brown onion. Add garlic and rice. Stir till rice looks transparent.
2. Pour in boiling stock. Stir and bring to boil. Seal and pressure cook for 6 minutes.
3. If rice has not absorbed stock allow it to cook in open pan for a minute or so. Stir in the cheese. Serve at once.

Variant with mushrooms:
Follow Risotto recipe. In a separate pan cook 120 g (4 oz) *finely sliced button mushrooms in oil.* Add this to Risotto just before serving. Serve Parmesan cheese separately.

Variant with chicken livers:
Follow Risotto recipe. In a separate pan gently fry 3 *thinly sliced chicken livers in oil* then lift out. Add the *juice of half a lemon* or 1 *tablespoon white wine* to juices in pan. Then add 140 *ml* ($\frac{1}{4}$ *pt*) *thickened brown or chicken gravy.* Adjust seasoning. Put back livers. Reheat without boiling. Serve in centre of rice.

Pilaff   **approx. 5 minutes**

170 g (6 oz) rice, 60 g (2 oz) butter, 2 tablespoons chopped onion, 570 ml (1 pt) hot chicken or veal stock, paprika, a clove of garlic, salt and pepper.

1. Remove trivet. Fry onion and garlic in butter. Add rice and mix well. Add stock and allow it to boil. Seal and pressure cook for required time (see tables) according to the type of rice being used.
2. Allow rice to separate by flicking it lightly. Arrange in a ring or a bed on the serving dish. The rice can be garnished with black olives and sliced hard-boiled eggs to make it a more substantial main dish.

Variant with celery: Add diced celery when frying the onions and garlic.

Accompaniments to Pilaff:
Tomato sauce (with chopped ham, wine and herbs).
Turkey in cream sauce. Rice garnished with bacon rolls.
Lamb or mutton in cream sauce. Rice mixed with raisins.
Duck in cream sauce. Rice garnished with orange slices or cooked, stoned prunes.

Paella   **15 minutes**

This is a pressure-cooked approximation.

Chicken pieces, patna rice, chicken stock, olive oil, garlic, saffron, peas, sweet peppers, chorizo (hard spicy Spanish sausage), raw shrimp, mussels or clams.

1. Pressure cook small-cut chicken pieces and rice in separators in usual manner (about 5 to 6 minutes depending on size of chicken pieces and type of rice).

2. Have ready a metal casserole that will fit inside pressure cooker. Heat oil and lightly fry garlic. Add rice and cook till brown. Put in pressure cooker.

3. Add hot stock, pinch of saffron, cooked chicken pieces, peas, diced sweet peppers and thinly sliced chorizo. Stock should barely be visible. Seal pan and pressure cook for 5 minutes. Open pan and correct seasoning.

4. Add shrimp and mussels and pressure cook a further 3 to 4 minutes. Depressurize carefully and serve.

GRAINS AND CEREALS

The types of grain and cereal sold vary widely not only from country to country but also from district to district. The table below covers a wide variety of types that you will find; if in doubt, choose the one that looks closest to the description for guidance about timings.

Wheats are available whole grain, cracked and creamed; Bulgar is cracked, steamed and toasted. Oats are available whole, rolled, and milled and also in 'instant' forms. Groats usually contain cracked wheat, buckwheat and oats; kasha is ground buckwheat and barley; hominy is fine-ground corn with the husk and germ removed – hominy grits, the stand-by of 'soul' cooking, is a coarser version; cornmeal is flour made from maize; farina is made from various fine cereal grains and sometimes some starchy roots; semolina is principally wheat which will not mill into flour; couscous is mixed cereal used in North Africa.

Grain/Cereal	Description	Weight	Water	PC time/ Normal time (minutes)
Barley (pearl)		170 g/6 oz	1·1 l (2 pts)	20/55–60
Cornmeal		120 g/4 oz	730 ml (1½ pts)	8/20–25
Cracked wheat		120 g/4 oz	500 ml (1 pt)	20/55–60
Farina meal	Meal made of cereal grains and starchy roots	90 g/3 oz	500 ml (1 pt)	3/10
Hominy	Dried sweet corn (maize)	120 g/4 oz	430 ml (¾ pt)	25/50
Hominy grits	Corn with husk and germ removed	120 g/4 oz	730 ml (1½ pts)	20/50
Oats				
quick	follow packet instructions; do not pressure cook			
rolled		170 g/6 oz	700 ml (1¼ pts)	10/30–45
meal		170 g/6 oz	1·1 l (2 pts)	15/45
porridge		170 g/6 oz	700 ml (1¼ pts)	5/15

For proprietary brands of *groats* (usually made from cracked wheat, buckwheat and oats), *kasha* (coarse-ground buckwheat and barley), and *couscous* (fine-ground flour or other cereal) follow instructions on packet and divide cooking time by 3. One cup by volume of a flaked cereal will absorb 2 to 3 times the volume of water. One cup of whole-grain cereal needs 3 to 4 times its volume of water and a granular cereal will be thickened and will absorb its own volume.

Cereal cooked for babies and invalids should have more liquid in them so that they become gruel.

GRAIN AND CEREAL RECIPES

Cornmeal Mush   **5–8 minutes**

170 g (6 oz) water-ground cornmeal, 140 ml ($\frac{1}{4}$ pt) cold water, 570 ml (1 pt) boiling water, salt, maple syrup, honey or molasses, water for cooker.

1. Combine the cornmeal, cold water and salt. Stir.
2. Remove trivet and add boiling water for cooker (about 570 ml or 1 pt).
3. Place the other 570 ml (1 pt) of boiling water in a separate pan and stir in the cornmeal mix gradually over a high heat for 2 to 3 minutes.
4. Remove this mixture to the separator and seal the cooker and bring to pressure for 5 to 8 minutes. Serve with maple syrup, honey or molasses.

Polenta

Cornmeal mush, paprika, red pepper, 120 g (4 oz) grated cheese, oil or butter; optional: tomato sauce and meat.

1. Prepare cornmeal mush as above. Just before pressure cooking add the spices to taste. Stir in the grated cheese after pressure-cooking time is over.
2. An optional method is to sauté the dish in olive oil or butter before serving.
3. Tomato sauce or meat can be served with the dish.

Cornmeal Dumplings

570 ml (1 pt) stock, 170 g (6 oz) cornmeal, 30 g (1 oz) all-purpose flour, 1 teaspoon baking powder, $\frac{1}{2}$ teaspoon salt, 2 whisked eggs, 140 ml ($\frac{1}{4}$ pt) milk, 1 tablespoon butter.

1. Combine the ingredients for the dumplings and let the batter stand for 5 minutes. Then roll into small balls.
2. Boil the stock in the pressure cooker. Drop the dumplings into the stock, seal and pressure cook for 5 minutes.
3. After cooking remove them at once from the stock.

Do not crowd the cooker by trying too many at once!

Refried Grains

This is a good recipe for left-over cooked grains and vegetables.

Cooked grain (see tables for cooking times), *onion, celery, carrot, peppers, egg, soy sauce, green onions.*

1. Cut vegetables into small pieces. Stir-fry them in the base of the pressure cooker. Add the grain and stir.
2. When grain is heated through add seasoning to taste. Make a space in the grain mix and drop in an egg or two. Quickly stir it in with the grain.
3. Serve garnished with sliced green onions, nuts or grated cheese.

Variants:

Seasonings: garlic, ginger, thyme, hot peppers, curry powder.
Garnishes: raisins, nuts, diced apple, toasted sunflower seeds.

Grain Soups

For basic soup cooking and timing see soup chapter p. 30.

170 *g* (6 *oz*) *grain* (see tables for water and timing), *salt, oil.*

1. Oil the pressure cooker and roast the grain a little. Add salt and water. Seal and pressure cook for required time.

2. For additional ideas about accompanying vegetables see soup chapter.

Basic Hot Cereal Recipe

170 g (6 oz) cereal, salt, oil or butter, water for cooker.

1. Sauté the cereal in the base of the pressure cooker in oil or butter. Remove from heat and allow to stand for a minute.

2. Add boiling water to the cooker. Stir well. Seal and pressure cook for required time (see table p. 234).

3. To vary the dish you can depressurize towards the end of the cooking period and add dried fruit, chopped nuts, sunflower seeds, nut butter to name but a few.

Kasha   **5 minutes**

230 g ($\frac{1}{2}$ lb) dry buckwheat, 1 lightly beaten egg, 430 ml ($\frac{3}{4}$ pt) boiling water, 2 tablespoons butter, salt and pepper.

1. Stir egg and buckwheat together. Put mixture in bottom of pressure cooker and stir over a high heat till grains are separate and dry.

2. Add the boiling water, butter, salt and pepper to taste. Stir again.

3. Seal and cook for $\frac{1}{3}$ the conventional time specified on the packet – usually about 5 minutes. Serve.

Couscous   **20 minutes**

170 g (6 oz) pre-cooked chick peas, 1 kg (2 lb) lamb, mutton or beef, 1 tablespoon olive oil, 2 tablespoons butter, 120 g (4 oz) minced onion, 2 teaspoons salt, $\frac{1}{2}$ teaspoon pepper, $\frac{1}{8}$ teaspoon *red pepper, ½ teaspoon turmeric, 2 tablespoons tomato paste, 450 g (1 lb) couscous (or semolina, cracked millet, cracked wheat or kasha), vegetables, 2 tablespoons orange-flour water, ¼ teaspoon cinnamon, ¼ teaspoon cloves, 2 knuckle bones.*

1. Prepare and cook chick peas (see vegetable chapter p. 104). Drain them.

2. Remove trivet. Cut meat into 10 to 12 pieces and brown in butter and oil. Add the minced onion during this. When onion goes clear add salt, pepper, red pepper, turmeric and tomato paste. Stir well.

3. Add knuckle bones and water to cover and vegetables of choice – potatoes, courgettes and marrow. Add chick peas. Add more stock if necessary. Seal and pressure cook for 10 to 15 minutes.

4. Depressurize and open cooker. Skim the fat from the surface of the stew and reserve 2 tablespoons of it.

5. Rinse the couscous (or cereal) and place in a separator. Reseal pressure cooker and pressure steam the cereal for 5 more minutes.

6. Drain stock and reserve. Take cereal from steamer and add to it the orange-flower water, cinnamon and cloves. Toss it in the 2 reserved tablespoons of fat and place in a serving dish. Pour 140 *ml* (¼ *pt*) of the reserved stock over the couscous dish. Place meat, vegetables and chick peas on top. Use remaining stock as a sauce. Serve very hot.

PASTA

Pasta is another way of eating grain, only this time it has already been processed and combined into shapes. The table lists most of the common types available. Cooking time is determined by the thickness of the pasta, so adaptation should be easy if you come across any strange varieties. The green or *verde* pasta has been coloured with vegetable dyes but is otherwise the same as ordinary pasta.

Remember to put the pasta into boiling salted water for best results. Long 'elbows' of spaghetti and vermicelli should be gently eased into the pan, pushing more in as the arms start softening under the influence of the boiling water.

Pasta	Weight	Water	PC time/ Normal time (minutes)
Macaroni			
5 cm (2 in) lengths	230 g/½ lb	1 l/(2 pts)	4–5/12–15
elbow	230 g/½ lb	1 l/(2 pts)	5–6/20–25
Noodles			
fine	230 g/½ lb	1 l/(2 pts)	2–3/6–8
medium	230 g/½ lb	1 l/(2 pts)	3–4/8–10
alphabet	170 g/6 oz	850 ml/(1½ pts)	3–4/8–10
small shells	170 g/6 oz	1 l/(2 pts)	3/9
Fettuccine	170 g/6 oz	1 l/(2 pts)	3/9
Spaghetti			
fine	230 g/½ lb	1 l/(2 pts)	3–4/8–10
regular	230 g/½ lb	1 l/(2 pts)	5–6/20–25
Vermicelli	230 g/½ lb	1 l/(2 pts)	3–4/8–10

Properly cooked pasta is not soggy but has a definite texture – the Italians call it *al dente*. If you wish to avoid overcooking, pressure cook for slightly less than the times indicated above, depressurize and finish off with an open pan at normal temperatures and pressures. You can then use your teeth to tell you about the degree of 'doneness' and can adjust salt and pepper seasoning if you wish.

PASTA RECIPES

Spaghetti Bolognaise   **15 minutes**

340 g (¾ lb) spaghetti, 3 tablespoons olive oil or butter, 1 onion, 120 g (4 oz) lean mince beef or 60 g (2 oz) each of mince beef and chicken livers, 60 g (2 oz) mushrooms, diced carrot and celery, lemon rind, bay leaf or basil, salt and pepper, nutmeg,

2 *tablespoons tomato puree or paste*, 140 *ml* ($\frac{1}{4}$ *pt*) *brown stock, clove of garlic, sugar*, 140 *ml* ($\frac{1}{4}$ *pt*) *dry white wine*, 2 *tablespoons grated Parmesan cheese.*

1. Remove trivet. Heat oil and brown diced onion. Add meat, chopped mushrooms and other vegetables if used. Stir for a minute or so.

2. Pour in wine and boil rapidly for a moment. Then add seasonings, pinch of sugar, tomato paste/puree, brown stock and stir. Seal and pressure cook for 10 minutes.

3. The sauce should then be heated gently in an open saucepan to reduce to a creamy consistency. Wash out the pressure cooker and cook the spaghetti under pressure for about 5 minutes in boiling water.

4. Drain the spaghetti and mix it with a little oil or butter while it is still in the hot cooker. Adjust seasoning of sauce and serve.

Spaghetti Milanaise   5–6 minutes

340 *g* ($\frac{3}{4}$ *lb*) *spaghetti*, 2 *tablespoons olive oil or butter*, 170 *g* (6 *oz*) *mixed cooked strips of ham and tongue*, 1 *tablespoon tinned mushrooms*, 2 *tablespoons tomato puree or paste*, 140 *ml* ($\frac{1}{4}$ *pt*) *brown stock, seasoning*, 2 *tablespoons grated cheese, chopped parsley.*

1. Cook spaghetti as above for 5 minutes under pressure.

2. Drain spaghetti and rinse with boiling water. Heat oil in cooker and return spaghetti and stir until coated with oil. Add the meat, mushrooms, tomato paste/puree and brown stock. Heat and stir thoroughly.

3. Adjust seasoning. Sprinkle with cheese and parsley. Serve.

Pressurized Pasta Sauce   **8–10 minutes**

450 g (1 *lb*) *Italian plum tomatoes, peeled, ½ chopped onion, 2 cloves crushed garlic, 2 tablespoons olive oil, ¼ green pepper, bay leaf, parsley, oregano, basil, salt, pepper, red wine.*

1. Heat oil and sauté the onion and garlic. Put tomatoes and green pepper in a blender and blend until liquid. Pour liquid into the cooker and add herbs and seasoning to taste. Stir.
2. Pour contents of cooker into a solid separator or small suitable container placed on bottom of pressure cooker. Simmer. Cook pasta in remainder of space in cooker.

Savoury Macaroni

230 g (8 *oz*) *macaroni, 2 tablespoons butter, 1 finely chopped onion, 4 tomatoes, strips of green and red pepper, 60 g (2 oz) sliced mushrooms, 140 ml (¼ pt) brown stock or gravy, 230 g (8 oz) cooked ham, meat, chicken or sausages, dash of Worcestershire sauce, salt and pepper.*

1. Cook macaroni (see tables). Pile on to a serving dish and keep hot.
2. Meanwhile melt butter in a pan and brown the onions, mushrooms and peppers. Add the quartered tomatoes. Stir in the liquid. Add seasoning and finally the cooked meat.
3. Simmer and cover. Leave on a low heat. Just before serving add a dash of Worcestershire sauce. Serve grated cheese separately as an optional dressing.

Pasta and Four Cheeses

150 g (5 *oz*) *each of cubed Gruyère cheese, Fontina cream cheese, and grated Mozzarella, 200 g (7 oz) grated Parmesan*

cheese, 1½ tablespoons flour, 60 g (2 oz) butter, 230 ml (8 fl oz) milk or single cream, 450 g (1 lb) shell macaroni.

1. Prepare all the cheeses as specified. Toss them all with flour except the Mozzarella which is to be kept separate.
2. Heat the butter with the milk or cream in the base of a heavy pan until the butter has melted. Gradually stir in the three cheeses until there is a smooth sauce. Keep hot over a low heat.
3. Cook the macaroni (see tables).
4. Drain macaroni and transfer it to a large warm bowl. Pour over cheese sauce and stir quickly using two spoons. Just before serving stir in the Mozzarella quickly. Pasta cools quickly so do not over-stir. Serve on heated plates.

Pasta e Fagioli

290 g (10 oz) pre-cooked haricot or pea beans, 11 tablespoons olive oil, bay leaf, 3 to 4 cloves garlic, 3 carrots, 2 celery stalks, 1 large onion, oregano, basil, 6 to 7 firm ripe tomatoes, 230 g (½ lb) shell macaroni, salt and pepper, chopped parsley, grated Parmesan cheese.

1. Soak beans overnight and cook (see vegetable chapter p. 104) with bay leaf, olive oil, 3 to 4 cloves of garlic. Drain and reserve stock. Discard bay leaf and garlic.
2. Clean vegetables. Dice the carrot, slice the celery, chop the onion. Sauté in hot olive oil. Add the remainder of crushed garlic, herbs and seasoning to taste. Add the tomatoes and cook thoroughly.
3. Cook the macaroni (see tables) and drain.
4. Combine the beans with the cooked vegetables and macaroni. Add about 280 ml (½ pt) of reserved bean stock to pan and adjust seasoning.
5. To serve, sprinkle the dish with chopped parsley. Serve Parmesan cheese separately.

Spaghetti-Stuffed Peppers **3 minutes**

4 green peppers, 1 l (2 pts) water, 120 g (4 oz) broken spaghetti, 120 g (4 oz) mushroom pieces, 230 g (8 oz) cooked ham or left-over meat, salt, pepper, crushed cereal flakes.

1. Wash and clean peppers and make 8 shells for stuffing.
2. Bring water to boil in the pressure cooker. Add spaghetti. Place peppers on top. Seal and pressure cook for 3 minutes.
3. Carefully remove peppers to avoid breaking. Drain upside down. Drain spaghetti and blanch with hot water and then mix with remaining ingredients, except cereal.
4. Fill pepper cups and top with flakes. Place on trivet, add water to cover bottom of pressure cooker. Seal and cook for 3 minutes. Serve with cream sauce.

Variant: This recipe also works if you use tomatoes in place of peppers.

10: FRESH AND DRIED FRUIT

For many purposes it is not worth using a pressure cooker for preparing fruit, particularly the fresh variety. Most fruit is at its best and most nutritious raw, but for variety and when preparing stewed fruit, fillings for pies, tarts and cakes, cooking is desirable. The pressure cooker, being an enclosed vessel, helps conserve the goodness of the fruit. The speed of the process can be slowed down either by leaving the weight/valve off so that the cooker functions as an ordinary saucepan with a well-fitting lid, or, if your cooker has a facility for adjusting the pressure, you could use a 5 *lb* (L) weight. If you cook without the valve the timings given below should be multiplied by 4 or 5 times; if you use a 5 *lb* weight, multiply by 3.

FRESH FRUIT

For most purposes you will want stewed fruit and the tables allow for this – you cook without the trivet or pannier. Stewed fruit is cooked in a syrup, a recipe for which is given. However, in certain cases you may prefer to pressure steam some sorts of fruit. I have never seen this suggested in any pressure-cooking book but I have found the technique useful in two cases: first, where one is going to stuff some hard fruit like an apple with a forcemeat of some variety – a recipe for a rapid 'baked' apple is given on p. 249; second, to make a filling for a pie or a tart. If you cook fruit in a syrup which you then drain away, most of the goodness goes down the sink with the syrup. A pressure-steamed fruit retains all the goodness. Add sweetness in the form of castor sugar or, if you prefer, golden syrup, after cooking and when you can judge the degree of tartness. Often, too, some lemon juice will bring out some almost hidden quality in a number of fruits.

In my own fruit cooking I rather like adding spices like cinnamon, nutmeg and cloves and using other additions like cochineal, rose water, almond essence and vanilla sugar (leave a pod of vanilla in a sugar jar for a few months and the taste will be subtly altered) but these are simply my own preferences.

You can also use your pressure cooker in the first stage of the making of jams, jellies, marmalades and chutneys. The fruit always has to be softened or pulped to release the pectin necessary for the proper 'setting' of jams and jellies and the pressure cooker is ideal for this. Then follow your own favourite recipes and techniques.

FRESH FRUIT RECIPES

Stewed Apples   **2 minutes**

This is a basic stew method for all recipes to be pulped or pureed for fillings, omelettes, fools etc.

Cooking apples, sugar to taste, piece of lemon peel; optional flavourings: *rose petals, rosemary, sprig of elder flower, orange-flower water, rose-water, cloves, cinnamon.*

1. Peel and core apples. Slice or cut up roughly.
2. If using optional flavourings remove trivet, add 140 *ml* ($\frac{1}{4}$ *pt*) water to cooker and boil with the flavourings for 3 minutes. Then lift out the flavourings.
3. Add the sugar and allow it to dissolve. If using orange-flower water or rose-water add it with the sugar. Stir until sugar dissolves then boil for 2 to 3 minutes.
4. Otherwise rinse the apples in cold water and add to cooker with sugar and lemon peel. Apples tend to froth when cooking so *do not fill the cooker more than $\frac{1}{3}$ full.* Bring to boil slowly in open pan until apple juices cover the bottom. Seal, bring to pressure and cook for 2 minutes.

[*continued* p. 249]

Fruit	Weight	Water	Sugar	Stewing/Steaming time	Instructions
APPLES					
Baked	1·4 kg/3 lb	140 ml/¼ pt	100 g/3 oz	4 mins/4–6 mins	Steam on trivet. Wash and core. Place in wet parchment on trivet in pan. Fill centres with sugar. Sprinkle with cinnamon.
Sauce	1·4 kg/3 lb	500 ml/¾ pt	200 g/6 oz	1½ mins	Quarter, core and pare. Stew without trivet and strain or leave as chunk sauce. Pack in layers sprinkling each with brown sugar and a strip of lemon peel. Nutmeg or cloves to taste.
APRICOTS					
Halves	1 kg/2 lb	140 ml/¼ pt	120 g/4 oz	3 mins/¾ min	Make syrup from water and sugar, add fruit, cover and stew.
Whole	2 kg/4 lb	500 ml/¾ pt	200 g/6 oz	3 mins/1½ mins	
BLACKBERRIES					
BILBERRIES }	2 kg/4 lb	140 ml/¼ pt	150 g/5 oz	1 min/1½ min	The berries can be cooked alone or with sliced apples. Add sugar to the fruit, add water, seal and cook.
BLUEBERRIES					
CHERRIES					
Black	2 kg/4 lb	140 ml/¼ pt	150 g/5 oz	¾ min/1 min	Both black and sour cherries can be cooked whole or stoned. Add sugar to fruit, add water. Seal and cook.
Red	2 kg/4 lb	140 ml/¼ pt	200 g/6 oz	½ min/¼ min	

Fruit	Weight	Water	Sugar	Stewing/Steaming time	Instructions
CRANBERRIES Jelly	2 kg/4 lb	500 ml/¾ pt	400 g/12 oz	3 mins	Add water and cook. Strain if desired. Add sugar. Boil 1 min without cover. Strain, add gelatin and pour into mould.
Sauce	2 kg/4 lb	280 ml/½ pt	230 g/8 oz	1½ mins	Stir sugar into water until dissolved. Add fruit, cover and cook. Bring to pressure slowly.
GOOSEBERRIES	2 kg/4 lb	280 ml/½ pt	230 g/8 oz	1½ mins/2 mins	To stew: stir sugar into water till dissolved. Add fruit, cover and cook. To steam: Add sugar after cooking.
GRAPES Juice for jellies	1·4–2 kg/3–4 lb	140 ml/¼ pt	—	¼ min	Wash fruit, place in pan with water and bring to pressure only. Strain juice for jelly making.
ORANGE Slices	1·4–2 kg/3–4 lb	140 ml/¼ pt	200 g/6 oz	3 mins	Wash, slice and remove seeds. Seal and cook. Add sugar and cook uncovered a few moments to glaze.
PEACHES Halves	2 kg/4 lb	280 ml/½ pt	100 g/3 oz	½ min/3 mins	Scald, peel and halve and remove pits. If stewing dissolve sugar in water and add peaches. Seal and cook. To steam add sweetening later.

Fruit	Weight	Water	Sugar	Stewing/Steaming time	Instructions
PEARS Halves (dessert)	2 kg/4 lb	280 ml/½ pt	100 g/3 oz	1 min/4 mins	Wash, pare and halve and core fruit. Dissolve sugar in water if stewing, add fruit, seal and cook. Add sugar later if steaming.
Hard (stewing)	2 kg/4 lb	280 ml/½ pt	100 g/3 oz	3 mins/8 mins	Cook in basic sugar syrup in container or in cooker without trivet.
PINEAPPLE	2 kg/4 lb	140 ml/¼ pt	200 g/6 oz	12 mins	Slice, pare and dice from core. Add water and cook. Stir in sugar after cooking.
PLUMS GREENGAGES DAMSONS	2 kg/4 lb	140 ml/¼ pt	120 g/4 oz	3 mins/3 mins	Cook whole, prick each one with a fork or halve and stone. Add sugar and bring to boil. *If whole, cook 4 minutes.*
QUINCE	2 kg/4 lb	280 ml/½ pt	120 g/4 oz	15 mins	Quarter, core, pare. Dissolve sugar in water, add fruit and cook.
RASPBERRIES	2 kg/4 lb	140 ml/¼ pt	230 g/8 oz	¼ min/¼ min	Bring water and sugar to boil. Add fruit, seal and bring to pressure only.
RHUBARB	1·4 kg/3 lb	140 ml/¼ pt	120 g/4 oz	¼ min	Wash and cut in lengths or short sticks. Add sugar and water. Seal and bring to pressure only.
STRAWBERRIES	2 kg/4 lb	140 ml/¼ pt	200 g/6 oz	¼ min/½ min	To stew: bring water and sugar to boil. Add fruit, seal and bring to pressure only. To steam: add sugar later.

5. If necessary strain off excess juice, then beat the apples vigorously. Adjust sweetening. Add a knob of butter. Stir.

Stuffed Apple   2 minutes

This is a rapid alternative to baked apple.

For each person: 1 *large cooking apple, currants, nuts, muesli, cloves, cinnamon, candied peel (or mincemeat), golden syrup or maple syrup.*

1. Core apples carefully and hollow out to leave shell.
2. Mix ingredients for filling, except syrup. Place in small bowl.
3. Arrange cored apples in bowl with filling on trivet (you can stack up if you wish). Place 280 *ml* ($\frac{1}{2}$ *pt*) water below trivet. Seal, bring to pressure and cook for 2 to 3 minutes.
4. Open cooker. Fill cooked apple shells with filling and pour over syrup. Serve with custard or single cream.

Chestnuts and Puree   10 minutes

1 *kg* (2 *lb*) *chestnuts,* 430 *ml* ($\frac{3}{4}$ *pt*) *milk,* 1 *teaspoon sugar, salt,* 7 *tablespoons butter.*

1. Slit chestnuts with a pointed knife and plunge them into boiling water for 5 minutes. Then shell them one by one.
2. Remove trivet. Put shelled chestnuts in pressure cooker and cover with sweetened milk. Seal and cook for 10 minutes.

To Puree:
Put cooked chestnuts through a vegetable masher. Add 7 tablespoons butter and beat vigorously to obtain a frothy puree.

Meringued Compote   **10–15 minutes**

1 *apple compote*, 2 *to* 3 *egg whites*, 2 *tablespoons sugar*.

1. Prepare compote of fruit by cooking a little longer than the time specified in table (about 10 minutes).
2. Beat egg whites stiff. Add a pinch of salt to whites before beating to speed up and improve the texture.
3. Pour the hot sweet apple compote into an ovenproof dish. Spread the beaten egg whites on top with the blade of a knife. Sprinkle with granulated sugar and leave in a medium hot oven for about 15 minutes. Allow to brown but not burn.

Rose Hip Syrup   **2 minutes**

1 *kg* (2 *lb*) *ripe rose hips*, 1 *l* (2 *pts*) *water*, 230 *g* (8 *oz*) *sugar*.

1. Remove trivet and boil up 570 *ml* (1 *pt*) water in the cooker. Immediately put the rose hips through a coarse mincer directly into the water. Seal, bring to pressure and cook for 2 minutes. Strain the liquid through a jelly bag.
2. Wash the cooker out and return the syrup to it. Add 570 *ml* (1 *pt*) water, then the sugar and allow to boil in the open cooker for 5 minutes.
3. This can now be consumed immediately or bottled in the usual way.
4. Once opened, the syrup will keep for about one week after bottling.

Spiced Oranges   **5 minutes**

4 *whole unpeeled oranges*, 120 *g* (4 *oz*) *brown sugar*, 60 *ml* (2 *fl oz*) *water*, ¼ *teaspoon cinnamon*, ¼ *teaspoon nutmeg*, 60 *ml* (2 *fl oz*) *corn syrup*, 350 *ml* (12 *fl oz*) *water for cooker*, *chopped nuts and dates*.

1. Pressure cook oranges for 3 minutes in 350 *ml* (12 *fl oz*)

water. Reduce pressure quickly. Drain, cool and peel oranges.

2. Mix remaining ingredients together and pour over oranges. Pressure cook for 2 minutes.

3. Put oranges in individual serving dishes. Boil the syrup in the open cooker to thicken. Pour over oranges.

4. Serve hot or cold. This dish can be either salad or dessert with cottage cheese or cream cheese on salad greens.

Spiced Caramel Pears   6–8 minutes

4 medium pears, 4 slices of pineapple, 140 ml ($\frac{1}{4}$ pt) double cream, 1 teaspoon castor sugar, pieces of cherry and angelica, chopped nuts for decoration, 280 ml ($\frac{1}{2}$ pt) water with lemon for cooker; for syrup: 140 ml ($\frac{1}{2}$ pt) water, 170 g (6 oz) loaf sugar, 1 clove, pinch of cinnamon, juice of 1 lemon.

1. Peel pears thinly and core. Put pears in suitably sized dish to fit in pressure cooker.

2. Heat and stir syrup ingredients in a separate saucepan till sugar dissolves. Then boil rapidly till thick and brown. Pour immediately over the pears.

3. Put water, trivet and dish of pears in pressure cooker. Cover dish with buttered greaseproof paper. Seal, bring to pressure and cook for 6 to 8 minutes.

4. Lift out dish, strain off juice and pour it back over the pears to coat them. Allow to cool or chill in fridge.

5. Whip cream till stiff then fold in sugar, cherries and angelica. Put a slice of pineapple on the base of each serving dish and place a pear on each. Fill the centre with cream mixture and decorate with chopped nuts.

Fruits Fool   2 minutes

450 g (1 lb) fruit compote, whipped cream; 280 ml ($\frac{1}{2}$ pt) milk, 2 teaspoons cornflour, sugar to taste, 1 egg (for custard) or 280 ml ($\frac{1}{2}$ pt) custard from custard powder.

1. Prepare any suitable fruit compote (see tables pp. 246–8). Chill.

2. Fold in stiffly whipped cream in proportions 1:1.

3. To make custard mix cornflour with a small amount of milk to make a paste. Boil the rest of the milk and then add cornflour paste. Return to heat and reboil. Stir in the yolk of an egg and cook for a minute without boiling. Add sugar to taste. Allow to cool.

4. Beat egg white stiff and stir it into the fruit and cream compote. Decorate with cherries, angelica, etc.

Apple Bread and Butter Pudding   25 minutes

8 *slices stale bread, 4 tablespoons sugar, 8 tablespoons butter, 140 ml (¼ pt) water, 2 tablespoons rum, 3 apples, cinnamon, cloves, 570 ml (1 pt) water for cooker.*

1. Cut bread into small cubes. Peel, core and slice apples.

2. Grease a suitably sized pie dish that will fit into the pressure cooker. Put a layer of bread cubes on the bottom.

3. Cover alternately with apple slices, sugar, spices. Then place knobs of butter on top. Fill the dish in this manner.

4. Press the mixture down firmly in the dish and pour over the rum and the 140 ml (¼ pt) water. Cover dish with grease-proof paper and a plate.

5. Place water for steaming in the cooker. Mount pie dish on trivet in cooker. Seal, bring to pressure in the usual way and cook for 25 minutes. Serve when warm.

Trinity Pudding   25 minutes

8 *sponge fingers, 4 beaten eggs, 6 tablespoons sugar, 700 ml (1¼ pts) milk, 120 g (4 oz) chopped candied cherries, 2 tablespoons rum, 570 ml (1 pt) water for cooker.*

1. Boil and stir milk and sugar together in a saucepan and pour into a bowl containing the sponge fingers. Reduce

sponge fingers to a puree. Add the beaten eggs. Stir well. Then add the chopped candied cherries and the rum.

2. Grease with butter a suitably sized soufflé dish that will fit in the pressure cooker and pour in the mixture.

3. Add water and trivet to cooker. Place dish on top. Seal, bring to pressure in the usual way and cook for 25 minutes.

4. Turn out pudding when cold. Serve chilled with fruit or custard compote.

Bread Pudding   15 minutes

5 slices stale bread, 430 ml (¾ pt) milk, 3 eggs, 5 tablespoons sugar, 2 tablespoons butter, salt, 2 tablespoons rum, 340 g (¾ lb) pitted prunes, 120 g (4 oz) chopped candied fruit, redcurrant jelly.

1. Prepare custard in the usual way adding 3 beaten eggs and rum.

2. Grease with butter a suitably sized soufflé dish that will fit in pressure cooker. Mix together chopped bread, prunes and candied fruit. Fill the dish. Gradually add the hot custard. Press mixture down in dish. Allow to stand for 10 to 15 minutes.

3. Cover the bottom of the cooker with water. Put in trivet and place soufflé dish on top covered with greaseproof paper secured by string or a rubber band. Seal, bring to pressure in the usual way and cook for 15 minutes.

4. Serve cold with redcurrant jelly or custard.

Variant: instead of bread use sponge fingers.

DRIED FRUIT

Pressure cooking is the best way to enjoy dried fruits. As with other foods that have been dehydrated – dried beans, grains and so on, pressure cooking offers the facility of forcing moisture into the fruit under pressure and as a result the finished dish is rather more juicy and tender than that obtained with more conventional stewing techniques.

Fruit is dried by laying out on racks either in low-temperature drying ovens operating at around 60 °C (140 °F) or simply by exposing to tropical sun. The drying prevents the enzyme and bacterial action which cause decay. In commercial practice a small amount of sulphur dioxide is used also, but you won't be able to taste it if the process has been properly carried out. 2·5 *kg* of fresh apricots make 450 *g* of dried fruit (5½ *lb* make 1 *lb*).

Quite a number of dried fruits are still fairly moist: decay is kept at bay by the presence of sugar in the fruit.

In the tables below the quantities of water suggested are average – there is obviously a world of difference between the dried fruit that emerges from a pack that has been neglected for six months in a suburban supermarket and the juicy specimens found in shops that specialize.

Stuffed Dried Fruits

450 *g* (1 *lb*) *dried apricots, prunes, dates or figs, nut meats or candied pineapple or candied ginger or marshmallows, granulated or powdered sugar or grated coconut.*

1. Pressure steam the dried fruits for required time (see tables opposite).
2. When cool, stuff the fruit with candied fruit or nut meats or marshmallows.
3. After steaming, the fruit can be rolled in granulated or powdered sugar or grated coconut.

Fruit	Weight	Water	Sugar	Stewing	Instructions
APPLES	450 g/1 lb	570 ml/1 pt	120 g/4 oz	8 mins	Add sugar to cooked fruit. If soaked reduce cooking time to 2 mins. Do not soak unless fruit is very dry.
APRICOTS	450 g/1 lb	570 ml/1 pt	120 g/4 oz	1–3 mins	Do not soak. Add sugar to cooked fruit.
CURRANTS	230 g/½ lb	280 ml/½ pt	—	5 mins	For use in cakes, desserts, etc.
FIGS	230 g/½ lb	500 ml/¾ pt	100 g/3 oz	10–12 mins	Soak overnight, if possible, and therefore reduce cooking time. Add sugar to cooked fruit.
MIXED, FOR PIES	230 g/½ lb	500 ml/¾ pt	60 g/2 oz	5 mins	Enough for an average-size pie. Soak if some fruit is very dry. Can be served as a fruit compote.
PEACHES	680 g/1½ lb	700 ml/1¼ pts	120 g/4 oz	5–10 mins	If soaked overnight add more water before cooking. No soaking necessary unless very dry; or cook longer. Add sugar to cooked fruit.
PEARS	680 g/1½ lb	280 ml/½ pt	100 g/3 oz	6 mins	No soaking necessary unless very dry. Add sugar after cooking.
PRUNES bulk	680 g/1½ lb	700 ml/1¼ pts	60 g/2 oz	10 mins	
packaged	680 g/1½ lb	570 ml/1 pt	60 g/2 oz	5 mins	
RAISINS seeded	230 g/½ lb	280 ml/½ pt		3 mins	Do not soak. Use in other recipes.
seedless	230 g/½ lb	280 ml/½ pt		5 mins	

Variant: GLAZED FRUIT

1. Pressure steam the fruit as above.
2. Pre-heat the oven to 120 °C (250 °F, GM ¼–½) and coat fruit in a meringue glaze made from 2 *stiffly beaten egg whites* to which you slowly add 120 g (4 *oz*) *sugar*, and ½ *teaspoon vanilla essence*.
3. Place fruit on a wire rack with a baking sheet beneath and sprinkle tops with grated coconut.

Egg Custard   **5 minutes**

2 *large eggs*, 430 *ml* (¾ *pt*) *milk*, *vanilla essence to taste*, *nutmeg*, 2 *tablespoons sugar or to taste*, 280 *ml* (½ *pt*) *water with lemon juice or vinegar for cooker*.

1. Beat eggs, sugar and vanilla essence together gently.
2. Warm the milk, then pour the eggs into the milk. Stir continuously.
3. Have ready a buttered soufflé or casserole dish that fits into the pressure cooker. Turn the egg mixture into it.
4. Put the water and trivet in the cooker and place the dish on top. Cover dish with a double thickness of grease-proof paper. Seal, and bring to pressure in usual way. Cook for 5 minutes.
5. To serve sprinkle the top of the egg custard with nutmeg. Serve hot or cold with stewed, bottled or tinned fruit, if wished.

11: CAKES, PUDDINGS AND BREAD

The cooking of steamed puddings and cakes at home has gone quite remarkably out of fashion. In the first place cakes and puddings in general are regarded as stodge, to be avoided by the figure-conscious. Secondly, if you use conventional cooking methods, making them is rather a long process.

The pressure cooker can take care of the second of these objections rather well, the pressure injection of steam is exactly what these foods need to cook them quickly and well. And as for the first worry, stodgy carbohydrates have their value in the diet of all normal healthy people – in fact we need them to give us energy and warmth. What counts is the overall intake of carbohydrates so, even if you are a little worried about your weight and health, provided you cut down in some other area, for example potatoes, there is no reason why you shouldn't try the occasional steamed pudding. Because what a delight they are – tasty, light and easy to digest and, once the basic methods are understood, capable of almost endless permutations. For families with young and growing children health-giving steamed puddings sweetened with stewed fruit, currants or jam are much better and much less of a threat to teeth than confectionery from the local sweet shop.

BASIC METHODS

The cooking of any steamed pudding takes place in two stages:

1. The flour and fat (and sometimes sugar) basic mix must be given something to make it rise and develop the characteristic open sponge-like texture.

2. The risen mixture must then be cooked solid so that

the flour and fat become edible and the open structure of the dough retained till the very end, when it is eaten.

In the sort of bread we normally eat, the raising agent is a yeast organism which starts multiplying rapidly at certain temperatures and giving off carbon dioxide. When the bread dough has been allowed to sit in the warmth and been kneaded, the bread loaves are transferred to an oven where the high temperature kills off the yeast to prevent any further activity and at the same time cooks the risen dough.

With steamed puddings the rising agent is baking powder and not yeast. In the United Kingdom it is quite easy to buy self-raising flour, but if you wish to use plain flour, then you add baking powder separately at the ratio of 3 level teaspoons to 230 g (½ *lb*) of plain flour (about 50 *g* to 1 *kg*). Baking powder gives off carbon-dioxide gas as a result of chemical reaction – the careful control of timing and temperature is necessary to ensure that the carbon dioxide is given off at just the right speed to provide a neat network of small holes throughout the cake or pudding.

The first or raising stage is normally carried out in an open steaming saucepan – that usually takes 15 minutes; and the second under pressure. Since the pressure cooker is providing more than just a higher cooking temperature but is injecting moisture, it is necessary to keep some control over this as well. As a result, most pressure-cooking experts now advise that steamed puddings should be cooked at low pressure – 5 *lb* (L) instead of the more usual 15 *lb* (H). This is to avoid an over-cooked outside or under-cooked inside.

In addition to the regular equipment with which your cooker comes to you, you will need a boilproof bowl – or a series of smaller ones and a bread tin. These are rested on the trivet or in the pannier. If you have any difficulty in removing the bowl or tin from the pan you should tie a string cradle round its neck. The bowl or tin is left open during cooking and is never filled to more than two-thirds – to allow for expansion in cooking. The top is merely covered with two thicknesses of greaseproof or parchment paper to prevent condensation on the top of the pudding.

Enough water is placed in the pressure cooker for the total cooking time – i.e. you will need 140 *ml* ($\frac{1}{4}$ *pt*) for each 15-minute period of cooking time. In fact, since these are steamed puddings, extra water will not come amiss.

GENERAL PROCEDURE

1. Pudding mix. Prepare pudding mix as per recipe and fill bowl up to $\frac{2}{3}$ full, to allow for rising. Cover bowl with greased greaseproof paper, tied down securely. Do not use containers with lids – the steam must be able to penetrate.

2. Pre-steaming. Place enough water in cooker for total cooking period, plus a little to spare. Place bowl on trivet or pannier. Close pan, but leave the weight/valve off. Bring to boil and allow gentle but persistent pre-steaming time as given in recipe. The heat should be low.

3. Pressure steaming. Now add 5 *lb* (L) weight, increase heat until pressure and internal temperature have been reached (the instruction booklet with your cooker will remind you about this). Then pressure steam for the time specified in the recipe on as low a heat as consistent with maintaining pressure.

4. At the end of cooking time, remove cooker from heat, and allow it to cool slowly to room temperature.

5. To serve: turn bowl upside down, loosen string on greaseproof paper, and serve garnished or smothered in sauce or syrup as appropriate.

6. Timings. Individual timings in minutes are given in the recipes but here is a rough guide:

Normal cooking time	Pre-steaming cooking time	PC at L (5 *lb*)	PC at H (15 *lb*)
30	3	5	$1\frac{1}{2}$
45	5	10	3
1–1$\frac{1}{4}$	15	25	8
1$\frac{1}{4}$–2	15	35	10–12
2–3	20	50–60	20

Note: Pressure cooking puddings at 15 *lb* (H) pressure is not recommended because of the unevenness of results. If your cooker does not have an adjustable pressure valve, then use the timings in the far column, but cook four smallish individual puddings rather than one big one. In the recipes that follow, all timings are for 5 *lb* (L) pressure. Divide pressure-cooking times by 3 if you have no alternative but to use full 15 *lb* (H) pressure.

If you are cooking in an extra-thick dish, e.g. an oven-proof glass one, up to 10 minutes' more cooking time will be needed.

7. In hard-water districts, add a little lemon juice to your boiling liquid.

Foundation Plain Pudding Mixture	**15 minutes pre-steaming** **30 minutes at L pressure** *or* **5 minutes pre-steaming** **10 minutes at H pressure** **(in individual cups)**

170 g (6 oz) *self-raising flour (or plain flour plus* 2½ *teaspoons baking powder), 90 g (3 oz) margarine or butter, 60 g (2 oz) sugar, 1 teaspoon mixed spice, salt, 1 egg, 3 tablespoons milk; for cooker: 850 ml (1½ pts) water.*

1. Rub fat into sieved flour, adding a pinch of salt, till mixture feels like fine breadcrumbs. Add sugar and spice. Beat in lightly the egg and milk until entire mix has a 'dropping' consistency.

2. Pour mix into greased bowl up to ⅔ mark so that it settles in evenly. Cover with greaseproof paper.

3. Pre-steam 15 minutes and pressure steam 30 minutes at 5 *lb* (L) pressure.

This recipe can be varied by (1) adding currants and other

chopped dried fruit, lemon; (2) omitting spices and adding ground ginger; (3) adding vanilla essence or almond essence; (4) pouring over jam, golden syrup, chocolate sauce, etc.

Foundation Rich Pudding	**15 minutes pre-steaming**
Mixture	**25 minutes at L pressure**

170 g (6 oz) self-raising flour (or plain flour plus 2½ teaspoons baking powder), 90 g (3 oz) margarine or butter, 90 g (3 oz) castor sugar, 1 large egg, salt, lemon rind, touch of milk, 850 ml (1½ pts) water for cooker.

This mixture as the name implies is sweeter than the plain one and the technique is different.

1. Cream the margarine or butter with lemon rind until quite smooth. Add the castor sugar and beat till the mixture looks white.
2. Add the lightly beaten egg dollop by dollop, to avoid curdling the mixture. Whisk well between each addition. Then fold in the sieved flour and a pinch of salt. You should again go for a 'dropping' consistency. A little milk may be used to help things along.
3. Then add to bowl and pre-steam and pressure steam as indicated above.

To this basic mix you can add any of the items mentioned for the plain mixture. To make a chocolate pudding, instead of the 170 g (6 oz) of self-raising flour substitute a mixture of 110 g (4 oz) of self-raising flour plus 80 g (3 oz) cocoa powder. A coconut pudding uses the basic mix with 50 g (2 oz) of desiccated coconut added.

Basic Suet Pudding   15 minutes pre-steaming
                                       30 minutes at L (5 lb)

This dough is an easy one to make: you use twice the weight
of self-raising flour to whatever quantity of shredded suet
you need, add a pinch of salt and enough water to make a
dough that will stretch when pulled, is not sticky and can
be rolled out easily. Any sweetening or spicy agent can be
added, depending on whether you are making a sweet
pudding or a savoury or a meat pudding (see p. 187).

To make a pudding, roll suet crust out thinly – 250 g (8 oz)
flour plus 125 g (4 oz) suet gives enough for the average-
sized pudding – and divide into two circles, one twice the
size of the other. The larger of the pieces fits into the bowl:
trim the edges around the top, leaving a small overlap.
Place your filling inside and use the second circle to act as a
top. Dampen the edges to make a good seal and press firmly
together. Cover with greased greaseproof paper to prevent
the formation of condensation during cooking. *Ingredients:*
use the fruit tables (pp. 246–8) for basic cooking times and
sprinkle castor sugar throughout as you layer the fruit in.
You should only need 1 tablespoon or so of water. Pre-
steam 15 minutes and pressure steam as above.

Bread   40 minutes pressure steaming

This recipe enables you to steam bread rather than bake it in
the traditional manner. The majority of commercial loaves
in most countries are steamed, and knowing how to steam
bread is useful when a hot oven may not be available.

Since the recipe uses yeast rather than a purely chemical
raising agent, you must let the dough rise naturally in a
warm place rather than encouraging it along with a pre-
steaming period. The pressure cooker is used solely for the
last stage of the operation.

12 g (½ oz) yeast, 1 teaspoon sugar, 300 ml (½ pt) hand-hot
water, 500 g (1 lb) strong white flour, salt.

1. Blend yeast in sugar (if using active dried yeast follow maker's instructions) and add half the warm water.

2. Shake flour and pinch of salt into warm basin and make well in the middle of the flour. Pour yeast mixture and remainder of water into middle and cover with a layer of flour. Put cloth over top of basin and leave in a warm place (e.g. kitchen, airing cupboard) until yeast bubbles through flour (about 10 minutes).

3. Mix yeast and flour well and turn on to a board, kneading it in the classic manner for another 10 minutes.

4. Place in floured basin. Cover again and leave in warm place till dough has doubled in size (this will take about 1½ hours). Turn out dough and knead again briefly to give uniform consistency.

5. Place mixture in bread tin and punch into shape. Leave in warm place for another 15 minutes. (You could divide the mixture into two smaller tins, if more convenient).

6. Now place tins, covered with greaseproof paper, in pressure cooker and pre-steam for 5 minutes before letting pressure mount. The yeast culture will now be killed off and cooking proper begins. Time at L (5 *lb*) pressure is 40 minutes.

The crust of this bread will be fairly pale and soft.

You can use a wholemeal flour instead of a strong white one – but do not use an ordinary plain flour.

Many of the traditional bread recipes that are usually baked can also be pressure steamed.

Christmas Pudding

The principles of cooking Christmas pudding are the same as for other steamed puddings only, mainly due to the density of the dish, it all takes much longer. In this case you use the full 15 *lb* (H) pressure. Timing is by weight.

Weight of mixture	Water for cooker	Steaming time	PC at 15 lb (H)
170 g/6 oz	850 ml/1½ pts	10 mins	50 mins
450 g/1 lb	1 l/2¼ pts	15 mins	1¾ hours
700 g/1½ lb	1·5 l/3 pts	20 mins	2½ hours
1 kg/2 lb	1·75 l/3½ pts	30 mins	3 hours

300 g (10 oz) *fresh breadcrumbs*, 230 g (8 oz) *soft brown sugar*, 230 g (8 oz) *currants*, 300 g (10 oz) *chopped seeded raisins*, 230 g (8 oz) *sultanas*, 60 g (2 oz) *chopped mixed peel*, 300 g (10 oz) *shredded suet*, ½ teaspoon salt, 1 teaspoon mixed spice, grated rind of 1 lemon, 2–3 teaspoons lemon juice, 2 large eggs, 140 ml (¼ pt) milk, 280 ml (½ pt) Guinness.

1. Mix the dry ingredients together in a large basin. Stir in the lemon juice, beaten eggs, milk and Guinness.

2. Grease the basins well and prepare the coverings. Weigh the mixture into the prepared basins and tie securely. Leave overnight. Next day give a final stir.

3. Refer to the table for the steaming and pressure cooking times. For a 1 kg (2 lb) pudding use 1·75 l (3½ pts) water. Pre-steam for 30 minutes and pressure cook for 3 hours at 15 lb (H).

4. If not eating the puddings immediately, cool, re-cover and store in a cool place. When required, steam for 30 minutes.

12: FREEZING AND PRESERVING

It is now possible to buy most forms of food at most times of the year. Sophisticated refrigeration, high-speed transport, high-grade commercial food processing and efficient marketing have all made home storage of food less necessary.

However, the pressure cooker can be used both as an aid to home freezing in the pre-cooking or blanching of food and it can also be used for the older techniques of bottling and canning. The advantage of the latter, of course, is that once fruit, vegetables or even meat have been bottled or canned, no further attention is necessary till they are eaten – you don't need an expensive freezer and you are independent of power supplies.

FROZEN FOODS

Most frozen vegetables behave better in the freezer if they have been blanched before packaging. The colour is better retained and enzyme action is slowed down. Most freezer manufacturers and writers of books on the use of home freezers recommend blanching in rapidly boiling water. The pressure cooker, however, gives you the alternative either of steam blanching (which minimizes the leaching away of vital juices) or of blanching in water that is much hotter than boiling water and where the process takes less time.

The British Ministry of Agriculture says that careful blanching is essential if losses of food value and taste are to be avoided. If you don't blanch brussels sprouts, they start deteriorating in three days, beans in three weeks to a month. However, if you immerse the vegetables for longer than necessary you start losing vitamin C. The pressure cooker seems to offer the best results.

INSTRUCTIONS FOR PREPARATION FOR FREEZING

1. Choose only the best vegetables and prepare them as you would do normally.

2. Unless otherwise stated the vegetables are steam blanched and are thus placed on the trivet, or in a separator, or in a pannier suspended over water. You should have 280 *ml* ($\frac{1}{2}$ *pt*) of water in the bottom. The base of the cooker can be up to two-thirds full.

3. The timings here are suitable for cookers with adjustable pressure – 10 *lb* (M) is the one selected, giving an internal temperature of 115 °C (240 °F). If your cooker is not adjustable, the blanching time will be approximately half the specified times.

4. Bring water to boil and fill the pan with steam before lowering the food rapidly on to the trivet. Seal pan and cook for specified period.

5. Have ready a colander and a large bowl of water into which the colander can be dipped. After cooking period is over, depressurize rapidly by cooling cooker under running water and empty vegetables into colander. Dip colander rapidly into large bowl of water for one minute in the case of small vegetables and two to three minutes in the case of larger ones.

6. Lift colander out of water and package vegetables rapidly in the usual manner.

Vegetable	Instructions	Blanching time/ minutes
ARTICHOKES (Jerusalem)	With trivet. Cut into cubes.	1
For puree	Cut small. Puree and cool before packaging.	8 – until tender
ASPARAGUS		To pressure only.
BEANS		
Broad		1
French or runner		To pressure only.
BEETROOT		
50 *g* (2 *oz*) whole	Remove trivet.	10
100 *g* (4 *oz*) whole	Remove trivet.	15

Vegetable	Instructions	Blanching time/ minutes
Sliced	With trivet.	7
150 g (6 oz) whole	Remove trivet.	20
Sliced	With trivet.	7
BROCCOLI		1
BRUSSELS SPROUTS		1
CARROTS		2
	To be ready for adding to prepared dishes.	6
CAULIFLOWER		
Flowerets	With trivet.	1
CELERY		
Young hearts	With trivet.	1
Stalks	To be ready for adding to prepared dishes.	5
CHICORY	With trivet.	1
LEEKS	Use separator.	1
PARSNIPS		
Sliced or quartered		1
For puree	Cut into slices or cubes. Puree. Cool and pack.	6
PEAS		1
POTATOES		
New/small		2
Old (for mashing)	Cut small. Mash. Use for duchesse and fish dishes.	6–8
SPINACH	Pack cooker as for fresh vegetable.	To pressure only.
SWEDES		
Diced/sliced		1
For puree	Cut small. Mash. Cool and pack.	6–8
SWEETCORN		2
TURNIPS		
Small whole		2
For puree	Cut small. Mash. Cool and pack.	6–8

For stocks suitable for freezing see the soup chapter, pp. 37ff.

BOTTLING AND CANNING

The basic techniques of bottling and canning are identical, only the vessels used for storing are different.

Food goes mouldy if it is not properly sterilized and sealed from the air. The aim of all bottling is to kill off moulds, yeasts, other micro-organisms and to deactivate enzymes in the food. At the same time the sterilizing process has to retain an acceptable texture and taste and avoid destroying too many nutrients.

Anyone seriously interested in bottling should get a specialist book on the subject or acquire *Home Preservation of Fruit and Vegetables* published by HMSO.

Bottles to be used for the preservation of food normally have a special seal which is not only airtight but enables a vacuum to be formed during the bottling process. As bottling proceeds the air is sterilized in the pressure cooker; the contents of the bottles cook and the air in the small amount of space above the food heats up and expands, forcing its way through the special one-way lids of the bottles. When the temperature is reduced the air in the bottle contracts and the outside pressure of the atmosphere effectively helps to keep the bottle sealed with a partial vacuum. Before using bottles and their lids, examine them for potential leakages. If rubber rings or seals are used, they should be blanched as well. Follow the instructions, with the type of bottle you are using, to the letter.

Canning requires special sealing equipment. Both bottling and canning have many pitfalls which would take some considerable space to explain in what is, after all, primarily a pressure cookbook. Some of the earlier books, available from public libraries if nowhere else, contain quite elaborate instructions; however, now in the late 1970s I can see little point in bulking this book out further. I do however consider the following observations important:

1. Only fruit is really worth bottling these days: it is also the easiest.

2. Vegetables demand similar techniques but some of them do not contain the natural acids necessary to inhibit bacterial growth.

3. Some of the older books contain instructions for bottling meat. Not only is this unnecessary today (butchers have freezers even if you don't) but such prolonged cooking time is required for bottling that the quality of the meat suffers considerably.

4. Do not try to bottle fish.

Appendix 1: HOW PRESSURE COOKING WORKS

The essence of pressure cooking is high-pressure steam. Nearly all forms of pressure cooking take place at a temperature of about 121 °C (250 °F) and at a pressure twice that of the atmosphere we normally breathe (and cook at). It is these unusual conditions that, by a combination of heat and steam penetration, give the rapid results. Heat gets to the heart of a lump of food more easily if moisture (either liquid or steam) helps to conduct it there, and the pressure helps to get it there even more rapidly.

The first person I ever saw using a pressure cooker used the equipment as though it was some sort of technological monster. Following the instructions blindly, she would fasten the lid down and then wait in trepidation to see, if by any chance, the results were palatable. Lots of cooks still use their pressure cookers in that same unthinking, ever-hoping fashion, and unfortunately the instruction books that come with the cookers rather encourage unquestioning obedience.

I've always enjoyed cooking if I've understood what was going on. It's made the actual activity more enjoyable and the results much better. In addition I now find it a lot easier to invent and adapt my own recipes. You can't really appreciate how best to use a pressure cooker unless you know a little about cooking techniques in general. In addition, if you are at all worried about the healthiness of the food you eat, you should know a little about what happens when various ingredients are heated.

HOW FOOD GETS COOKED

The simplest – and most misleading – description of cooking is the application of heat to food. A cooking encyclopaedia could easily identify more than *twenty* sorts of cooking, and if you thought about it yourself, you'd find you knew and used most of them. Different levels of heat, different combinations of air and water and steam, the presence of fat, both solid and liquid, even the type of cooking vessel and the source of heat, all contribute to the taste of the various sorts of food we eat. A potato can be fried, baked, boiled, steamed, roasted, sautéed, mashed, combined with milk or cheese, sprinkled with herbs and spices ... it can even be first boiled, then mashed and seasoned before frying or baking ... and in each case the taste will be quite different while still obviously being a potato.

What we admire in food is its taste, its texture and its appearance. Increasingly, too, we are concerned about its effect on our health. Most of us know by instinct what cooking method to use in each case but only a few of us can actually explain what is going on. Some of the fear that the pressure cooker arouses comes, I am sure, because instinct doesn't seem to help and everything goes on inside beneath a firmly sealed lid. In fact the rules of cooking don't alter that much.

I was fortunate that, when I was finally free of home and college and was sharing a house in West London, one of my friends had done a proper *cordon bleu* course – but in Jamaica – so that added to the traditional grande cuisine menu were Caribbean specialities bought in the Portobello Market which we used to watch him cook with interest. As he operated over the stove, he would murmur to himself what he was doing to the food, how it was changing in colour and taste, how juices were flowing in and out and how each ingredient affected the next ... that's how I really began cooking ...

The two variables in cooking are the make-up of the original food and the method of applying heat. We need to heat certain foods in order to be able to digest them in our systems. We need to cook certain foods simply to improve their taste – we eat more if we like what we eat. In some cases heating destroys them, at least partly. You have to make a choice.

THE BASIC COMPONENTS OF FOOD

Our diet consists of five components: Carbohydrates, Fats, Proteins, Minerals and Vitamins.

No one eats these pure ingredients by themselves, so any application of heat to a given piece of raw food has a variety of effects – we have to trade-off the loss of certain nutrients in return for releasing others and making the entire result more palatable. This is what happens when heat is applied to the various basic components listed above:

Carbohydrates – the sugars, if they are solid, melt very easily and become more sweet to the taste. If they are heated above a certain point they start to turn yellow and caramelize. Sugar eventually turns a light brown and then gets black and burned. You can watch the process happen if you fry carrots or onions (in fact onions make a good colouring agent for stocks and soups, as well as a flavour, if used in this way – fry an onion clear for a white well-flavoured stock, and fry it dark brown for a dark stock).

The other edible carbohydrate – starch – is inedible unless cooked. The starch in uncooked flour, potato, rice and so on is locked up in a series of packages that resist the stomach juices. Cooking breaks down the packages so that the digestive system can reach the edible starch. Over-cooking results in a breakdown of the shape of the food itself – and while that is not bad nutritionally, the texture is mushy and that offends us.

Fats – heating fat melts it. Whether one has to heat it at all depends on the type of fat and is really a matter of what you happen to like. Most people will cheerfully spread butter on bread, but not lard. If over-heating occurs, the fat burns and produces fatty acids. Butter burns at 137 °C (278 °F), beef suet at 180 °C (356 °F), lard at 200 °C (372 °F), vegetable oil at about 260 °C (500 °F), and olive oil at 290 °C (554 °F).

Proteins – on heating, protein coagulates and hardens – watch what happens to egg white. We can digest cooked protein rather more easily than uncooked – which is why raw eggs are not always as health-giving as is sometimes claimed. A raw egg can slip through your digestive system without having very much of its protein absorbed! Protein is located in the fibres of meat, which is why meat can taste tough or stringy if not carefully treated. The only meats that can put up with violent exposure to heat are the very soft-textured ones like steak. Otherwise they have to be physically cut up (as in hamburgers and meat loaf), marinated in wine or vinegar to soften the fibres chemically, or cooked slowly at a low heat. Rare beef is 'done' at 65 °C (150 °F) and fresh pork and poultry at 87 °C (190 °F), those being the final temperatures at the centre.

The hardening of the protein fibres also causes shrinking of the meat and a squeezing-out of the juices which contain other forms of goodness. Cooking of protein in general – and meat in particular – is quite possible in a pressure cooker, but obviously needs a bit of thought. A lot of people waste meat using perfectly 'normal' techniques! Excessive heat breaks down protein.

Minerals – there are no general rules. The calcium in milk becomes a little less available if it is heated, but if greens are boiled in hard water (not normally a good idea), then more calcium becomes ready to be digested. Iron is normally more easily picked up after cooking (a lot comes from cast-iron cooking pots!), and salt is unaffected by heat. However, a lot of minerals are lost if they are allowed to soak or leach away into cooking fluid (water or gravy) which is then thrown away. For this reason boiled vegetables are in general not a good idea, unless use is made of the vegetable water. Steaming is far better as the vegetables retain all their fluids and very little water is involved in the process. Pressure cooking is high-pressure steaming, of course.

Vitamins – vitamins A and D are unaffected by baking and boiling, though vitamin A is destroyed at the high temperatures used for frying. Vitamin B (or rather the various sorts of vitamin B) can be destroyed by high heat; but more importantly, they are soluble in water which means that losses can take place in the same way as for minerals.

The real problem vitamin is C. Vitamin C can be destroyed in five ways – by prolonged cooking, by heating in the presence of air (and that can include keeping meals hot), by dissolving in water (keep those cooking fluids!), by plant enzymes (the living plant protects the vitamin C from its own enzymes but ceases to do so when it is cut – that's why shredding lettuce for salad too long before eating is a bad thing), and finally vitamin C can be destroyed by the presence of copper.

But really, all cookery results in pluses and minuses in nutritional value. Potatoes, which in the raw state contain Vitamin C, have to be cooked if the starch in them is to become edible by which time the vitamin C is destroyed ... the plant enzyme that breaks down the vitamin C in a dead plant is killed off by temperatures in excess of 60 °C (140 °F), so that in certain circumstances cooking green vegetables is definitely a good thing ...

In practice most of the techniques we use are reasonably sane and safe. Pressure cooking, whatever the critics may tell you, in fact preserves far more in the way of essential nutrients than most of the traditional techniques. Further, because the techniques are a little different and unusual, it forces us from time to time to think carefully about our diet – are we getting enough of the right sort of ingredients, or too many of others!

THE TECHNIQUES OF HEATING

The other half of the cooking conundrum is the question of heat, and the way in which it is applied. Professional cooks and domestic-science teachers tend to distinguish between two types of heat – dry and moist.

The 'purest' form of *dry* heating is old-fashioned roasting on a spit in the open air. The heat is entirely radiant and progresses from the outside of the food to the middle relatively slowly – as each particle of food gets heated up it passes on some of the heat to the next particle further inside. If you place your food too close to a strong source of heat like a grill the outside will start to burn before the inside has started to cook at all. We do this to good effect when we toast bread, but if you place a 3 *in* (sorry 75 *mm*) steak under the same grill, then the outside will be charred and the inside raw. Microwave cooking is also a 'dry' heat.

With *moist* heat the heat is transferred not only from particle to particle of food but is transported by molecules of liquid or steam. If you are stewing or boiling, then the heat is carried through by stock or water; if you are steaming or pressure cooking, then the heat is conducted through the food by molecules of steam. With pressure cooking it is possible to make the steam hotter than it normally would be and also (unlike other forms of cooking), because everything happens under pressure, the heated steam is forced into the heart of the food much more quickly.

Critical to both forms of heating is the *size* of the piece of food to be heated. Meat minced or ground fine enough will cook almost instantly if put in fairly hot stock or fat. An enormous potato baking away in an oven for a long period may look gorgeous from the outside and still be raw on the inside. Every cook with only a little experience knows this. Pressure cooking is no exception – food cut up suitably small will always cook more rapidly than great chunks.

However, cooking is much more than bringing the ingredients to the right temperature so that the appropriate chemical changes can take place. Reading through the last few pages as one does when one is writing I fear I may have sounded too obsessed with cooking processes and biochemistry. I'm glad to be able to turn to more familiar material. Moving away from the biochemistry lab and back into the kitchen, we ought to return to those things that we admire in food: taste, texture, appearance, and nutrition.

Whatever the domestic-science theorists say, it's these that count and the clear-cut distinctions between dry and moist forms of heat are not always so easy to make when we look at what cooks actually do. One of the classic British ways of 'roasting' a joint consists of setting the meat in a tray of fat and then placing it in a pre-heated oven. Periodically the fat is basted over the joint to keep it moist. Then, at the end of cooking time, the joint is removed and put on a carving dish and the juices collected at the bottom of the pan are made into gravy by adding a little cornflour and heating fiercely. If the theorists were to break down this cooking process, they would say that you weren't *really* roasting at all; the bottom of the joint would actually be frying (a form of dry heat because moisture is absent); after the first few minutes of heating, the water in the joint of meat will turn to steam. If the joint were really being roasted, in the open air, the water vapour would disappear into the atmosphere but, in fact, since the whole process is taking place in an oven, the steam collects and becomes a vehicle of cooking itself, in the form of moist heat which then reaches the centre of the joint rather more quickly than 'pure' dry heating does. Add to this the spurting fat, the hot juices flowing over the meat as they bubble out and are then basted over . . . and you get your classic dish, but with what technique? Now with pressure cooking, there's nothing inherent in the process which would give us anything like that result. So if we want effects similar to the ones we are used to we have to replace them in various ways.

If this sounds alarming, that is in fact what all the recipes in this book (and most of the ones that you are likely to find elsewhere) try to do.

A pressure cooker cannot:

FRY – but you can fry the outside of meat and then pressure steam the inside to give a similar though juicier result (see pp. 130, 132, 157, 161, 165, 207).

ROAST – but you can pot roast, giving meat a delicious outside crust, either by searing or by using burnt sugars and then pressure steaming the inside far more rapidly than any traditional roasting method and with far less loss of intrinsic goodness (see pp. 142, 169, 177).

GRILL, or BAKE, or FLAMBÉ, or BARBECUE, or SMOKE, or DEEP (FAT) FRY.

SLOW CASSEROLE – but it can take the same ingredients and produce something equally interesting.

Neither will your pressure cooker play cassette tapes, speak your weight, or take off into orbit in outer space.

However, in addition to acting as a pressure cooker your appliance has other culinary uses:

1. Quite obviously it is a superb *saucepan* with the ideal characteristic of spreading heat evenly round the bottom and sides due to the thickness of the metal. You could even *deep fry* in it if you wanted to.

2. It is a well-designed *steamer* at ordinary temperatures and pressures (you just don't use the weights or valve). Steaming is a marvellous way of cooking vegetables and fish. One way in which this book differs from any other you're likely to come across is that I sometimes suggest it is silly to pressure-steam foods that cook rapidly anyway – who needs to have spinach ready in one minute?

3. Most pressure cookers can be adapted to become *double boilers*. You rest a smaller pan or bowl on the trivet and then fill the outer pan with water which you heat in the normal way to 100 °C (212 °F). The contents of the inner bowl will keep just below that temperature – ideal in fact for making delicate sauces. The French name for this contraption is *bain-marie*.

THE PHYSICS OF PRESSURE COOKING

To complete this appendix, I will explain how a pressure cooker works. The temperature at which water becomes steam depends on the pressure of the surrounding air. The higher the pressure the higher the temperature at which the water boils. Conversely, several hundred metres up a mountain, water will boil below 100 °C (212 °F).

Water in an open pan at sea level (15 *lb/in²* or less familiarly 101·325 *kg/m²*) boils normally. Close the pan, let the air escape and the steam builds up pressure inside, just like a steam engine. By letting a little of the steam at a time out of the pan, you can control the pressure inside. Normally this is done by means of weights or a spring-loaded valve and usually the pressure is kept at twice atmospheric pressure. (Most pressure cookbooks call this 15 *lb* pressure, though the latest ones, in deference to metrication, call it H pressure). Under these conditions the boiling point of water becomes 122 °C (252 °F) and the cooking is achieved by means of higher heat and a forced 'injection' of steam, which sounds more horrific than it actually is.

Many pressure cookers enable you to lower the internal pressure somewhat by using different weights or adjusting the valve. The comparable pressures and temperatures are as follows:

1½ atmospheres	5 *lb* (L)	108·5 °C (228 °F)
1⅔ atmospheres	10 *lb* (M)	115·3 °C (239·8 °F)

Very occasionally you may find an extra-powerful model that has provision for a 20 *lb* weight:

2⅓ atmospheres	20 *lb*	126 °C (259 °F)

However, for most purposes, you will actually be cooking at:

2 atmospheres	15 *lb* (H)	122 °C (252 °F)

The Tefal Safety Cooker is an exception in that it operates at $1\frac{1}{2}$ atmospheres ($7\frac{1}{2}$ lb). Vegetable cooking times are the same, more or less, as with cookers working at 2 atmospheres. Meat, however, requires longer. Tefal produce their own instruction book, which should be read along with this.

In conclusion . . .

Since this book is being written to appeal to a large number of different cooks with varying interests, commitments and levels of experience, I've really no way of knowing how useful any individual reader may have found the above explanation. I realize that there are plenty of cooks who learn simply by practice. If you've found some of this appendix a little intimidating – don't worry, there's nothing essential in it.

Most 'ordinary' cooking, when broken down and subjected to the question 'what is actually going on in there?', turns out to be *fairly* complicated – we just do certain things by instinct, and that's the way it'll happen for you with pressure cooking.

Appendix 2: SPECIALIZED USES

THE PRESSURE COOKER AND ROASTING

Pressure cookers that are of especially thick construction may be used for roasting. In chapter 6 all the meat recipes are variations on pressure steaming (pot-roast or braising) or pressure boiling (steaming or boiling) and rely on the presence of water throughout the cooking process.

There is, however, an alternative technique which works by placing a small quantity of fat in the bottom of the cooker, bringing up to twice the atmospheric pressure (15 *lb*), and then relying on the natural juices of the meat and the accompanying vegetables to do the cooking. This method is not recommended unless the manufacturers' instruction book specifically says it may be used. With pressure cookers of thin metal construction the dangers of burnt fat, uneven cooking and a warped base to the appliance are very great. In any case, satisfactorily cooked meat and poultry are possible using the techniques already described.

However, if you wish to try pressure roasting, this is how it is done:

1. Use cooking oil with a high burning point and place 1 to 2 tablespoons in the bottom of the cooker. Heat. Place joint or chicken in cooker and brown all over making sure there is no chance of sticking. Add vegetables if wished but *no* water.

2. Close pressure cooker and heat slowly until 15 *lb* (twice atmospheric) pressure is reached. (The appliance must have some form of indication that the pressure is at that point – a gauge, a whistle, a revolving top, etc.) Lower the heat so that 15 *lb* pressure is maintained.

3. Cooking time now commences:

Beef	5–8 mins/*lb*	6–9 mins/500 *g*
Mutton	8–10 mins/*lb*	9–11 mins/500 *g*
Veal	10–12 mins/*lb*	11–13 mins/500 *g*
Pork	10–12 mins/*lb*	11–13 mins/500 *g*

The shorter cooking period is for under-done meat and the longer time is for well-done.

4. Reduce pressure after cooking time. This method with the right appliance will give good results for the experienced cook.

THE PRESSURE COOKER AND DEEP FRYING

Most pressure cookers, with the great depth and turned-over rims, are well suited to the ordinary techniques of deep fat frying. You will need a frying basket which will fit easily into the bottom of the pan and a flat wire gauze anti-spatter tool.

The cooker is half to two-thirds filled with cooking oil and is heated to the appropriate temperature – your conventional cookery book will give you instructions. The food is placed in the frying basket in the ordinary way with the anti-spatter wire gauze preventing splashes. The pressure-cooker lid is not used. Using your pressure cooker in this way saves purchasing a separate deep fat fryer.

THE PRESSURE COOKER AS A DOUBLE-BOILER

A number of cooking processes require the use of a *bain-marie* or double-boiler, which ensures that the temperature of the liquid to be cooked never goes above boiling point. It is particularly important in the case of delicate sauces which might curdle or separate, or dishes like zabaione.

Your pressure cooker can easily be converted into a *bain-marie*. Place the trivet or rack in the bottom of the pan and fit on top a bowl or handleless saucepan. Surround with sufficient water to reach half-way up the outside of the inner pan.

THE PRESSURE COOKER AND STALE BREAD

The sort of white loaves most people buy are more likely to go stale than mouldy. The pressure cooker can be used to freshen-up a dried-out loaf or part of a loaf. Place loaf on trivet or in basket with 140 *ml* ($\frac{1}{4}$ *pt*) water below. Cover top of bread with greaseproof paper. Bring to pressure and pressure steam for 2 to 3 minutes. Then remove loaf and place in hot oven 220 °C (428 °F, GM 7) for 5 to 10 minutes.

THE PRESSURE COOKER AS STERILIZER

Medical instruments, baby's bottles (if heatproof) and dressings can all be sterilized in the pressure cooker. Use trivet with 300 *ml* ($\frac{1}{2}$ *pt*) water beneath. Place object to be sterilized on trivet (or in tray on trivet) and seal pan. Make sure steam is issuing freely from vent (so that all air and the micro-organisms in it are expelled from the cooker) and then close valve/weight. Allow 20 to 30 minutes steady pressure steaming. Depressurize and remove lid and then apply heat to base of cooker to allow it to dry out completely. Watch carefully while you do this.

THE PRESSURE COOKER AND CAMPING

The traditional idea about cooking and camping is a roaring driftwood fire with an iron pot brewing an aromatic stew while potatoes, sausages and wild animals are delicately roasting. The prosaic truth is that most cooking on camping holidays is on a butane- or propane-gas stove. These stoves give out little heat (unless the bottle of gas is large). Even the sort of stove you find in a caravan trailer gives out heat less efficiently than a domestic mains-connected gas stove or an electric one.

The pressure cooker is a boon to the camper from several points of view. It requires very little heat to keep it going and the results are quick. Many of the recipes for main meals in this book can be prepared *in toto* in 10 or 15 minutes. Intelligent use of the separators and the trivet means that whole meals can be cooked at the same time in the same spot. Steaming ensures that flavours do not mix.

It is also possible to make considerable use of dried foods, as the pressure cooker is particularly good at rehydrating. Dried foods are useful both because they store easily and for a long period and also because a small quantity of each goes a long way. Small portions of dried beans, TVP chunks, freeze-dried vegetables and stock cubes can be accommodated in any rucksack or back-pack. A caravan that is left unattended for long periods can also hold quantities of dried foods, while you can be secure in the knowledge that they won't go bad.

Small, light-weight pressure cookers for campers and hikers are available, but some of the smaller ones intended for domestic use are just as effective. Remember that you can store things inside your pressure cooker as you carry it about – with sensible packing you need hardly notice it is there.

Appendix 3: SPECIAL DIETS: INFANTS AND INVALIDS

More than one brand of pressure cooker has been sold as a 'health cooker'. There is little doubt that, used properly, the pressure cooker does maximize the nutritional value of foods.

INVALIDS

The great dietetic requirement for invalids is a supply of nutritious but easily digested foods. Pressure cooking is an exceptionally 'pure' and in most cases fat-free method of cooking. In pressure steaming little except the basic raw material itself forms the final dish. It is easy to omit strong spicings.

The method of cooking fish – steaming – avoids the dangers of fatty foods to weak hearts that come from frying. Meat cookery, in the version explained in chapter 6, works best with relatively fat-free meats. It is also widely believed that roasted foods may contain carcinogenic agents.

The speed with which pressure cooking works means that many of the cereals – like tapioca and barley which have a good supportive role for weakened constitutions – can be prepared with little difficulty. Further, by slight overcooking of any ingredients it is possible to produce nourishing food tender enough to slip down constricted throats and capable of being digested by delicate stomachs.

Finally, the speed works to the benefit of anyone who has to look after a sick person in the home. Special meals and diets become less of a distinct chore because the pressure cooker is rapid and efficient.

Your doctor should be able to give precise advice and you should know that you will be able to carry it out.

INFANTS

Between the ages of four months, when a baby gives up a milk-only diet, until the age of twelve to eighteen months, a special pureed diet is called for. The diet, which concentrates on cereal foods, pureed fruit and vegetables, egg yolk and very finely chopped meat, prevents over-loading the young alimentary canal. As little sugar as possible is incorporated in these foods.

A whole baby-food industry, based on tins and jars, has grown up to satisfy the requirements of busy mothers. By and large the foods offered are of a high standard, though tinned vegetables in particular can never be as good as fresh. The main problem is that the tins and jars themselves are very expensive, and much of the mother's money goes simply into the cost of the packaging and marketing.

The pressure cooker, in conjunction with the blender, or even a simple sieve, enables the mother to prepare her baby's foods from fresh products – often the same foods the rest of the family may be eating. In cooking foods for a baby the instructions given throughout this book should be followed but with these modifications:

1. Cooking time is shortened if the foods are minced down in their raw state before cooking. In the case of vegetables, more vitamin C can be preserved if root and leaf vegetables are minced down and then cooked for only 1 to 2 minutes.

2. Over-cooking (by normal standards) ensures a tender meal.

3. Several foods may be cooked simultaneously: tea-cups may be stood on the trivet and used both as cooking and serving vessels.

4. Do not use too much sugar or salt: you are cooking for a baby, not for an adult taste.

Appendix 4: QUICK REFERENCE TABLES

All vegetables to be cooked with the trivet and with 250 *ml* ($\frac{1}{2}$ *pt*) water in the bottom unless otherwise specified. The timings are varied according to the size and age of the ingredients.

Vegetable	Cooking Time (*mins*)	Cooking and Serving Instructions
ARTICHOKE (French, Globe) Small Large	6 10	Wash, remove discoloured leaves, cut stems short, stand heads upright on trivet. Serve with melted (browned if preferred) butter, lemon juice and salt – or with Hollandaise sauce (see recipe p. 76).
ARTICHOKE (Jerusalem)	4–5	Wash, peel, cut into uniform pieces (quarters if large, halves if small). Serve with: melted butter, white sauce and golden egg crumbs. Pepper and salt.
ASPARAGUS Tips Cut	1 2–3	Wash and cut up. Serve with melted butter or Hollandaise sauce. The cut pieces may take 4 minutes or more and should be saved for soups or stocks.
Whole stalks*	2	Arrange in bundles of 6 to 8 in perforated container which should stand in 10 *cm* (3$\frac{1}{2}$ *in*) water. The bundles should be placed on the slant, stems in the water. Using this method, which approximates the classic culinary technique, the stems are super-*boiled* and the tips super-*steamed*. Serve with melted butter or Hollandaise sauce (see recipe p. 76).
AUBERGINES (Egg-plant)	1–2	Wash but leave purple skin intact. After cooking, lift from trivet, dry lightly on kitchen paper and fry in

* Remove the trivet.

Vegetable	Cooking Time (mins)	Cooking and Serving Instructions
		hot butter or olive oil. The pressure cooking ensures a juicy interior.
BEANS		Shell. Older beans will need longer
Broad		cooking time. Serve with butter or
On trivet	2	herb sauce.
In container	4	
French, runner,		Slice on the slant. Remove the strings
String, snap, princess		from older beans. Young beans will
On trivet	2–4	need hardly any cooking at all. Serve
In container	4–5	with butter. A sprig of mint will add variety.
Soya (Fiskeby), see SOYABEANS		
Lima	1–2	Shell. Serve with butter or a sauce made from vegetable water and *roux*.
BEET		Wash well leaving some stem.
Tiny, whole	10	Remove trivet. Cook. Remove skins.
Large, fresh	15 or more*	Serve buttered, spiced or cold in salads with vinegar and sugar.
Greens	2–3	Treat like spinach. Until recently this was purely an agricultural crop; it is now sometimes called leaf-beet or perpetual spinach.
BROCCOLI	2–4	Wash, season with salt and place on
White		trivet. Separate from other vegetables
Purple sprouting		with greaseproof paper. Serve with butter or Hollandaise sauce (see recipe p. 76).
BRUSSELS SPROUTS		Wash. Remove wilted yellow leaves.
On trivet	2–3	Season with pepper. Serve with
In container	3–4	melted butter or sauce made from vegetable water and *roux*. Alternatively, take cooked sprouts and lightly toss in hot butter so as to crisp-fry the outside.
CABBAGE		Remove discoloured pieces. A quar-
Green		tered cabbage will take 5 minutes –
White		older cabbages still longer. Serve
On trivet	2–3	well peppered and with melted
In container	3–4	butter.

* The very large ones may take 30 minutes: if cooking time exceeds 15 minutes remember to add another 150 *ml* ($\frac{1}{4}$ *pt*) or so of water.

Vegetable	Cooking Time (mins)	Cooking and Serving Instructions
CABBAGE (cont.)		
Red		Cook separately. (See recipe p. 80.)
On trivet	2–3	
In container	3–4	
CARROTS		Remove tops. Peeled carrots look cleaner, scraped carrots are more health-giving. Cut into matchsticks (very short cooking time required) or thin circles and ovals instead of the usual chunks. Serve with butter, gently fried in butter or with *velouté* sauce.
Cut	2–3	
(depending on age or size)		
Whole	4 or more	
CAULIFLOWER		Remove all except inner leaves. Separate from other vegetables with greaseproof paper. Serve with butter, with parsley sauce, with cheese sauce or quick crisp-fried on outside.
Flowerets	4	
Quartered	4	
Whole	4	
Leaves	2–3	Treat like asparagus (p. 286).
CELERIAC (Celery-Turnip)	3–4	This is the root of the celery plant. Peel thickly. Cut into 2 *cm* (1 *in*) thick slices. Drip lemon juice over. Serve with white sauce garnished with crumbled hard-boiled egg.
CELERY	3–4	Scrub, remove leaves (save for garnishing soup or putting into stock), de-string tough stalks. Cut into allumettes or crescents. Serve with white or parsley sauce or *roux* and juice.
CHICORY (Endive)	4–6	Do not cut as this makes for a bitter taste. Cook alone in the cooker without trivet. Melt 50 *g* (2 *oz*) butter with 2 tablespoons of water, 1 tablespoon of lemon juice. Cover with buttered greaseproof paper. Cook over low heat for 4 to 6 minutes. To serve, remove endive and reduce cooking liquid to make sauce.
CORN, see SWEETCORN		
COURGETTES (Zucchini, Baby marrow)		Leave skin on. Serve with melted butter or crisp-fry in melted butter. Add garlic and tomato puree for an Italian taste.
Whole	4	
Sliced	1–2	

Vegetable	Cooking Time (mins)	Cooking and Serving Instructions
CUCUMBER	1–2	Use older fruit. Slice lengthways and remove pips. Or dice. Serve with a white or onion or parsley sauce. Large cucumbers can be stuffed like a marrow. Paprika can offset the taste. Can be sautéed after pressure steaming.
DANDELION LEAVES	Cook to pressure only	Use only very young leaves. Toss in butter with light seasoning.
KOHL-RABI		Select small ones: remove leaves and
Sliced	4	cut into very thick matchsticks.
Whole	8	Serve with cheese or Hollandaise sauce or deep fry as for French fried potatoes. Can also be baked with sour cream sauce, or stuffed. They taste like turnip cabbages.
LEEKS	4–6	Cut off roots and most of green leaves. Very large leeks are tasteless. Serve with white, cheese or parsley sauce or paprika. Leaves can be used in soup or for garnish.
MARROW (Squash, Gourd)	4	Skin and slice. Serve with white or cheese sauce or *roux* and vegetable water.
(for COURGETTES, see separate entry)		
Stuffed	10–12	Gouge out centre and fill with cooked minced meat, add onion and vegetable. (See recipes pp. 92ff.)
Vegetable spaghetti	8–10	(See recipe, p. 114.)
MUSHROOM	1–3	The smallest (button) mushrooms need hardly any cooking at all. It is doubtful if it is worth cooking mushrooms by themselves.
OKRA (Lady's Fingers)	3–4	Choose tender young pods. Remove stems and cut into 15–20 mm ($\frac{1}{2}$–$\frac{3}{4}$ in) slices. Wash well. Serve with butter and seasoning. Or fry in butter till crisp.

Vegetable	Cooking Time (mins)	Cooking and Serving Instructions
ONIONS		Steamed onion avoids bad smells. Remove the outer skin to preserve clear colour. The pre-cooking period is for when onions are to be finished off with a roast.
Sliced	3–4	
Quartered	6	
Whole	8–10	
Pre-cooking	4	
PARSNIPS		Parsnips need careful cooking and flavouring if they are to be more than just starch and roughage. Fry lightly in butter to finish, adding garlic, nutmeg or cinnamon for an unusual 'medieval' taste. Parsnips to accompany a roast should be pressure par-boiled for 2 minutes.
Sliced } On trivet	3	
Whole } On trivet	10	
In water beneath trivet	3–4	
Pre-cooking	2	
PEAS		Shell and cook with mint and a few pods (and a bit of sugar if peas are very old). Serve with butter or mixed with other vegetables, e.g. carrots, sweetcorn.
In perforated container	2–4	
In solid container	5	
Mange-tout	2	Mange-tout are cooked whole in their pods – some people even prefer them raw!
PEPPERS (Bell peppers, Capsicum)	5	Slice off tops at stalk and remove pips and centre. Peppers can either be cut into short strips or into very long continuous ones. See separate recipe for stuffed peppers (pp. 92ff).
Green or Red		
PLANTAIN	6–8	These are the large yellow or green bananas used in West Indian, African and 'soul' cooking. Remove skin and fibrous strings. Can be rapidly fried after cooking to crisp up. Serve with crackling or with streaky bacon.
POTATOES		Large potatoes should be sliced. Make sure all pieces are roughly the same size. Leave the skin on for better health. You can toss in hot butter or fry or roast afterwards. Add mint or dill or parsley and pepper for flavour.
Sliced	4–6	
Whole	6–10	
Sweet, see SWEET POTATOES		
PUMPKIN	10–15	Longer time is for chunks of whole pumpkin. The inner flesh is for pumpkin pie.
RUTABAGA, SWEDE (Yellow Turnip)		This is a root crop usually served mashed with salt, pepper and butter.

Vegetable	Cooking Time (mins)	Cooking and Serving Instructions
RUTABAGH (cont.)		
Quartered	12	It can be served diced with a cream
Whole	20*	sauce.
SALSIFY (Vegetable oyster, Scorzonera)		Soak salsify in water to remove earth from root – then peel skin. *Either* pressure steam and serve with butter
On trivet	25*	or sauce. *Or* remove trivet, place
in water	15	1 *l* (1¾ *pts*) water in bottom and boil up with 1 tablespoon of flour and 1 tablespoon of lemon juice. Add a pinch of salt. Pressure cook for 15 to 20 minutes and then serve with butter or bechamel sauce.
SORREL	Bring to pressure only	This spinach-like leaf is very strong-tasting and is seldom cooked by itself but can be mixed with other green leaves. It needs hardly any cooking. Serve tossed in butter.
SOYABEANS (Fiskeby)		Soyabeans have an unusual number of 'animal protein' amino acids and
In pods	2	so are prized by vegetarians. Varieties
Shelled	1	that grow in temperate zones are now more readily available. The problem of blandness of taste remains. Serve younger specimens in their shells, older ones as individual beans. Toss with butter and experiment with herbs like chervil, parsley, tarragon, mint, depending on what else is to be eaten at the same time.
Textured, Spun, see MEAT SUBSTITUTES		Soyabeans can be processed to make meat substitutes; for handling – see pp. 219 ff.
SPINACH	Bring to pressure only	Wash well and remove the spines from the thickest leaves. If you forbear from draining the leaves you needn't add any water at all to the base of the cooker. It is however doubtful whether pressure steaming is worthwhile. I use the pressure cooker without the weight and steam for 2 to 3 minutes – a little longer if the spinach is to be pureed.

* Use 350 *ml* (¾ *pt*) water.

Vegetable	Cooking Time (mins)	Cooking and Serving Instructions
SPINACH (cont.)		Serve with melted butter or pureed in a small quantity of pre-cooked mashed potato and butter.
SPRING GREENS (Kale, Beet tops, Brussels tops, Chard, Turnip tops)	4	Wash, tear to shred. Serve tossed in butter with plenty of pepper. Experiment with herbs as suitable combinations.
SQUASH, see MARROW		
SWEDES, see RUTABAGA		
SWEETCORN (Corn, Sugar Corn)		Remove leaves and stalk; top and tail. Serve with melted butter, salt and pepper; cinnamon for variety.
Loose	1	Loose sweetcorn can be served like
On cob: small	3	peas, perhaps in a sauce made of
On cob: large	5	vegetable water and *roux*.
SWEET POTATO		Peel after cooking – it is much easier.
Whole large	12–15	Sweet potatoes can be mashed with
Whole thin	8	butter or milk and butter. Cinnamon
Halves	8–10	can sometimes be added.
Slices	5–7	
TOMATOES		It is usually not worth pressure
Juice	½–1	cooking tomatoes by themselves unless for juice. Remove skins by immersing briefly in boiled water. Puree result in sieve or blender. Serve with salt, pepper and, optionally, sugar. Basil is the traditional herbal accompaniment.
Stewed		
Whole		
TURNIPS		Wash and peel. Serve with butter.
Whole	4–5	Turnips are best mixed with other
Sliced or diced	4	vegetables like peas, carrots and sweetcorn.
YAMS		Cook unpeeled. Serve either mashed
Sliced	10–12	and seasoned, or slice and sauté. Yams benefit from adventurous seasoning: brown sugar, cinnamon, lemon juice, sherry, grated orange or lemon rind, etc. They can be flambéed in brandy!

Frozen Vegetables

Timings are given for vegetables both wholly frozen and part-defrosted.

Vegetable	Cooking Time (mins) (Frozen)	Cooking Time (mins) (Part-defrosted)	Cooking and Serving Instructions
ASPARAGUS			Break up carefully before cooking to allow steam to circulate. Serve with creamy butter or sauce.
Pieces	3½	1	
Tips or stalks	3	Pressure only	
BEANS Broad, French, Runner, Snap, Wax, Soya, Lima	4	2	Break up solid blocks.
BEET Red	5	2	Usually only very small beet are frozen by commercial undertakings. Break block carefully.
BROCCOLI	4½	1½	Partial defrosting is recommended. If vegetable looks soggy – serve in *velouté* sauce.
BRUSSELS SPROUTS	4	3½	Break up block carefully. Cook in a separator, lowering into pan when water is already boiling and pan filled with steam. Sprouts should be crisp.
CARROTS	3	1½	Break block. Serve with butter or sauce. Some commercial types are sold already in a sauce, in which case, cook in solid separator for 3 to 4 minutes.
CAULIFLOWER Flowerets	3	1	Partial defrosting recommended – the flowerets are easily damaged.
MIXED VEGETABLES (Carrots, Peas, Beans, Sweetcorn, Turnip)	4	2	Break up roughly. If provided with a frozen sauce, cook in solid separator for 4 to 5 minutes.

Vegetable	Cooking Time (mins) (Frozen)	Cooking Time (mins) (Part-defrosted)	Cooking and Serving Instructions
PEAS	2½	Pressure only	Break up roughly. Commercial frozen peas are often very sweet and sometimes have mint added. Go easy on the seasoning.
SPINACH	4	Pressure only	Break block up. Leaf spinach is usually a waste of time frozen as it ends up pureed.
SWEETCORN			Corn on the cob should be completely defrosted and then just brought up to pressure.
Loose	1½	Pressure only	
On cob		Pressure only	

Dried Vegetables

Timings are on soaked and non-soaked ingredients: in each case the weight of dried vegetables is 175 g (6 oz) – enough for four servings.

Vegetable	Dried (mins)	Pre-soaked (mins)	Instructions
CHICK PEAS (Garbanzos)	80	30	Use 750 ml (1½ pts) water. It is much better to soak, preferably for 24 hours. If used for thickening – grind up beans in pestle or coffee grinder while still dry. Cooking time is then 5 minutes.
HARICOTS (Butter, Blackeye, Kidney, Red)	60	20–30	Use 500 ml (1 pt) water. Larger specimens need the longer time.
LENTILS (Green or Red)	45	20	Use 750 ml (1½ pts) water. Red lentils don't keep their form and go mushy fairly easily – neglect to pre-soak and they will certainly do so. Use them as thickener for soup and 'meat' loaf. Green (or brown) lentils retain their shape more readily and taste nicer.

Vegetable	Dried (mins)	Pre-soaked (mins)	Instructions
LIMAS (and NAVY)	45–55	30–45	Use 700–1000 *ml* (1½–2 *pts*) water. These are the beans sometimes used for baking. Big, hard specimens may need longer cooking periods. Unsoaked beans tend to have a mealy texture.
MUSHROOMS (Chinese, Polish)	15–25	5	Pre-soaking is strongly recommended unless you are merely adding a few mushrooms to a whole mix of things to make a casserole. Chinese dried mushrooms are expensive but so strongly flavoured that a few will go a long way. You'll need 500 *ml* (1 *pt*) water for every 125 *g* (4 *oz*) of mushrooms (1 *pt* to 4 *oz*) but 25 *g* (1 *oz*) of mushrooms may be enough!
SPLIT PEAS (Yellow and Green)	15–20	To pressure	Some split peas require no soaking. You'll need only 125 *ml* (¼ *pt*) water.
SOYA BEANS	45	30	Use 750 *ml* (1½ *pts*) water. Note that this refers to the actual dried bean, not to the textured meat substitute.
TAPIOCA	15	5	Tapioca is used in desserts and it is better to use fruit juice instead of water. Use water plus milk if wished. Remember to boil any liquid first before adding the tapioca. You'll need 750 *ml* (1½ *pts*).

Dehydrated Vegetables

It is usually not worth cooking these freeze-dried vegetables by themselves in a pressure cooker as they already take so little time to cook. However, if you are adding them, as I do, to other ingredients, as in a soup or casserole, you need to know that the notional pressure cooking time is 3 *to* 4 *minutes.*

Fish

The tables give the basic cooking times, though allowance should be made for the size of individual pieces. Many fish are prepared in similar ways and you rely on the inherent difference in the flavour of the flesh and a wide assortment of sauces and garnishes to give variety.

In each case you need 140 *ml* ($\frac{1}{4}$ *pt*) of water for the cooker unless the pressure cooking time is 15 minutes or more, when you should have 250 to 300 *ml* ($\frac{1}{2}$ *pt*) water. You can use fish stock instead of water but it is not really important if you are merely pressure steaming.

Fish	Type	Cooking time (mins)	Serving
BREAM	freshwater and sea	5–7	Sea-bream is the better, more delicate fish, the freshwater fish is rather coarse. Sold whole. Clean, open up and serve either simply or with a savoury stuffing (increase cooking time by 1 to 2 minutes for this).
BRILL	sea	4–6	Comes in steaks, tails or middle cut, or whole. Remove skin and bone after cooking. Serve with contrasting sauce.
CARP	freshwater	4–6 8 for large fish	Comes whole and is farmed. Remove heads, tails, fins and innards before cooking. Diced it can be used in Quenelles (or Gefilte fish).
COD	sea	4–6	Comes in fillets and steaks. Remove skin and bone after cooking. Can be pre-fried or served with contrasting sauce.

Fish	Type	Cooking time (mins)	Serving
COLEY	sea	4–6	A 'grey' fish, unattractive in the raw state. Usually sold filleted. Takes on a firm texture when cooked. Can be fried or served with contrasting sauce.
EEL	freshwater or sea	6–8	Eel is usually sold live or already cooked. The jellied form is a British working-class delicacy. It is best pressure poached or stewed.
FLOUNDER	sea	6–8	Sold either whole or filleted. Treat like cod, or can be pre-fried.
HADDOCK	sea	4–6	Comes in fillets, steaks or tails. Remove skin and bone after cooking. Serve with contrasting sauce.
SMOKED HADDOCK (Haddie, Finnan)		4–6	Comes in fillets – best served simply with melted butter.
HAKE	sea	4–6	As for Cod and Halibut.
HALIBUT	sea	4–6	As for Cod, but steaks more usual.
HERRING	sea	5–8	Can be cooked whole, when it is best to begin by browning the outside in hot butter. Or should be opened up on the lower side, the bones (of which there are many) removed, and the fish flattened and then cooked, possibly with herbs. Herring are rather oily; lemon juice and fennel can counteract the taste.
HUS	sea	4–6	A 'grey' fish, unattractive in the raw state. Usually sold filleted. Takes on a firm texture when cooked. Can be 'fried' or served with contrasting sauce.
JOHN DORY (St Peter's Fish)	freshwater	6–8	Sold whole. Remove head and tail. Skin is quite attractive left on. Serve simply with

Fish	Type	Cooking time (mins)	Serving
JOHN DORY (cont.)			
			butter and a slice of lemon or contrasting sauce.
KIPPER	smoked	5–8	Sold either as fillets or whole fish, opened out. Serve simply with melted butter. This can be a breakfast dish as well as one for supper!
MACKEREL	sea	6–8	Usually sold whole, sometimes filleted. The biggest mackerel may need 10 minutes. Can be cooked whole, de-boned and flattened out, or can be filleted. Mackerel is rather oily and lemon juice, fennel or a tart contrasting sauce are the best accompaniments.
MULLET Grey Red	sea	6–8	Sold whole and cooked whole. The grey fish are larger, cheaper and less interesting than the red ones. May be cooked on or off the bone. Grey mullet usually needs a contrasting sauce, while red mullet is fine with melted butter and lemon juice.
PIKE	freshwater	6–8	Usually not sold much but often obtained from amateur anglers. Treat like John Dory.
PLAICE	sea	6–8	Sold either whole or filleted. Treat like Cod, or can be pre-fried.
ROACH	freshwater	6–8	Sold whole and now being farmed in Europe. Flesh sometimes turns reddish when cooked. Clean out, leaving head and tail on for decoration. Serve with a simple sauce.
ROCK SALMON	sea	6–8	Not related to salmon. Sold usually as boned fillets. Serve 'fried' or with contrasting sauce.

Fish		Cooking time (mins)	Serving
SALMON Salmon-Trout	freshwater or sea	Steaks: 6–8. Tails or middle cut: 7 mins per 500 g (6 mins per *lb*)	Sold whole and in steaks. Can be steamed or poached. Serve simply, as this expensive, superb dish needs very little help. To serve cold: remove from cooker and wrap in muslin or parchment paper to keep moist.
SARDINES	sea	3–4	Sold whole. Should be browned in butter before pressure cooking, though it is doubtful whether pressure cooking is of much benefit.
SKATE	sea	6–8	Sold filleted. Treat like Cod.
SOLE FILLETS Lemon sole	sea	6–8	Treat like Plaice.
SQUID/ OCTOPUS Calamari	sea	6–8	Cut up. Do not attempt to pressure steam, but serve in a stew.
SWORDFISH	sea; not usually available in Europe	4–6	Comes usually in steaks and has a closer, meatier texture than most fish. Pressure steam and then finish in a pan of melted butter for a classic treatment.
TUNA	sea	25–30	Tuna fish is difficult to obtain fresh but is best used in stews.
Tinned		3–4	Tinned tuna fish is already cooked and is usually preserved in olive oil. Serve with vegetables and herbs to make a tasty instant fish stew.
TURBOT	sea	6–8	Superlative and expensive white fish sold in steaks or large pieces. Should be steamed plainly and served with simple sauce. Or can be browned in butter before pressure cooking.
WHITEBAIT	sea	—	Too small to be worth pressure cooking – grill or fry in butter instead.
WHITING	sea	6–8	Treat like Herring.

Fish	Type	Cooking time (mins)	Serving
SHELLFISH Lobster Crab Crawfish	sea	10	These shellfish are best cooked when just killed – drive a sharp skewer through the brain! Or just drop alive into boiling water if you are not squeamish. Remove trivet and separators. Bring 1½ *l* (2½ *pts*) of water to boil. Plunge shellfish in. The pressure-cooking time is 10 minutes.
Mussels Prawns Shrimps Fresh Scampi	—		Cooking time is so short I do not recommend pressure cooking – use your pan open. 3 to 4 minutes is usually enough, 5 minutes for the larger ones.

Meat

You need a minimum of 140 *ml* (¼ *pt*) plus 140 *ml* (¼ *pt*) for each 15 minutes of cooking time for pressure steaming – more if pressure boiling. Do not use joints weighing more than 1·4 *kg* (3 *lb*).

By type of meat

Meat	Method	Preparation	Time mins/ 500 g	mins/ lb
BEEF:				
Topside, brisket, rolled rib, flank	Pot-roast (pressure steam)	Use trivet/pannier. Trim, remove fat. Weigh. Brown in hot fat in open pan. Season.	13–16	12–15
Brisket, silverside	Boiling (pressure boiling)	No trivet. Trim, remove fat. Weigh. Fill cooker with water to half-way mark.	16	15
Chuck, rump	Braise (pressure steam)	No trivet. Trim, weigh. Brown in hot fat. Cook over *mire-poix*. Add liquid to cover vegs.	11	10

Meat	Method	Preparation	Time mins/ 500 g	mins/ lb
BEEF (cont.)				
Oxtail	Braise (pressure steam)	No trivet. Fry onions in hot fat – then fry joints – half cover joints with stock, approx. 750 *ml* (1½ *pts*).	40	
	Stew (pressure boil)	No trivet. See recipe p. 188.	40	
Stewing steak (fillets or pieces)	Braise (pressure steam)	No trivet. Season and cover with flour. Brown in hot fat on both sides. Lay on *mire-poix* and use water and tomato juice according to length of cooking time.	20 25 30	2½ *cm* (1 *in*) 5 *cm* (2 *in*) 7½ *cm* (3 *in*)
Mince	Stew (pressure boil)	Mince can be stir-fried: cooking will take 3 to 4 mins in hot oil. Cook further in stock with other ingredients.	3–4	
Meat loaf	Pot-roast or braise (pressure steam)	See recipe p. 185.	20–25	
Salt beef (corned beef)	Boil (pressure boil)	Leave in clear water overnight. Drain most off. Weigh. Cover with water. Add potatoes, turnips, carrots and pepper. No salt needed.	27	25
Tripe	Boil (pressure boil)	Add minced macaroni. Cover with water.	15	
VEAL:				
Stuffed shoulder, loin	Pot-roast (pressure steam)	Brown in hot fat. Drain. Place on trivet with required amount of liquid.	13–15	12–14

Meat	Method	Preparation	Time mins/ 500 g	mins/ lb
VEAL (cont.)				
Knuckle	Boil (pressure boil)	Half-fill cooker with water. No trivet.	11	10
Rolled, stuffed breast	Braise (pressure steam)	Roll tightly round stuffing and cook over *mire-poix* plus liquid.	13	12
Pieces, stew	Stew (pressure boil)	Fry lightly in butter but do not brown. Add vegs 5 mins before end.	15	
LAMB AND MUTTON:				
Stuffed, rolled breast	Pot-roast (pressure steam)	Standard method.	11–13	10–12
Chops, cutlets	Braise (pressure steam)	Standard method.	10	
Best end of neck	Stew (pressure steam)	Cut into pieces.	10–12	
Shoulder, stuffed breast	Braise (pressure steam)	Remove fat and skin. Rub with garlic clove. Season, brown and braise with standard method.	10–12	
Leg	Boil (pressure boil)	Standard boiling method.	17	15
Hearts	Stew (pressure boil)	Clean out and fill with stuffing – then standard stew method.	30	
Liver	Stew (pressure boil)	Standard stew method.	5	
Kidneys	Stew (pressure boil)	Brown in bacon fat – use only 280 *ml* (½ *pt*) liquid.	7	
PORK:				
Chops	Braise (pressure steam)	Standard braising method.	10–12	

Meat	Method	Preparation	Time mins/ 500 g	mins/ lb
PORK (cont.)				
Pickled leg, hand, belly	Boil (pressure boil)	Standard boiling method.	20	18
Pig's trotters	Boil (pressure boil)	Use 200 *ml* ($\frac{1}{4}$–$\frac{1}{3}$ *pt*) each of cider or wine vinegar and water.		30

By cooking method

Method	Meats
Pot-roasting (with trivet) Pressure steaming	Beef: topside, brisket, rolled rib. Veal: stuffed shoulder, loin. Lamb/Mutton: stuffed, rolled breast.
Braising (without trivet but using *mire-poix* of vegetables) Pressure steaming	Beef: chuck, rump, Swiss steak, oxtail, rolled rib roast. Veal: rolled, stuffed breast. Mutton/Lamb: chops, cutlets, neck, shoulder, hearts, liver, kidneys. Pork: chops, stuffed, gammon slices.
Boiling (without trivet) Pressure boiling	Beef: brisket, silverside, salt beef. Veal: knuckle. Mutton: leg, breast, neck. Pork: pickled leg, hand, belly. Ham: gammon, hock, collar, flank. Heads: pig, sheep, calf. Pig's trotters.
Stew (without trivet) Pressure boiling in stock	Beef: pieces, mince, oxtail, tripe. Veal: pieces. Mutton/Lamb: best end of neck, scrag end.
Stuffing	Beef: rolls. Veal: rolls, shoulder, breast, chops. Lamb/Mutton: shoulder, breast. Pork.

Meat Temperatures

If you have a meat thermometer, use it to check the degree of 'doneness' according to this table. Most meat thermometers do not like being immersed in water, so do not leave the instrument in the pan while you are cooking.

	°C	°F
Beef: rare	60	140
medium	70	160
well done	77	170
Cured Pork, Bacon, Gammon etc.	77	170
Veal	77	170
Lamb, Mutton	82	180
Rabbit, and small game	82	180
Fresh Pork	88	190
Poultry	88	190

Chicken

Age and Size	Preparation and Use	Pressure-Cooking Time
Baby (under 1 kg/2 lb)	Halved or jointed	4–7 mins depending on size
Roasting (1–1½ kg/2–3 lb)	Whole, stuffed or jointed	6 mins/500 g, 5 mins/lb 5–6 mins
Boiling (1½ kg+/3½ lb+)	Whole, stuffed Whole, marinated Halved Jointed	12 mins/500 g, 10 mins/lb 10 mins/500 g, 8 mins/lb 20 mins 12 mins

Frozen joints, even if defrosted, require less cooking time than fresh ones – take 10% to 15% off the timing above.

Game

Animal	Preparation	Cooking Time
Duckling	Whole	13–16 mins/500 g 12–15 mins/lb
	Jointed	12 mins
Duck and Goose	Whole	15–17 mins/500 g 13–17 mins/lb
	Jointed	15 mins
Partridge Pheasant Guinea Fowl Pigeon	Whole, in casserole or braised	7–12 mins
Hare	Jointed	35–40 mins
Rabbit	Jointed	12–15 mins

Meat Substitutes (Textured Vegetable Protein)

Rehydration: follow manufacturer's recommendations.
Mince will not need pressure cooking; chunky styles can be
rehydrated in one-fifth to one-quarter of the time recommended for normal purposes by manufacturer – usually
within five minutes. Do not pressure cook chunky styles for
longer than fifteen minutes. TVP needs to absorb twice its
volume of water in order to be reconstituted.

Rice

Rice type	Description	Weight	Water	PC time/Normal time (minutes)
Basmati	Long grain Top quality polished	170 g/6 oz	570 ml (1 pt)	5/15
Patna	Long grain	170 g/6 oz	570 ml (1 pt)	5/15
Risotto	Short grain Pudding	170 g/6 oz	570 ml (1 pt)	4–5/12–15
Brown	Unpolished Nutritious	170 g/6 oz	650 ml (1¼ pts)	20/45–55
Wild	Sold largely in U.S.A.	170 g/6 oz	650 ml (1¼ pts)	20/45–55
Pre-fluffed	Parboiled to avoid stickiness	170 g/6 oz	1 l (1¾ pts)	8–9/25
Pre-fluffed brown	Parboiled to avoid stickiness	140 g/5 oz	1 l (1¾ pts)	16–18/50

Grain and Cereal

Grain/Cereal Description	Weight	Water	PC time/Normal time (minutes)
Barley (pearl)	170 g/6 oz	1·1 l (2 pts)	20/55–60
Cornmeal	120 g/4 oz	730 ml (1½ pts)	8/20–25
Cracked wheat	120 g/4 oz	500 ml (1 pt)	20/55–60

Grain/Cereal	Description	Weight	Water	PC time/ Normal time (minutes)
Farina meal	Meal made of cereal grains and starchy roots	90 g/3 oz	500 ml (1 pt)	3/10
Hominy	Dried sweet corn (maize)	120 g/4 oz	430 ml (¾ pt)	25/50
Hominy grits	Corn with husk and germ removed	120 g/4 oz	730 ml (1½ pts)	20/50
Oats				
quick	follow packet instructions; do not pressure cook			
rolled		170 g/6 oz	700 ml (1¼ pts)	10/30–45
meal		170 g/6 oz	1·1 l (2 pts)	15/45
porridge		170 g/6 oz	700 ml (1¼ pts)	5/15

For proprietary brands of *groats* (usually made from cracked wheat, buckwheat and oats), *kasha* (coarse-ground buckwheat and barley), and *couscous* (fine-ground flour or other cereal) follow instructions on pack and divide cooking time by 3. One cup by volume of a flaked cereal will absorb 2 to 3 times the volume of water. One cup of whole-grain cereal needs 3 to 4 times its volume of water and a granular cereal will be thickened and will absorb its own volume.

Pasta

Pasta	Weight	Water	PC time/ Normal time (minutes)
Macaroni			
5 cm (2 in) lengths	230 g/½ lb	1 l (2 pts)	4–5/12–15
elbow	230 g/½ lb	1 l (2 pts)	5–6/20–25
Noodles			
fine	230 g/½ lb	1 l (2 pts)	2–3/6–8
medium	230 g/½ lb	1 l (2 pts)	3–4/8–10
alphabet	170 g/6 oz	850 ml (1½ pts)	3–4/8–10
small shells	170 g/6 oz	1 l (2 pts)	3/9
Fettuccine	170 g/6 oz	1 l (2 pts)	3/9

Pasta	Weight	Water	PC time/ Normal time (minutes)
Spaghetti			
fine	230 g/$\frac{1}{2}$ lb	1 l (2 pts)	3–4/8–10
regular	230 g/$\frac{1}{2}$ lb	1 l (2 pts)	5–6/20–25
Vermicelli	230 g/$\frac{1}{2}$ lb	1 l (2 pts)	3–4/8–10

Fresh Fruit

Fruit	Weight	Water	Sugar	Stewing/ Steaming time	Instructions
APPLES					
Baked	1·4 kg/3 lb	140 ml (¼ pt)	100 g/3 oz	4 mins/4–6 mins	Steam on trivet. Wash and core. Place in wet parchment on trivet in pan. Fill centres with sugar. Sprinkle with cinnamon.
Sauce	1·4 kg/3 lb	500 ml (¾ pt)	200 g/6 oz	1½ mins	Quarter, core and pare. Stew without trivet and strain or leave as chunk sauce. Pack in layers sprinkling each with brown sugar and a strip of lemon peel. Nutmeg or cloves to taste.
APRICOTS					
Halves	1 kg/2 lb	140 ml (¼ pt)	120 g/4 oz	3 mins/¾ min	Make syrup from water and sugar, add fruit, cover and stew.
Whole	2 kg/4 lb	500 ml (¾ pt)	200 g/6 oz	3 mins/1½ mins	
BLACKBERRIES **BILBERRIES** **BLUEBERRIES**	2 kg/4 lb	140 ml (¼ pt)	150 g/5 oz	1 min/1 min	The berries can be cooked alone or with sliced apples. Add sugar to the fruit, add water, seal and cook.
CHERRIES					
Black	2 kg/4 lb	140 ml (¼ pt)	150 g/5 oz	¾ min/1 min	Both black and sour cherries can be cooked whole or stoned. Add sugar to fruit, add water. Seal and cook.
Red	2 kg/4 lb	140 ml (¼ pt)	200 g/6 oz	¼ min/½ min	

Fruit	Weight	Water	Sugar	Stewing/Steaming time	Instructions
CRANBERRIES Jelly	2 kg/4 lb	500 ml (¾ pt)	400 g/12 oz	3 mins	Add water and cook. Strain if desired. Add sugar. Boil 1 min without cover. Strain, add gelatin and pour into mould.
Sauce	2 kg/4 lb	280 ml (½ pt)	230 g/8 oz	1½ mins	Stir sugar into water until dissolved. Add fruit, cover and cook. Bring to pressure slowly.
GOOSEBERRIES	2 kg/4 lb	280 ml (½ pt)	230 g/8 oz	1½ mins/2 mins	To stew: stir sugar into water till dissolved. Add fruit, cover and cook. To steam: Add sugar after cooking.
GRAPES Juice for jellies		140 ml (¼ pt)	—	¼ min	Wash fruit, place in pan with water and bring to pressure only. Strain juice for jelly making.
ORANGE Slices	1·4–2 kg/3–4 lb	140 ml (¼ pt)	200 g/6 oz	3 mins	Wash, slice and remove seeds. Add sugar and cook uncovered a few moments to glaze.
PEACHES Halves	2 kg/4 lb	280 ml (½ pt)	100 g/3 oz	½ min/3 mins	Scald, peel and halve and remove pits. If stewing dissolve sugar in water and add peaches. Seal and cook. To steam add sweetening later.

Fruit	Weight	Water	Sugar	Stewing/Steaming time	Instructions
PEARS Halves (dessert)	2 kg/4 lb	280 ml (½ pt)	100 g/3 oz	1 min/4 mins	Wash, pare and halve and core fruit. Dissolve sugar in water if stewing, add fruit, seal and cook. Add sugar later if steaming.
Hard (stewing)	2 kg/4 lb	280 ml (½ pt)	100 g/3 oz	3 mins/8 mins	Cook in basic sugar syrup in container or in cooker without trivet.
PINEAPPLE	1	140 ml (¼ pt)	200 g/6 oz	12 mins	Slice, pare and dice from core. Add water and cook. Stir in sugar after cooking.
PLUMS GREENGAGES DAMSONS	2 kg/4 lb	140 ml (¼ pt)	120 g/4 oz	3 mins/3 mins	Cook whole, prick each one with a fork or halve and stone. Add sugar and bring to boil. *If whole, cook 4 minutes.*
QUINCE	2 kg/4 lb	280 ml (½ pt)	120 g/4 oz	15 mins	Quarter, core, pare. Dissolve sugar in water, add fruit and cook.
RASPBERRIES	2 kg/4 lb	140 ml (¼ pt)	230 g/8 oz	¼ min/¼ min	Bring water and sugar to boil. Add fruit, seal and bring to pressure only.
RHUBARB	1·4 kg/3 lb	140 ml (¼ pt)	120 g/4 oz	¼ min	Wash and cut in lengths or short sticks. Add sugar and water. Seal and bring to pressure only.
STRAWBERRIES	2 kg/4 lb	140 ml (¼ pt)	200 g/6 oz	¼ min/½ min	To stew: bring water and sugar to boil. Add fruit, seal and bring to pressure only. To steam: add sugar later.

Dried Fruit Tables

Fruit	Weight	Water	Sugar	Stewing	Instructions
APPLES	450 g/1 lb	570 ml (1 pt)	120 g/4 oz	8 mins	Add sugar to cooked fruit. If soaked reduce cooking time to 2 mins. Do not soak unless fruit is very dry.
APRICOTS	450 g/1 lb	570 ml (1 pt)	120 g/4 oz	1–3 mins	Do not soak. Add sugar to cooked fruit.
CURRANTS	230 g/½ lb	280 ml (½ pt)	—	5 mins	For use in cakes, desserts, etc.
FIGS	230 g/½ lb	500 ml (¾ pt)	100 g/3 oz	10–12 mins	Soak overnight, if possible, and therefore reduce cooking time. Add sugar to cooked fruit.
MIXED, FOR PIES	230 g/½ lb	500 ml (¾ pt)	60 g/2 oz	5 mins	Enough for an average-size pie. Soak if some fruit is very dry. Can be served as a fruit compote.
PEACHES	680 g/1½ lb	700 ml (1¼ pts)	120 g/4 oz	5–10 mins	If soaked overnight add more water before cooking. No soaking necessary unless very dry; or cook longer. Add sugar to cooked fruit.
PEARS	680 g/1½ lb	280 ml (½ pt)	100 g/3 oz	6 mins	No soaking necessary unless very dry. Add sugar after cooking.
PRUNES bulk	680 g/1½ lb	700 ml (1¼ pts)	60 g/2 oz	10 mins	
packaged	680 g/1½ lb	570 ml (1 pt)	60 g/2 oz	5 mins	
RAISINS seeded	230 g/½ lb	280 ml (½ pt)		3 mins	Do not soak. Use in other recipes.
seedless	230 g/½ lb	280 ml (½ pt)		5 mins	

Appendix 5: INTERNATIONAL CONVERSION TABLES

The weights and measures used throughout this book are based on British Imperial standards and metric. However, the following tables show you how to convert the various weights and measures simply.

International Measures

Measure	U.K.	Australia	New Zealand	Canada	U.S.A.
1 pint	20 *fl oz*	20 *fl oz*	20 *fl oz*	20 *fl oz*	16 *fl oz*
1 cup	10 *fl oz*	8 *fl oz*	8 *fl oz*	8 *fl oz*	8 *fl oz*
1 tablespoon	$\frac{5}{8}$ *fl oz*	$\frac{1}{2}$ *fl oz*	$\frac{1}{2}$ *fl oz*	$\frac{1}{2}$ *fl oz*	$\frac{1}{2}$ *fl oz*
1 dessertspoon	$\frac{2}{3}$ *fl oz*	no official measure	—	—	—
1 teaspoon	$\frac{1}{3}$ *fl oz*	$\frac{1}{8}$ *fl oz*	$\frac{1}{3}$ *fl oz*	$\frac{1}{6}$ *fl oz*	$\frac{1}{8}$ *fl oz*
1 gill	5 *fl oz*	—	—	—	—

Conversion of fluid ounces to metric

1 *fl oz*	= 2·84 *ml*
35 *fl oz* (approx 1¾ Imperial pints)	= 1 litre (1000 *ml* or 10 *decilitres*)
1 Imperial pint (20 *fl oz*)	= approx 600 *ml* (6 *dl*)
½ Imperial pint (10 *fl oz*)	= 300 *ml* (3 *dl*)
¼ Imperial pint (5 *fl oz*)	= 150 *ml* (1½ *dl*)
4 tablespoons (2½ *fl oz*)	= 70 *ml* (7 *cl*)
2 tablespoons (1¼ *fl oz*)	= 35 *ml* (3½ *cl*)
1 tablespoon ($\frac{5}{8}$ *fl oz*)	= 18 *ml* (2 *cl*)
1 dessertspoon ($\frac{2}{3}$ *fl oz*)	= 12 *ml*
1 teaspoon ($\frac{1}{3}$ *fl oz*)	= 6 *ml*

(All the above metric equivalents are approximate)

Conversion of solid weights to metric

```
2 lb 3 oz = 1 kg (kilogramme)
1 lb      = 453 g (grammes)
12 oz     = 339 g
8 oz      = 225 g
4 oz      = 113 g
2 oz      = 56 g
1 oz      = 28 g
```

U.S. Equivalents

In converting American recipes for metric or Imperial use, note that the U.S. pint is 16 *fl oz* (454·6 *ml*) against the Imperial pint of 20 *fl oz* (568·3 *ml*). Americans tend to use cups (8 *fl oz*) for measuring quantities of solids, like flour, beans, raisins, even chopped vegetables. If you own a number of American recipe books, invest in a U.S. cup measure as well.

Oven temperatures

Description	Electric Setting	Gas Mark
Very cool	225 °F (110 °C)	$\frac{1}{4}$
	250 °F (130 °C)	$\frac{1}{2}$
Cool	275 °F (140 °C)	1
	300 °F (150 °C)	2
Very moderate	325 °F (170 °C)	3
Moderate	350 °F (180 °C)	4
Moderately or	375 °F (190 °C)	5
fairly hot	400 °F (200 °C)	6
Hot	425 °F (220 °C)	7
	450 °F (230 °C)	8
Very hot	475 °F (240 °C)	9

These temperatures are only an approximate guide as all ovens vary slightly, according to the make and country of manufacture.

INDEX